ENTERTAINMENT INDUSTRY

Selected Titles in ABC-CLIO's
CONTEMPORARY
WORLD ISSUES
Series

Books in the Contemporary World Issues series address vital issues in today's society such as genetic engineering, pollution, and biodiversity. Written by professional writers, scholars, and nonacademic experts, these books are authoritative, clearly written, up-to-date, and objective. They provide a good starting point for research by high school and college students, scholars, and general readers as well as by legislators, businesspeople, activists, and others.

Each book, carefully organized and easy to use, contains an overview of the subject, a detailed chronology, biographical sketches, facts and data and/or documents and other primary source material, a directory of organizations and agencies, annotated lists of print and nonprint resources, and an index.

Readers of books in the Contemporary World Issues series will find the information they need in order to have a better understanding of the social, political, environmental, and economic issues facing the world today.

ENTERTAINMENT INDUSTRY

A Reference Handbook

Michael J. Haupert

CONTEMPORARY WORLD ISSUES

ABC-CLIO

Santa Barbara, California • Denver, Colorado • Oxford, England

HOT TOPIC
791.43
H374
2012

Library of Congress Cataloging-in-Publication Data

Haupert, Michael J. (Michael John)
    Entertainment industry : a reference handbook / Michael J. Haupert.
      p. cm. — (Contemporary world issues) (World issues)
    Includes bibliographical references and index.
    ISBN 978–1–59884–594–5 (hard copy : alk. paper) — ISBN 978–1–59884–595–2 (e-book) 1. Performing arts—United States—History—20th century. I. Title.
PN2266.H382   2012
791.430973—dc23   2012020108

ISBN: 978–1–59884–594–5
EISBN: 978–1–59884–595–2

16 15 14 13 12   1 2 3 4 5

This book is also available on the World Wide Web as an eBook.
Visit www.abc-clio.com for details.

ABC-CLIO, LLC
130 Cremona Drive, P.O. Box 1911
Santa Barbara, California 93116-1911

This book is printed on acid-free paper ∞

Manufactured in the United States of America

Contents

Preface

This book serves as an entryway into the fascinating world of the economics of the entertainment industry. It begins with a brief history of the evolution of the industry, primarily over the twentieth century, when it experienced its greatest period of growth. The second chapter discusses the major issues that confront the industry today, and the third chapter takes a broad look at the industry from a global perspective.

Chapter 4 is a timeline of the most important events in the industry. Chapter 5 consists of brief biographies of three dozen individuals who have had a profound impact on the entertainment industry. No attempt was made to pick the most important people, however that might be defined, but rather to single out a small number who through their actions had a major impact. This list includes executives like David Sarnoff, who rose to power at RCA and had a profound influence on the way in which radio and television evolved; Jackie Robinson, the first African American to play major league baseball after a half century of segregation; and Mary Pickford, the actress and entrepreneur who captured the hearts of American moviegoers on the big screen and helped revolutionize the movie industry with her business acumen.

Chapter 6 includes a selected list of information covering the industry in an effort to put some of the types of entertainment, and entertainment's place in our economy, into perspective. It is certainly not an exhaustive list, but it does serve to illustrate some of the issues addressed in the text. I have also included a directory of major firms and organizations in the entertainment industry (in Chapter 7). Most of these have websites, which I have noted so that you can more easily explore the current makeup of the industry. This directory includes major producers in every type of entertainment I have discussed, as well as labor organizations and professional associations representing the entertainment industry's major players.

Finally, I have included in the reference chapter a list of works that I found especially helpful in writing this book, and that you will likely find helpful in your future studies of the entertainment industry. The references are annotated to help you get an idea of the scope and focus of the research. In this way it will be easier for you to quickly search out sources that will provide you with the information you want. The list should be useful to anyone who wishes to delve more deeply into the business and history of entertainment.

As consumers, we view entertainment as a pastime and a way to relax during our precious free time. For those involved in the production of entertainment, however, it is—and always has been—a business. And that business has experienced its share of turbulence as a result of the fluctuating economy, evolving tastes of consumers, and technological progress.

As you will see in the first three chapters, the common thread across time and venue in the entertainment industry has been the impact of technology on both the supply and demand of entertainment. Some types of entertainment have been affected more than others. Indeed, one of those featured types, vaudeville, faded out of existence largely due to its inability to adapt to the changes of technology, primarily in the form of talking pictures. Technology is no less a presence today. Whether it be 3D or computer animated movies, HDTV, digital music, or file sharing, the impact of technology is still present.

Entertainment is amusement. Its purpose is to create a relaxing, enjoyable environment in which to temporarily escape the stresses of daily life. It has taken countless forms over the centuries, ranging from recreational amusement such as jogging or painting to passive entertainment like watching television or listening to music. Entertainment can also take the form of everyday activities, for example, gardening or cooking. In fact, the list of activities that could be considered entertainment is virtually endless and differs from person to person. The realm of possibilities is so grand as to make it impossible to cover the subject thoroughly in one volume.

The six specific forms of entertainment to which I devote most of my time in this book are vaudeville, recorded sound, movies, radio, television, and spectator sports. They all share some aspects in common. They were, or are, all consumed by large numbers of Americans. All are, or were, accessible to a wide variety of income classes, in virtually any community, and they are all easily recognizable as entertainment. Television, radio, and recorded sound are all primary forms of entertainment that are available widely and cheaply in most homes and that appeal to all ages and income levels in every geographic area of the country. While they may be consumed alone or in small groups in the home, the fact that the same program is entertaining millions at the same time makes them eligible for inclusion as mass entertainment.

Technology is another common thread in each of these forms of entertainment. It defines some of them (radio, television, movies, and recorded sound) and has had a profound impact on all of them. While vaudeville and spectator sports existed before the dramatic technological advances of the twentieth century, these advances redefined both industries when they did come along. Spectator sports thrived by strategically exploiting radio and television. Vaudeville, on the other hand, was displaced by the technological advances that produced radio, television and the movies.

The sports industry is certainly older than all but perhaps vaudeville (or its stage antecedents, such as Greek theater). It bears less similarity to the other types of entertainment discussed here. The other formats are clearly derivations of one another, while sports is less so, even though spectator sports do share a lot in common with the other means of entertainment, and there certainly is crossover. Sports owe their explosion in popularity and profitability to television and radio broadcasts along with the hefty fees that come with them. Vaudeville regularly featured prominent sports heroes on their bills, and the first highlights of sporting events debuted on the weekly newsreels at the movies in the pretelevision days.

Entertainment is a fascinating industry, with colorful personalities, intriguing origins and, at the bottom line, a straightforward business model. Despite the glitz and glamour often associated with the various types of entertainment, they are businesses designed to make a profit.

I use economics as a lens through which to view the broad historical evolution of various segments of the entertainment industry. However, this book does not presume a prior level of expertise in economics. Economic jargon is kept to a minimum, and where I felt it necessary to use economic terms and concepts, I have taken care to define them.

The growth of the American economy has been the primary factor in the growth of the American entertainment industry.

The growth of the economy, which decreased work hours and increased income, and its concomitant technological improvements, which both decreased the cost of providing entertainment as well as increased the amount of leisure time available to consume that entertainment, was the catalyst. Technological improvements contributed to increased labor productivity, shorter workweeks and increased wages. At home, that technological revolution decreased the amount of time needed to finish household chores, thus freeing up time for entertainment. It is the increased wealth measured by both income and free time that has allowed for the explosion in demand for entertainment.

Over the course of the twentieth century, the average American saw a 33 percent decrease in the number of hours on the job, enjoyed an inflation-adjusted income increase by a factor of 25 (after taxes, no less) and responded by nearly tripling their expenditures on entertainment. Add to this the decreased amount of time needed to accomplish household chores such as cooking, the impact of the automobile on personal mobility, and the increased ability to be entertained at home made possible by radio, television and recorded music, and the elements are all in place for the consumption of entertainment on a mass scale. The result, as you will see, was a century of spectacular growth and innovation.

There is no absolute demarcation between these various types of entertainment. It is not always clear where one ends and another begins, nor even where they might be separated. As a result, the coverage of the entertainment industry requires some knowledge of one medium in order to understand the other. Entertainment is an industry that brings joy to millions. It continues to be a growing sector of our economy, generating billions of dollars in revenue and employing millions of workers. I try to provide an overview of that industry and a launching point for you to explore it in greater detail.

1

Background and History

Introduction

On its surface, the entertainment industry seems surreal. It is defined by tabloids, television gossip shows, glamour, and glitz. Behind the scenes, however, it is a business, indistinguishable in many ways from any other industry. Like any manufacturing plant, goods are produced. Like a financial adviser or hair stylist, services are provided. In each case, the market for these goods responds to the basic principles of economics: primarily supply and demand. The market then operates to allocate the goods, whether they be automobiles or videocassettes, haircuts or theater performances, from sellers to buyers. In many ways, however, these industries are different from those that provide manufactured goods or haircuts.

There are some properties of the entertainment industry that do not necessarily apply to other markets. These include uncertain product characteristics, producers who have an unusually high personal attachment to their product (think *art* as opposed to *commerce*), and goods that cannot readily be inventoried.

The quality of entertainment goods is seldom known in advance. What is more, no two are alike, so it is hard to predict exactly what the quality will be the next time they are produced. As a result, more so in entertainment than other industries, consumers rely on signals for quality indicators. In the movie industry, for example, the quality of a movie cannot be determined until it has been seen. To try and avoid buying tickets to bad movies, consumers rely on the opinions of critics and word-of-mouth reviews from friends who have already seen the movie to give them an indication of its quality.

Live performances, such as concerts and vaudeville, share certain characteristics. In particular, they cannot be inventoried, that is, produced now and then stored for sale at a later time. The consumption of their product takes place at the same time as its final production, and customers must come to it, as it cannot be shipped to them or an intermediary middleman for resale. Over time, technology has blurred these lines of distinction since a live performance can be recorded and sold like any other commodity. However, while a taped version of a concert or play is a substitute for the live performance, the degree of substitution is highly debatable. Listening to a high quality digital recording of a concert may, for example, be a closer substitute for the concert than would be a similarly high quality video recording of last night's big championship football game. The high prices commanded for some live events suggest that the substitutability is far from perfect.

The standard economic explanations for demand are equally applicable to the entertainment industry. People usually demand a greater quantity of a good when its price decreases. They are also likely to buy more of the good if their income goes up or there is a change in the price of related goods. For example, if the cost of parking at the movie theater goes down, more people are likely to attend.

Demand for goods is also affected by the number of potential buyers as well as their tastes and preferences. In larger cities, more tickets are likely to be sold to an event than in smaller cities. While tastes and preferences are difficult to explain, their impact on demand is straightforward. When a hit song is recorded, buyers clamor for it. What *makes* it a hit song, however, is difficult if not impossible to explain.

Americans saw their after-tax income increase by a factor of 25 over the course of the twentieth century. This increase in income allowed Americans to purchase more entertainment. The percentage of personal consumption expenditures Americans devoted to recreation and entertainment rose from 3 percent at the end of the nineteenth century to more than 10 percent by 2010.

The decrease in the length of the workweek also contributed to an increase in leisure consumption. The average workweek decreased by one-third over the century from 59 hours to 39 hours, freeing up a tremendous amount of time for leisure pursuits. Additional time for leisure has also been made available by inventions, which have led to the reduction of the amount of time needed for household chores such as laundry, cleaning, and cooking (Bowden and Offer 1994, Costa 2000, Hunnicutt 1980, Maoz 2010, Vandenbroucke 2009).

The population of the United States increased from 76 million in 1900 to 280 million in 2000. By itself, this increase in population made for a larger market, thus leading to an increase in demand for entertainment. It is not just the growth of the population, however, but how it grew that is significant. The dramatic shift of population from the country to the city is also an important factor in explaining the growth of the entertainment industry. The cost of pursuing entertainment is lower for city dwellers because of the closer proximity of venues such as theaters and stadiums. There is also a greater supply of entertainment opportunities in the city.

The automobile has broadened the horizon of potential forms of entertainment for Americans. It is one of the most important reasons for the increase in out-of-home types of entertainment. By creating a more mobile society, the automobile increased the scope of possible entertainment venues and lowered the cost of reaching them (Clevinger and Vozikis 2007, Shaw 1986).

Technology also changed the supply of entertainment, progressing from live theater to the movies for public consumption and adding home entertainment in the form of recorded music, radio, television, and ultimately the internet. The American entertainment industry responded to the demands of the public and adapted the latest technologies in an effort to capitalize on the growing demand for entertainment services.

The unknown quality of many forms of entertainment causes problems not only for consumers, but it can be a challenge for the producers as well. Consider the movie industry as an example. The success of a movie is almost impossible to predict. Even after a movie smashes box office records, it may not be clear as to why it was so much more popular than other films. Even knowing what made one movie, play, television show, or recording popular usually adds nothing to the predictive ability of what will make the next one popular. No actor is a guaranteed box office hit every time, and no genre of film has proven to be eternally popular. Without really knowing what factors influence the quality of the final product, producers are at an extreme disadvantage, and the final result is the volatile movie industry we see today.

The skills of those producing entertainment goods are highly variable, and in many cases are not identifiable before hiring. For example, not all athletes are the same quality. In fact, there is a huge discrepancy in talent (defined here only as ability to generate revenue, usually through ticket sales). This leads to a market with high salaries for the few who are most easily identifiable as high quality workers (i.e., superstars). However, that still does not guarantee high quality. Even an award-winning actor can make a bad film or a star athlete can have a bad season. This leads to a division of the marketplace into "superstar" and "secondary" employees. The difference is not in the known outcome of the quality of their product, but rather the likelihood of the quality being high. A superstar actor (a recent Tony Award winner, for example) is more likely to produce a high quality acting job (and high box office revenues) than is a "secondary" actor (Berri, Schmidt, and Brook 2004, Berri and Schmidt 2006, Frey 1998, Hausman and Leonard 1997, Jung and Kim 2010, Rosen 1981, Walls 2010).

The time value of money is an issue in the entertainment industry as it is in many industries. For example, when a studio produces a movie costing $100 million, the money is entirely spent before any income can be earned on ticket sales. That means the $100 million cannot be used by the studio for anything else—another movie, paying off debts, or simply earning interest in the bank. The longer the time lag between spending the money and earning any income to pay it back, the more expensive the investment becomes in terms of foregone income. The problem with this lag is exacerbated by the difficulty in storing entertainment goods. For example, while a movie can be inventoried, some movies do not hold up well because of their topical nature or their lower quality due to technology. As a result, there is little opportunity to earn income on many previously produced films.

Vaudeville

The first real mass entertainment medium of the twentieth century was vaudeville. Before technology made entertainment a packaged and stored commodity, live entertainment ruled the industry. This took the form of staged shows: opera, symphony, theater, burlesque, and vaudeville. The former were attended primarily by the well educated and upper class. Burlesque was mainly a saloon-based form of entertainment, appealing to the male working class. Of these early forms of mass entertainment, only vaudeville appealed to the mass audience.

Simply defined, vaudeville was a live variety show. While it usually contained acting and music, it differed from theater, opera, or symphony performances because it contained so much more. Vaudeville was more like a talent show; it contained a little bit of everything—basically, anything that might entertain an audience. Big-time vaudeville was the top of the entertainment pyramid and featured the greatest entertainers in the world.

Vaudeville flourished in America for the first two decades of the twentieth century and spawned many of the early actors who went on to propel the movie and television industries to their current positions in the entertainment industry. Like theater and opera, vaudeville was performed live. Unlike theater and opera, however, it was neither as formal nor as exclusive. Vaudeville also contained elements of the circus and appealed to a broader customer base than did the theater, opera, or symphony (Taubman 1965, Toll 1976).

A typical vaudeville show lasted about two hours and featured as many as 10 different acts, ranging from the stars of opera and Broadway to acrobats and animal acts with the occasional appearance of the famous and bizarre. Prices were low compared to more formal stage shows, and the acts traveled from city to city, usually on a weekly basis. Thus, the local theater provided great variety, and the vaudeville acts performed before a wide range of audiences.

While vaudeville in America had its roots in the burlesque and variety shows performed in saloons, it differed in its targeted audience and hence the type of acts it featured. Vaudeville was family entertainment. Burlesque and variety were aimed at working men. The performances were initially used as bait for customers to draw them into beer halls. The first true American vaudeville hall was built by Tony Pastor, a saloon owner who opened a separate theater for entertainment in New York City in 1881. That marked a clear demarcation from the beer hall environment. Pastor's theater provided entertainment that was appropriate for women and children as well as appealing to men. The concept soon spread to other cities along the eastern seaboard (Di Meglio 1973, Erdman 2004).

After Tony Pastor, the vaudeville mantle was picked up by Benjamin Franklin Keith and Edward F. Albee. Keith is often referred to as the father of American vaudeville. Along with Albee, he assembled the most impressive string of theaters and monopolized the booking of vaudeville talent, ultimately establishing nearly total control over the industry before his death in 1914 (Snyder 2000).

Vaudeville was certainly not the only staged live entertainment available at the beginning of the twentieth century. The "legitimate" stage was also strong. This included musical revues and plays. Symphony orchestras and opera companies also existed. These were considered "classical" entertainment, whereas vaudeville was "mass" entertainment. The difference for the biggest stars was not so much salary as status. Along with that status came a reduced work and travel schedule and better perks, such as private dressing rooms and first class travel and accommodations paid for by the theater company. In contrast, typical vaudeville stars seldom played in any town for more than a week, perhaps two for a major booking. On a typical 40-week touring circuit, a vaudevillian could expect to play in more than 30 venues.

The relationship between the "legits" and the vaudevillians was mixed. Stage actors tended to look down on vaudevillians as classless entertainment, while the vaudevillians saw their counterparts as snobs. However, each benefited from the existence of the other. The legitimate theater was the goal for many vaudevillians, and the appearance of a Broadway star on the program would often pack the house, improving the situation for all. For Broadway actors, vaudeville served as an easy way to make some serious money in between shows, where they were typically headliners playing to adoring audiences, most of whom would have no chance to see them otherwise. It also served as a training ground for actors. Some Broadway shows were broken into one act shows and tested on the vaudeville circuit before opening.

Vaudeville reached its peak in terms of organization, and perhaps quality, in the early 1920s, about a decade before the entire industry collapsed under the weight of competition from talking pictures. At the time, there were over 15,000 theaters in towns of every size. It was the most popular form of mass entertainment in America. It was easily accessible, affordable, and appropriate for the whole family. The bill changed on a weekly basis, and the most famous names eventually landed in even the smallest of theaters, adding a sense of commonality to it all.

When the movie industry grew into a major entertainment force in the 1910s, movie moguls predicted that the motion picture would replace vaudeville. However, vaudeville adapted, including silent films as part of the program throughout the 1920s. It was not until the advent of sound in motion pictures that vaudeville was dealt a fatal blow (Allen 1979).

The larger theaters in the biggest cities, like the Palace Theater in Manhattan, continued to feature live entertainment with motion pictures, but by 1935, the industry had disappeared from the American entertainment scene, never again to reappear. It was not that vaudeville failed to adjust or misread the future, it was simply a victim of forces beyond its control. Evolution in technology and consumer tastes, and better alternatives for the best entertainers, victimized vaudeville.

Vaudeville was a victim of the technology on both the demand and the supply side of the equation. The demand for vaudeville shows fell off as the quality of movies and radio programming improved. In addition, talent was drained from the stage to the big screen. Performers preferred the higher paychecks and reduced travel schedule offered by national radio networks and the movie industry. Finally, venues disappeared as theaters were converted from presenting vaudeville shows to the more profitable motion pictures.

Despite being gone from the entertainment landscape for more than a decade, the imprint of vaudeville was evident in the early days of television. Television variety shows in the 1940s and 1950s were patterned after vaudeville, and some even starred vaudeville performers, such as Milton Berle's *Texaco Star Theater*. Berle had been in vaudeville since childhood. The show was actually called *The Texaco Star Theater Vaudeville Show* when it debuted on June 8, 1948.

The demise of the Keith-Albee empire is symbolic of the decline of vaudeville. In 1927, Keith-Albee merged with Orpheum to form the Keith-Albee-Orpheum circuit. In 1928, Joseph P. Kennedy, patriarch of the Kennedy political clan, bought controlling shares in Keith-Orpheum and merged it with his own Film Booking Office (FBO). Kennedy had no interest in vaudeville; he just wanted the theaters, which he planned to convert to movie houses for the film booking interests he ran in cooperation with Radio Corporation of America (RCA). He merged Keith-Albee-Orpheum with RCA to form the film company Radio Keith Orpheum (RKO).

Radio was another threat to vaudeville but not a significant one until nationwide networks debuted in the late 1920s. Two factors affected vaudeville in this regard: the ability to stay at home and listen to radio instead of going out and the exodus of stars from the stage to the microphone, especially comedians.

It is no coincidence that the final deathblow for vaudeville came during the Depression. Though the industry was well on its way to oblivion by the early 1930s, the prevailing economic conditions ensured that it would not survive. The demand for shows fell sharply amidst the dire economic conditions, and theater owners resorted to cheaper fare. Straight films, absent any live acts, were much cheaper for theaters to supply. The result was the dramatic growth of the double feature and the extinction of the vaudeville show.

As vaudeville faded away, so did its thousands of performers who disappeared into the forgotten realms of history. A few, however, succeeded wildly by successfully transferring their act to new entertainment media. In fact, some of the best-known radio acts were little more than sound versions of vaudeville comedy and singing acts. George Burns and Gracie Allen, Jack Benny, and Fred Allen all transformed their comedy skits to the airwaves. Milton Berle and Ed Sullivan hosted variety shows that resembled vaudeville in style, if not form: a variety of performers, changing weekly, gathering together to entertain an audience. The difference, of course, was that the audience now numbered millions, and the act, once played on television, was pretty much played out. There wasn't much of a market left for it once it had been played to a national audience in one broadcast. A successful performer now had to have fresh material every week. This was too much for most, and the new venue killed off more. Not all performers could translate their act from the big stage to the small screen. Some were unable to adapt to the new methods required by the new medium—the different type of audience, the different type of sound and camera needs, and the fact that for television they were not a life-size act, but an eight-inch picture. On the radio, of course, actors who relied on facial and physical expressions to express themselves were unable to survive.

Recorded Sound

Prior to mass production of the phonograph, the piano had been the main source of music in the American home. Because of its size and cost, the piano was limited primarily to middle and upper income households. When the phonograph first debuted, it too was marketed at upper income households. Its price dropped rapidly, however, and it soon found a place in American homes of all income ranges, largely displacing the piano along the way.

The talking machine debuted to great fanfare. Demonstrations were arranged by the Edison Speaking Phonograph Company in and around New York City and were attended by thousands of curious souls who paid an admission fee to witness the latest invention from the Wizard of Menlo Park. The success of the demonstrations led to national tours of the machine, which was leased out to local entrepreneurs who charged for similar demonstrations in their towns. These lease arrangements were commercially successful early on, but ultimately the novelty of simply hearing a recording wore off. This meant that a different kind of marketing strategy was needed. The result would be the recording industry we know today, centered primarily around music (Gelatt 1977, Millard 1995, Sanjek 1996).

Inventor Eldridge Johnson founded the Victor Talking Machine Company in 1901. He had perfected his trade working for the Berliner company, an early rival of Edison's in the phonograph business. While it was Edison who invented the phonograph, it was Johnson's Victrola that became synonymous with the evolution of the industry.

The phonograph went through many changes, most in response to the demands of the marketplace. For example, as interest in recorded music grew, the demand for higher quality recordings grew. This led to a bifurcation of the market. Those producing the machines focused on increasing the quality of the sound and volume. Others focused on producing the recordings.

Standardization was the next important frontier. After getting machines into general usage, it was necessary to standardize the recordings so that they could be played on any machine. Initially, manufacturers believed that controlling the supply of recordings was the key to long-term profitability. To that end, they found it worthwhile to create a system in which recordings were machine dependent, that is, they could not be played on rival machines. This required that the manufacturer also be a recording studio (Hull 1998).

Manufacturers scrambled to sign up talented musicians to exclusive contracts in order to help sell their machines, which would then be the only source for the masses of listening to the music of world famous talents such as opera star Enrico Caruso.

Caruso is credited with turning the recording machine from the business application originally foreseen by Edison into a source of home entertainment. His first recordings for Victor, on their exclusive Red Seal label in 1902, proved to be so popular that they raised the status of the talking machine to the level of a musical instrument. It began to be sold in high end music stores along with pianos and violins, and was purchased by discriminating consumers who could afford it.

The recording industry began to decline in the 1920s, and from production to sales, the industry flagged. The basic problem was too many companies competing in a market that was already saturated. In 1914, 18 companies, with sales of $27 million, manufactured phonographs. Less than five years later, the industry had expanded to 166 companies with $158 million in sales. The expanding market and profit potential was only one factor enticing entrepreneurs. Another was the availability of patents, most of which had expired by 1917, thus removing a serous barrier to new entrants.

By the end of World War II, the number of recording companies would be drastically reduced, and by the end of the century, the industry concentration of global publishers would be so tight it would undergo several close looks by antitrust investigators. The production of phonographs has given way to CD players and electronic music devices, such as the iPod.

Recorded music and radio suffered through a love hate relationship. On the one hand, they competed against one another for the entertainment time and dollar of the American public. Early radio broadcasts were most likely to be live performances. This, however, was an expensive pursuit and as the availability and quality of recorded music improved, recorded music became more prevalent. This occasionally led to legal wrangles. Record companies objected to radio stations playing their discs on the air, which they clearly labeled "not licensed for radio broadcast." On the other hand, it was free publicity for their new songs, so the protests were often faint, as negotiations between the record companies and radio stations regarding the payment of rights fees would ultimately show. The industry would learn to see radio as a strong complement, eventually going so far as to eventually pay radio stations to play their music.

Radio and recording went from being substitutes for one another to complements in the entertainment industry. Each found that it profited from the other. Recordings were cheaper and more efficient than live performance as a source of entertainment for radio broadcasters, and radio broadcasts became the primary method of advertising a recording to its potential audience. A song gained popularity through repeated play over a wide network of radio stations and became a "must have" for the American buying public, which then sought out a copy of the recording for their own personal library (De Long 1980).

Radio stations began to move away from live and into recorded music as early as the mid-1920s. As technology improved the quality of transmitting recorded music, it eventually led to the elimination of stations employing musicians to provide live music. The lack of royalties grated on performers and publishers for decades, even after they saw the benefits radio had on their record sales (Douglas 1987).

The radio became the in-home entertainment choice during the Depression. The number of households with radios more than doubled from 12 million homes in 1930 to 25 million in 1935, whereas only about 500,000 phonographs were purchased during the decade ending in 1935. While cost considerations of the Depression first gave rise to the use of prerecorded entertainment by radio stations, it was the drafting of large numbers of performers for World War II that really pushed its use into the mainstream. With the paucity of performers available for live broadcasts, radio stations were forced to rely on prerecorded music only. What they discovered was that as long as the quality was good, listeners could not tell the difference, so they did not care (Fones-Wolf 1999, Lewis 1992).

The arrival of talking pictures in 1927 had a greater impact on the recording industry than just introducing new technology. It also changed the market structure of the industry. The movies produced popular music, which recording companies wanted to sell. The rights to the music now in demand by the public belonged to the movie companies, which soon recognized a good market opportunity, and instead of partnering with the record producers, they took them over. Warner Brothers purchased a recording studio in 1930, consolidating the process. It now owned the music performed in its films, and it produced the recordings the film-going public grew to love. In turn, it promoted its music on its radio stations, just in case somebody had not already heard it in the movie theater. Warner Brothers grew from a nearly bankrupt $10 million company in 1927 to a $230 million corporate behemoth three short years later.

With the dawning of the Depression, more radio stations were willing to use recorded music in place of the more expensive live versions, though the two national networks at the time, CBS and NBC, held out longer in their policy against "canned music." The first crack in their defense was the recording of shows. which originally aired live on their stations. They tended to record these on discs, as they were convenient, durable, and easily transportable to other stations. It also provided for a cheap way to rebroadcast popular shows at a later time and even turn them into a source of income by leasing them to non-network stations in the future. During the 1930s, the radio networks became the major users of recorded sound technology. Today, little music is broadcast live on the radio.

During the 1940s, the prominence of recorded entertainment grew to the point where 75 percent of all broadcasts over radio were recordings. This era gave birth to the "disk jockey," the live broadcaster who chatted to, or sometimes with (via call-ins), the audience in between introducing recorded songs to play. This format still exists today in most markets, although it has been replaced in some stations with totally prerecorded entertainment, without the benefit of any actual person in the studio (Eliot 1989).

The role of local disc jockeys increased in importance through the 1950s. They were the source of most of the new music heard by the consumer. This market shift led easily from providing free music to radio stations to directly paying disc jockeys to favor certain recordings on the air. This "payola" scheme involved cash and material goods, spread to thousands of disc jockeys, cost the publishers millions of dollars, and ultimately led to restraint of trade charges against the major publishers (Mol and Wijnberg 2007).

Paying for the privilege of getting a song performed did not originate with radio. "Plugging," as it was known, was a scandal in the vaudeville industry. Performers were paid to include certain songs in their acts. Among publishers, the popularity of plugging eventually became a Frankenstein monster. The price of popularizing a song could exceed its total sales revenue if a bidding war for popular talent erupted and the song did not catch on as hoped. If plugging was not purchased, the song would be less likely to achieve "hit" status. Plugging, however, did not guarantee a hit. It just meant that more of the publisher's profits were being paid to performers.

The military was the source of many new techniques in recording technology. Its efforts to improve communications, preserve messages, and capture sounds from the enemy were valuable defense tools during World War II and were transferred to profitable improvements in home and theater entertainment after the war. Among the many innovations that owe at least their genesis to the military was magnetic tape recording, which in time became the music industry's cassette tape. Cassettes were first produced commercially in the 1940s, shortly after the end of World War II.

The Phillips Company introduced the compact cassette in 1964 and did not protect it as a proprietary technology. The cassette recorder became the technology of choice in the mid-1970s. It remained a mainstay and central feature of stereo systems until the compact disk (CD) began to replace both it and records. Currently, CDs are being replaced by electronic music, which can be directly downloaded onto computers and hand held devices like the iPod and smartphones.

The introduction of MTV in 1981 created a new era in sound. Now music became a video show as well. The cooperation of Time-Warner and American Express created it as one of the first dedicated cable television channels catering to a small but homogenous audience. Television took over where movies and radio had preceded it in the promotion of musical tastes, and it proved to be much more powerful. Because of its reach and its audience of baby boomers prone to buy music, MTV turned good songs into hits virtually overnight.

Like the radio stations that received free records in return for publicizing music, MTV did not pay to produce or broadcast its videos. The videos were provided by the artists and publishers. The cost of a music video was much greater than a record, but the results could be fantastic. A 1982 survey of retail record dealers by *Billboard* found that new acts debuting on MTV could expect an immediate 10 to 15 percent increase in album sales.

The success of MTV led to imitators, such as VH1 and the Nashville Network. Some were 24-hour dedicated music channels; others featured music video programming. The market became more competitive and a familiar pattern emerged. Established artists could now sell their videos to television stations and then benefit additionally from the sale of their music promoted by the video. A new artist would pay to finance his own video and then through a major distributor hope to strike a deal that would get it aired on television just to get the exposure that would give him the break he needed.

The CD debuted in 1982 as an expensive, upper end alternative to records. It featured higher quality sound, and the standard 4.5-inch disc could hold much more music, up to 75 minutes, than a record. The absence of physical contact during playback meant the discs would never wear out. By the end of the twentieth century, less than 10 percent of recorded music sales were long play record albums (LPs). Most of it was CDs. Not only had the CD made record albums obsolete, it was in danger of being eclipsed itself by music stored directly onto electronic devices. There is nothing to record on, just a collection of electrons stored for personal use. And the vast quantities of music that can be stored on these pocket-sized devices is virtually limitless.

Digital sound has come to the forefront of the industry, and the greatest challenge facing it is how to retain control over the recorded product once it is produced. Computer file sharing systems like Napster and handheld devices like the iPod have revolutionized the industry. Listeners can share music files over the internet and download libraries of music onto their computers and handheld devices, bypassing the marketplace altogether. While this type of music sharing violates U.S. copyright laws, it is difficult to enforce these laws and expensive to monitor the sharing of music (Liebowitz 2006).

Despite changes in the types of music preferred by the listening public and the different means of delivering music, the industry looks remarkably like it did a century ago. The main issues are still the same. Manufacturers seek to push the envelope and deliver the highest quality sound possible. Performers still strive to express themselves through their art. Producers compete for the opportunity to promote and distribute the best-selling stars, and consumers clamor for the best equipment on which to listen to the best music. Despite all the advances in technology, or perhaps because of them, the same problem besets all the players in the industry: how to control the rights to the final product. The dawning of the computer age in the recorded sound industry is not likely to solve this problem, only to complicate it.

The Movies

At the dawn of the twentieth century, the movie industry was dominated not by movie stars, directors, and producers, but by inventors and businessmen. Since then, while the power in the industry has ebbed and flowed from the stars to the studio executives to the agencies, the spotlight has never faded from the movie stars who have captured the imagination and adulation of the public eye.

On April 14, 1894, the first Kinetoscope parlor opened in New York City. It was a machine that allowed one person to peer through what looked like a pair of binoculars to view a short moving picture with no sound. Within a year, Kinetoscopes were popping up in storefronts of their own and as attractions in stores, hotels, and saloons in major cities across the country and abroad.

Within two years, the motion picture projector was simultaneously introduced by the Lumiere brothers in France and by Thomas Edison in the United States. Edison put his, called a Vitascope, to a public test for the first time on April 23, 1896. The projector began displacing the Kinetoscope and quickly transformed the industry into what we would recognize today as a "movie," at least in form if not content.

Businessmen, particularly the inventors themselves, were quick to recognize the commercial promise of the Kinetoscope. They moved to monopolize the potential profits by tying up the technology necessary for making and displaying the pictures. The early years of the movie industry were dominated by patent battles and lawsuits. The industry paid little attention to the actual movies that were made, focusing instead on controlling the means of making and displaying them. In fact, such little regard was given to the quality and substance of the movies themselves that they were sold by the foot. Films were valued only by how long they ran and how new they were, not by the actual content.

The first distribution companies appeared in 1902. They dealt in films; not producing them, but simply distributing existing films among theaters to maximize the profitability both of the film, by ensuring it got the widest circulation possible, and the exhibitors, by ensuring that they got a steady supply of fresh material. Within five years, about 150 such distributors were in business across the country. Within two decades, a mere eight would control the entire film industry.

Once a steady stream of films could be ensured, permanent theaters appeared. Harry and John Davis opened the first one in Pittsburgh in 1905. Within a year, more than 1,000 opened across the country, and by 1910 there were more than 10,000.

Films were demanded by consumers because they were new and had not yet been seen, not because they had exciting storylines or featured favorite actors or special effects. As new films were released, interest in older films decreased. These films were then sent to smaller theaters, in smaller towns, where they had yet to be viewed. To this day, that is how the release schedule of films works. New films open in the largest theaters in the biggest markets, where they can play to the greatest number of people, at the highest possible prices, in the shortest period of time. After they have exhausted the demand in these markets, they move on to successively smaller and more remote markets. The difference now, of course, is that films are marketed for their plot, stars, and special effects, not simply because they are new.

The increasing sophistication and size of the market quickly led to specialization and division of labor, which are key ingredients in efficient and cheap production. The industry soon could be divided into the three major sectors that still exist today: the production of films, the distribution of films, and the exhibition of films.

The legal battles involving patents came to a head in 1908 with the organization of the Motion Picture Patents Corporation (MPPC). It was formed through a horizontal merger of 10 major companies that held most of the important industry patents.

In 1910, a vertical merger combined the production and distribution levels of the industry. The MPPC purchased 68 distribution companies and merged them into one company, called the General Film Company (GFC). This created a virtual monopoly in the production and distribution sectors of the industry. The exhibition level of the industry was still extremely competitive, with more than 10,000 theaters in operation. The theaters were forced into exclusive dealings with the GFC out of fear of being blackballed if they were caught showing films from one of the few remaining independent distributors.

The film trust composed of the MPPC and GFC, however, did not last long. Innovation is not the strongpoint of a monopolist, and it certainly was not for the film trust. Their failure to anticipate market changes ultimately led to their demise. Primary among those changes was the evolution of the movie star system, the use of famous actors to market a film, and the metamorphosis of the industry from a novelty, showing generic motion pictures, to one telling stories. In addition to a changing market, the MPPC was found to be in violation of antitrust law and was dissolved in 1918 (Thomas 1971).

By this time the industry had matured. The films being produced were more than mere motion pictures. They had grown into feature films with compelling plots and well-developed characters, that featured recognized movie stars, and that were created by well-known directors. The film talent was now in a position of power, able to extract economic concessions from the front office businessmen. In short, the system looked much like it does today. Stars were in high demand by both the public and the film studios seeking to employ them in profitable films. One major difference between the industry in 1920 and today was the absence of sound. Until 1927, all pictures were silent. Dialogue could be read but not heard.

The first commercially successful combination of sound and film, known as synchronized sound because it was produced along with the picture and not accompanied by a pianist or orchestra in the theater, was in *Don Juan*, produced in 1926. The soundtrack consisted of orchestral music only, no talking. It was, however, a harbinger of things to come. Once the technology was perfected to allow for the synchronization of sound and picture, adding the live voices of actors was next. The red-letter day for sound in the movie industry was October 6, 1927. On this day, the first movie with spoken dialogue debuted. *The Jazz Singer*, produced by Warner Brothers, featured only limited dialogue but had a cataclysmic impact on the industry. Al Jolson proved to be prophetic when he uttered the first spoken words heard in a movie: "Wait a minute, you ain't heard nothin' yet." Sound quickly took over the industry. In just two years, the number of sound movies released outnumbered the number of silent films, and by 1932, 98 percent of all films had sound. A new era had dawned for movies, and it forever changed the landscape of the industry.

Sound was only one of the cataclysmic changes at the end of the 1920s that dramatically changed the industry, swinging the balance of power once again in favor of the executives at the expense of the actors. Only the largest studios could afford the conversion to sound, which required huge capital outlays. As a result, mergers occurred or smaller distributors simply went out of business. The studio era had dawned (Eyman 1997).

Vertical integration of the movie industry was beginning to reappear. This time, it focused on the exhibition end of the industry as well as the production end. Distribution companies were purchasing movie theaters so that they would have a guaranteed market for their product. By 1928, the top eight studios owned over 1600 movie theaters. While this represented only a fraction of the total theaters in the industry, it was a majority of the first-run theaters in the largest cities. Independent theater owners, who were primarily located in smaller, second-run markets, could not afford to gamble that sound was more than a fad. They had to wait until the turning point came, when it was obvious sound was here to stay. In the meantime, they were only able to show silent films (Balio 1993, Gomery 1980, Hanssen 2010).

The return to an integrated industry was made possible by a number of factors, among them the economies of scale resulting from technological changes in the industry, the shift in the balance of power from actors back to studio executives as a result of sound, and the economic hardships of the Depression.

The change in the balance of power and the onset of the Depression changed the status of contracts with actors. Instead of being signed to make individual pictures with various companies depending on their time and interest, actors were signed to long-term contracts with studios, who then used their stable of stars to produce pictures built around the talent at hand. These actors and directors were paid annual salaries, and their contracts often specified a minimum and maximum number of films they would be required to make. The actors became fixed costs in a production process. This was a much better deal for the studio executives than for the actors, who lost their bargaining power. Actors sought comfort in long-term contracts, which protected them from the uncertainty of the new talking picture format as well as the cruelty of the Depression. This was no small concession during a period when up to 25 percent of the labor force was unemployed (Pokorny and Sedgwick 2001, 2010, Sedgwick and Pokorny 2005).

Double features were popularized during the Depression as a way to get more patrons in the theater. Prior to this, the typical format was a feature film, a newsreel, and a few shorts. In 1931, about 10 percent of theaters showed double features; by the end of the studio era in 1947, more than 60 percent did.

It was the rise of television that spelled the end for the double feature and the B movie. The mid-1950s also saw the return of antitrust legislation, which forced diversification of the major studios and dissolved the contract arrangements they had with the stars. As the era of "free agency" in talent returned, the B picture was priced out of the market. Finally, with so many entertainment options opening up in the postwar boom, consumers began to demand quality instead of mere quantity for their dollar. The cost of supplying B pictures increased, their demand waned, and a chapter of American movie history drew to a close. The industry was going through another major organizational shift, the last one of the century.

However, the distribution arm of the industry was what remained in control of the studios, and ironically, it was what kept the industry an oligopoly. As the market shrank in the face of changing American entertainment patterns, the presence of the distribution arm became more important, and it was more difficult for a newcomer to enter the industry. While the number of independent producers increased over time, the number of distributors did not. By the mid-1970s, the major studios had captured 90 percent of total box office revenues, approximately the same percentage as they controlled during the studio era. Today the top six studios account for more than 80 percent of box office revenues.

By the 1970s, the industry had evolved into its present-day form, with the major studios operating essentially as bankers and distributors. They provide the financing to independent producers in return for the rights to distribute their pictures. Some own production stages that they lease or use primarily for television production. While they do not control the industry from top to bottom as they once did, distributors still represent the least competitive sector of the industry. Few of them exist, and until a method of distributing films is developed that can bypass the old studios, all producers and theaters must deal with them.

The movie industry is one of prognostication. A typical studio will release an average of 30 to 40 movies in a year, and its fortunes usually rest on one or two blockbusters. Without one, it is unlikely the studio will make a profit. With an *Avatar*, bonuses will flow and careers will be made. Hot new actors and directors will emerge, with agents commanding and earning higher salaries for them in their future pictures. Nobody has yet been able to predict the film market on a regular basis. Eventually the hot actor or director will turn out a film the audience simply does not like, and the studio holding the bag will pay (De Vany and Walls 1999).

A movie is generally released in theaters before it is available on demand or DVD because the theater is the way to generate the greatest amount of revenue in the shortest amount of time. In the movie business, time is money. The entire cost of a movie is borne before any tickets can be sold. With an elapsed time from beginning until release of one to two years, it is critical that the studio recoup the money it invested as quickly as possible. As technology evolves and the availability of on-line movies reaches a greater percentage of American households, it is likely that on-demand viewing will become a more important source of income, perhaps displacing the theater as the quickest and best source of revenue for studios (Jozefowicz, Kelley, and Brewer 2008).

The arrival of television was at first thought to be the death knell for the movie industry. Television was seen as a substitute for the movies, and since it was much cheaper and more convenient, it was felt TV would completely displace movies. Television was a substitute in some ways, but not completely. In many ways, it has served as a complement to the movie industry. Network and cable television have become havens for recycled older movies. Pay per view and movie channels (HBO, Showtime, etc.) have become alternate outlets for movies just off the theater circuit. While there is a segment of the market for which television and the theater are close substitutes, there are always people who are not willing to wait and will go to the theater, in large part because the movie theater is part of a social experience and an evening of entertainment (Balio 1990, Epstein 2005).

The motion picture industry has matured from a fledgling storefront curiosity to a multi-billion dollar entertainment industry over the course of the twentieth century. In the process, it has embedded itself into the culture and fabric of American life. Over the course of roughly 100 years, technology has changed the movie industry, and the movie industry has changed American culture. The industry has survived a depression, two world wars, and the technological revolutions of sound, color, television, and the computer. Each has only added an outlet to the industry and strengthened it, rather than diminished it. The movies are an everyday part of our lives and are likely to continue as such, adapting to future technological changes as readily as they have in the past.

Radio

Radio changed America in the twentieth century the way the computer has revolutionized it today. It brought an immediacy to the news that had heretofore not existed. The telegraph wire reduced the time it took for news to travel from point to point, but it still had to be gathered by newspapers and converted to print before being distributed to the general public. Radio brought the news directly into the homes of listeners.

Three men are largely responsible for the development of the radio industry: Two inventors, Lee de Forest and Howard Armstrong, along with David Sarnoff, an RCA executive. De Forest invented the audion tube, which made radio transmission possible. Armstrong invented the superheterodyne, which increased the amplitude of the broadcasts and turned AM broadcasts into a national industry. Armstrong also invented FM radio, although he never lived to see its commercial success. While Sarnoff did not invent any hardware, he essentially invented the industry. He was responsible for organizing and marketing the radio and television industries, from the construction and sale of sets to the broadcast of programs and the invention of improvements. Even though he was not an engineer, Sarnoff was arguably the most influential man in the radio industry (Lewis 1991).

The advantage of wireless communication was the ability to bypass wires. The drawback was that it was not completely private because anyone with a receiver tuned in to the specific frequency of the transmission could receive it. The inventions of de Forest and Armstrong exploited this drawback and created the concept of "broadcasting" a signal to a wide audience. From this concept evolved the word *radio*, which signifies the radiation of waves from a transmitter. A new era and a new social construct were soon to be born. Radio would revolutionize the world (Aitken 1985).

Armstrong and de Forest were antagonists. While both of their inventions were necessary for the development of wireless communication, and radio in particular, and the inventions were symbiotic, neither man liked the other. They spent most of their lives and much of their fortunes in court fighting over patents. By the time the Supreme Court finally found in favor of de Forest, much to the incredulity of the scientific community, the patents had long expired, and both men had exhausted huge amounts of money. While the inventors fought, RCA, under the direction of Sarnoff, reaped the profits by shrewdly acquiring the licenses to the competing claims. By the time the fight ended, de Forest was ruined financially and Armstrong was ruined emotionally.

Armstrong would ultimately commit suicide 20 years later after losing another patent case, this one to RCA.

David Sarnoff built RCA into the dominant firm in the radio industry by purchasing all of the important patents. Some have likened Sarnoff to a self-aggrandizing thief, but he did oversee the most powerful media company in the first half of the twentieth century and pioneered its growth from a small participant in the electronics industry to an industry giant. By the early 1920s, RCA controlled the radio industry, holding more than 2,000 key patents. No radio could be made or sold in the United States without using RCA technology. In fact, over 90 percent of the world's radios were sold under license to RCA. In addition to radio, RCA would eventually play a leading role in television and the movies, launching the National Broadcasting Corporation (NBC) as one of its many progenies (Lippmann 2007, McChesney 1993).

The radio allowed Americans access to news and entertainment from the privacy of their living rooms. No longer was it necessary to go out to the crowds or travel great distances (made greater by the primitive transportation and more rural population of 1920s America) to be entertained. Now it was available from home, and at no cost beyond that of the initial price of the radio. Commercial broadcasting was a liberating innovation for millions of Americans, and it changed the pattern of life. At once, the radio made it possible to unify the country as a whole as well as emphasize its differences. This was accomplished when the population listened to the same things. Much of the country listened to Amos and Andy together at the same time each week. On the other end of the spectrum, cultural differences became popularized. Bluegrass music, for example, moved out of Kentucky to the rest of the country via radio broadcasts. Idealists saw the radio as the great equalizing medium. It would allow for the education of the masses via the broadcast of cultural events such as lectures, operas, and classical concerts to those previously unable to gain access to them.

The commercialization of radio was the brainchild of Walter Gifford, president of AT&T. In an effort to establish a foothold in the broadcasting business, AT&T used its considerable telephone muscle. It first established a high watt radio station, WEAF in Manhattan, and then used its telephone model to finance the station. When a telephone call was made, the caller paid for the time used, and AT&T applied the same principle to the radio waves. AT&T set up its station and invited any and all to come and rent airtime, to say what they wanted during a broadcast that would reach hundreds of thousands of potential listeners. Customers flocked to the idea called "toll broadcasting," among them Macy's and Gimbel's department stores. To fill the empty time between paid broadcasts, Gifford hired people to sing, play piano, lecture, and otherwise entertain. The model for radio, and eventually television broadcasting, was set: scheduled interruptions of paid advertisements.

The concept of networking was slightly ahead of the technology necessary to fully exploit it. As AT&T increased its broadcast business by adding more stations, they pioneered another innovation: the synchronized broadcasting of programming over multiple stations. The technology for relaying signals through the airwaves had not yet been perfected, but AT&T overcame this problem by sending the signal over its phone lines, where the stations picked them up for broadcast locally. In this way, the first true network was born. As technology improved, the phone lines were ultimately rendered obsolete, and synchronized broadcasting through the airwaves became the norm.

Government oversight of the airwaves began before the commercialization of the medium into the broadcasting industry we know today. Even so, government regulation of the airwaves came to Europe far earlier. The first international treaty governing use of the airwaves was signed by European nations in 1903. The United States did not consider such regulation necessary and refused to sign the treaty. The wireless industry was in flux, with seemingly continual groundbreaking inventions coming forth. It was possible technology might solve the problem for the politicians. Moreover, a thorny issue was raised: How does one regulate and assign property rights to airwaves?

The United States passed the Radio Act in 1912. This law required that all operators of radio equipment be licensed, wavelength access be allocated between users, distress calls be given preferential treatment, and the secretaries of commerce and labor be empowered to grant licenses and make other necessary regulations as they saw fit. Amateur radio operators were allowed to listen in on any frequency but could broadcast only on the lowest wavelengths, heretofore considered useless.

This government involvement determined the direction radio would take. The allocation of airwave space clearly favored military and commercial interests over those of amateurs. Amateurs were allocated the least desirable wavelengths and were

forced to share them among the great number of operators in existence at the time. Thus, the allotted amateur band was over-
crowded. The next step was to allocate power maximums. In
1923, Congress divided radio stations into three classes: high,
medium and low power. The high power stations went to the
major corporations for their broadcasts. These were the most
desirable and least congested, and they consequently became the
dominant stations. AT&T, General Electric, and Westinghouse,
not surprisingly, benefited the most from this allocation. This pattern of regulation perpetuated by the regulated companies continued with future legislation, which inevitably benefited the
large commercial broadcasters to the detriment of the small
broadcasters. The nature of the history of radio broadcasting
was thus largely determined by the large corporations. This was
the result of the tendency of government to consult closely with
the experts in the field when making regulatory decisions, and
those experts invariably included the leaders of the most prominent firms in the radio industry. As a result, the likes of David Sarnoff played an important part in determining the regulations
under which RCA was governed (Kruse 2002).

The radio industry changed the way Americans communi-
cated, relaxed, received their news, and ultimately lived. It has
survived changing lifestyles and revolutionary technology, and
it still thrives today. According to the Bureau of Labor Statistics
(BLS), nearly $8 billion is spent on radio advertising each year
on approximately 10,000 stations broadcasting over the airwaves
and computers. It appears that reports of its demise in the face
of modern technology are greatly exaggerated.

Television

Television is ubiquitous. It shapes our lives: whether it is influenc-
ing the outcome of elections, bringing the horror of catastrophe
into our living rooms, entertaining, or educating us. It has made
an indelible mark on American society. Television changed the
concept and availability of entertainment. Americans could sit at
home and choose from several television shows to entertain them.
Over time, the number of choices grew to the hundreds. Not until
recently, with the increasing popularity of home computers and
high speed internet access, has a technology impacted entertainment the way television did.

The invention of television was essentially a two-man race between Philo Farnsworth and Vladimir Zworykin. Farnsworth, working with a small staff in a ramshackle laboratory in San Francisco, received the first patent in 1927 for electronic television, which would eventually become the industry standard. At the same time, scores of other inventors and corporate research teams were trying to develop a television device. Most of them, however, were pursuing a mechanical approach, as opposed to the Farnsworth electronic system. None of them were to prove workable (Barnouw 1968).

The other major player was the Radio Corporation of America (RCA). Their television research team was headed by Vladimir Zworykin, a Russian immigrant and a scientific genius. Farnsworth and Zworykin spent nearly two decades in a technological race to perfect television. It was a classic matchup, pitting the underdog Farnsworth, a self-taught tinkerer, against Zworykin, a model of the well-financed twentieth-century corporate research machine. While Farnsworth would ultimately come to be recognized as the Father of Television, this outcome was far from certain at the time. He overcame RCA in the laboratory by developing a workable television and battled them in the courtroom over the rights to the patents covering his inventions.

In 1935, Farnsworth scored his biggest legal victory when he successfully sued RCA for patent infringement. In July of that year, the patent courts sided with him, proclaiming him the true inventor of television, acknowledging that his patents superseded those of Zworykin and RCA. This victory acknowledged the accomplishments of Farnsworth but did not stop RCA's commercialization plans.

In 1947, Farnsworth's most valuable patents expired, and his ability to receive royalties from them disappeared as well. He still held over 100 television-related patents, but none as valuable as his original patents, which were now public domain. His chance at cashing in on untold riches from his invention expired just as the television craze was about to begin.

Both NBC and CBS began regularly scheduled commercial broadcasts on July 1, 1941, and it appeared the television industry was set to take off. However, it ground to a halt with the bombing of Pearl Harbor and was mothballed until after the war as the government suspended most television broadcasting in the spring of 1942.

Networks were established in the 1920s for radio and were transformed into television networks in the 1940s and 1950s. Each of the three major networks had about 200 affiliates by the end of the century. The relatively newer Fox and WB network have about half as many. The networks no longer dominate the industry. Their share of the audience has decreased from over 80 percent as recently as 1980 to less than 30 percent by the early twenty-first century.

Bill Paley, the first president of CBS, invented the affiliate system that now prevails in both the radio and television industries. The early model, pioneered by NBC, was for the network to charge affiliates to receive its programming. The affiliates could then air popular shows produced by the network, attract listeners, and sell local advertising. Paley took the opposite approach. He attracted greater numbers of stations to the CBS network by paying the affiliates to receive broadcasting exclusively from CBS. Paley then sold national advertising to national brands, which were able to reach vast audiences provided by the large numbers of local stations that Paley attracted. The local stations also set aside time to sell their own advertising. The system was carried over to television when it was commercialized and prevails to this day (Baughman 1997).

American Broadcasting Corporation (ABC) was formed by a divestiture of the NBC radio network, when RCA was forced by the Federal Communications Commission (FCC) to divest itself of one of its two networks. Edward J. Noble, chief executive officer (CEO) of Beech-Nut Life Savers, Inc., branched into broadcasting with the purchase of the network in 1943.

DuMont formed a television network in 1945. DuMont was originally a firm that manufactured television sets. It was a relative newcomer to the industry, having been founded only in 1931. When the FCC began accepting applications for television broadcast licenses, DuMont diversified into the broadcasting business.

DuMont and latecomer ABC fought for the dubious distinction of being the third viable weak sister in the network scheme (which allocated three stations to the largest markets, UHF being the third in 60 percent of the largest 50 markets). ABC gained a better position when they merged with United Paramount Theaters, the chain of theaters sold off by Paramount during the divestiture move of the late 1940s. DuMont, which did not have the radio relationships the other three networks used to sign up affiliates, finally ceased to operate in 1955, leaving the television landscape settled for the next generation, until the technology of cable and satellite created the next upheaval.

In the early years of television, production was concentrated in New York City. Hollywood was still primarily focused on movies. In fact, the predominant attitude at the movie studios was that TV was a fad that would soon go away. Little if any television production took place in Hollywood, and few movie actors crossed over to television. Movie theaters neither cooperated with TV stations nor did business with them. They viewed television as a potential competitor but not a serious one likely to last long.

The growth of original television programming was due in part to the reticence shown by Hollywood toward television. Studios prevented networks from rebroadcasting original films on television. The result was the growth of original dramatic programming on the television networks. With a need for programming, the networks clamored to hire writers, creating an entire new industry niche for television writers, one that would eventually flourish into a specialty of its own.

Early shows tended to be supported by a sponsor in their entirety, rather than selling commercial time piecemeal. The first successful situation comedy (sitcom) was *Mama*, airing on CBS for eight years beginning in 1949. Before becoming a successful television show, it was a hit on Broadway and in the movie theater as *I Remember Mama*. The show was sponsored by Maxwell House Coffee, and as was common in those pioneering days of television, the show sponsor had more control over the content of the show than did the network.

Another standard of television is the newscast. The first regular newscast was launched in 1949. The *Camel News Caravan*, anchored by John Cameron Swayze, began its nightly 15-minute broadcasts from New York City, still the center of network news broadcasts (Conway 2009).

Along with the growth of television newscasts came the growth of live news events. It is difficult to imagine, in this day of 24-hour news networks and on-the-spot reporting, that live coverage of major events was ever novel for television. However, only in 1951 did the first live coverage of a congressional hearing take place, when cameras were allowed in the Senate chambers for the first time to televise Senator Estes Kefauver chairing the committee investigating organized crime. Even more dramatic, in 1954, the same cameras elevated Senator Joseph McCarthy to national celebrity in his crusade to oust communists from America. The power of television to make and break celebrities virtually overnight is commonplace today, but it was a new and powerful force in its infancy, one that was only beginning to be understood.

The Eisenhower administration realized the vast potential for television to aid the president in communicating his message to the American public. Eisenhower held the first live presidential press conference in 1956 in San Francisco, where he announced he would run for reelection later that year. While the power of television was understood, it was not yet mastered. Perhaps the most famous example of the power of television in a political race is the 1960 presidential debates between John F. Kennedy and Richard Nixon. Kennedy used the medium well, while Nixon did not, and the difference has often been cited as an important factor in the close Kennedy victory.

Politicians were not the only ones who could be turned into instant stars. Before television, an entertainer had to work his or her way up from the bottom, working local circuits and vacation resorts before eventually landing a spot in the big vaudeville revues. By the time the top was reached, the act was practiced and refined, and the entertainer was a veteran of the circuit. With television, all that changed. Now a green performer, thrust onto television in the *Ed Sullivan Show* or the *Amateur Hour* could suddenly capture the attention of the nation in one brief moment. Careers could now be launched with one good appearance, where the performer would command a larger audience than a lifetime of vaudeville circuits could ever provide. The meteoric rise and decline of stars became commonplace. Some, like Elvis Presley, would rise and stay at the top. Others, like Julias La Rosa, a young Brooklyn singer who rocketed to fame on *Arthur Godfrey and His Friends*, burned brightly and briefly before fading into obscurity. This trend continues with the brief celebrity status enjoyed by participants on today's reality shows.

In the 1950s, most television broadcasts were live. As the ability to record shows became economically feasible, live broadcasts quickly faded in favor of videotape. In 1953, more than 80 percent of all television broadcasts were live. By 1965, only 25 percent of broadcasts were live, and these were dominated by newscasts. By 1974, 90 percent of all prime-time television viewing originated on video. Aside from sports and news programs, videotape is the industry standard today, though it is being replaced by electronic storage. This will change the method of storage but not the fact that little on television is broadcast live anymore.

Another change brought about by the transformation to videotape was the creation of reruns. By the beginning of the 1960s, summer reruns, as we know them, were the norm. While regular programs today are rebroadcast during the "summer rerun period," that was not originally the case. During the summer break, replacement shows were offered instead of reruns of the season originals.

Interestingly, early critics and network executives were convinced that television was different than radio and the movies in its attractiveness to audiences. They were sure that its success lay not in imitating radio, with regular weekly shows centered around the same theme, setting, or characters as radio had done, but rather with live, spectacular shows, more like vaudeville or a concert. This "big events" philosophy was perceived to be the key that would sustain television.

Not all executives thought this way, and it was CBS, behind its president Frank Stanton, that first pioneered the regular weekly broadcast. Stanton correctly predicted that regular broadcasts of the same show on the same day and time each week would become events around which people would plan their entertainment schedules. This was not exactly a novel idea, as it had been the format successfully used by the radio networks (owned by the same companies). For nearly 20 years, the *Jack Benny Show* had been a staple on Sunday night. It led all other radio shows in the ratings in the postwar years until Benny eventually moved to television, where he proved a success as well.

Cable television's roots go back to the 1940s, when it served as a means for communities in geographically remote areas to receive a better signal. Television signals do not travel far, and they cannot go through mountains. This created reception problems in certain areas. The answer was a signal delivered through a cable instead of over the air.

The earliest cable systems were created in towns where the geographic terrain made over-the-air reception difficult or impossible. Early cable bore little resemblance to today's multichannel offerings. It offered little more than a retransmission of over-the-air network broadcasts, with the occasional addition of a local access channel and perhaps a text channel, such as the Associated Press (AP) scroll or an early weather channel that broadcast pressure and temperature along with wind gauges for current local conditions. Cable remained small and insignificant for a number of years. The total number of cable TV subscribers did not reach 1 million until 1963. Intense lobbying from the networks kept cable a small and unimportant player in the market through various FCC regulations that, for example, restricted the distance that signals could be transmitted for relay over cable systems and prohibited carrying movies less than a decade old or sporting events that had been broadcast by the networks in the previous five years (Batten 2002, Comstock 1989, Eisemann 2000).

In 1970, Ted Turner introduced the concept of the super station, when he convinced cable systems outside of Atlanta to carry his independent Atlanta station, WTCG (Watch This Channel Grow). He felt a larger audience would make it easier to sell advertising. Distant cable systems took interest in his channel because they had excess capacity to carry additional broadcasts. Imitating the success of Turner, who ultimately renamed the station TBS (Turner Broadcasting System), were WGN of Chicago, owned by the Chicago Tribune newspaper, and then the ultimate cable innovation, HBO (Home Box Office), which for the first time sold premium television subscriptions to movies and other broadcasting without commercial interruption.

The distribution of signals to the local cable operators was originally via microwave, and they were neither high quality nor reliable. As a result, cable operators were eager to move into the newest technology: satellite distribution. Local cable systems function like local stations in that they provide access to the signal, which they receive via satellite. A local cable system makes the physical hookup to the household and delivers a digital signal to the household. The household then receives a variety of cable network programming, as well as digital versions of broadcast network shows.

Cable evolved as a local monopoly because most municipalities did not want competing cable systems to duplicate overhead wires or tear up streets on multiple occasions so that each could lay its own cable. Instead, most cities granted a local monopoly to one cable system. In return, the local government received some concessions, such as a percentage of the gross revenues and local access channels.

Since it was a government-granted monopoly, the cable system was heavily regulated from the beginning. Subscription rates, access, quality and quantity of service, and channel authorization were all subject to government oversight. In 1984, cable companies lodged a protest against what they claimed was unfair regulation. They cited the increased competition in the television industry from other technologies, such as television signals carried by telephone companies, over-the-air broadcast networks, and home satellite systems. At this time, the broadcast networks still dominated the airwaves. They had more than 73 percent (ABC, CBS, and NBC represented 73%) of the market, in part because cable was not available in about half the country, including several of the largest cities where over-the-air broadcasts were readily available.

After the passage of the Cable Communications Policy Act of 1984, which deregulated service pricing, the cable industry was the dominant television provider in America, with over half of all homes with televisions subscribing to some sort of cable service. Subscription fees today represent 80 percent of cable's revenue, with only 20 percent coming from advertising. In recent years, satellite television has begun to grow to a point where it now controls about a quarter of the market. Like cable, satellite is a subscription service. The only difference is how the signal is transmitted: through a cable, or via the airwaves.

In 1987, the cable companies received the deregulation they requested. The FCC ruled that any city where three or more over-the-air broadcast stations could be received was sufficiently competitive to allow for deregulation. This involved 97 percent of U.S. households. Since deregulation, consumer complaints have risen. Cable revenue has more than doubled, as have rates. Less than 1 percent of households are located in a market with competing cable systems. The most feared competitor has not been over-the-air broadcasters, who now account for less than a third of the market, but satellite dish systems, which now control about a quarter of the market.

Deregulation of the cable industry has not been all bad. While rates skyrocketed, so did the number of available channels. The average cable system increased its offerings from 27 to more than 200 channels. The per-channel cost of subscription has actually decreased slightly when adjusted for inflation. On the down side, several of the channels in any system are purely advertising, or infomercial channels, like the Home Shopping Network and QVC. Many subscribers do not consider such channels positive additions to their packages. Competition does work. In markets with competing cable systems, the cost of subscribing is just over half that found in systems with no competition.

Regulation returned to the industry in 1992. Exclusive contracts between cable companies and cable networks were prohibited. In addition, the definition of the competition needed to avoid reregulation was changed from three over-the-air broadcast stations to six, significant competition from another television system, or "good behavior" by the cable company. Cable companies side-stepped rate regulation by offering tiered service. The basic cable package included the over-the-air networks and a small selection of less popular cable stations and was regulated, while the tiered packages of "extras" generally escaped regulation. These tiers included the most popular cable networks, such as CNN, ESPN, and TBS, not to mention the numerous specialty networks like the History Channel, Food TV, and MTV.

As a science, television is complex. As a business enterprise, it is rather straightforward; it is an advertising medium. Networks and local stations sell airtime to national and local advertisers and in return deliver viewers. Nielson, the television ratings service, measures the number and demographic details of the viewers. This is valuable information to advertisers looking to buy commercial time on television broadcasts. Ultimately, television programming is little more than scheduled interruptions of advertising messages, rather than the other way around.

The movie and television industries enjoy a symbiotic relationship. The movie industry supplies much of the talent and facilities used to produce television shows, and television serves as an important ancillary market for the movie industry. Movies are shown on television as pay-per-view, pay cable, cable, and network broadcasts at various times in the life cycle of a motion picture.

Although they do compete with one another for the leisure time of consumers and the advertising dollars of firms, they are also complementary in many ways. Studios lease their sound stages to television producers to make films. In some cases (e.g., Fox), they own television networks themselves. Television is also an important outlet for motion pictures, usually after they have enjoyed a run in the theaters. Motion pictures are also made directly for television or cable. Many stars successfully cross over from television to movie success and back again, as do writers, directors, and other off-screen talent. Of course, television also serves as a handy advertising medium for the movies.

Television competes with other leisure time activities for entertainment dollars, advertising dollars, and time. Because of the convenience of being located in the consumer's home, it enjoys the advantage of easy accessibility. The downfall of TV is that it does not provide an opportunity to get out of the house and break from the daily routine. For that reason, it never displaced the movie theater as a source of motion pictures as the industry initially feared it would. Of course, there is a difference in quality between seeing a movie on the big screen with surround sound and watching the same movie on a television set.

Spectator Sports

Sports are big business. From payroll to ticket sales, they bring in billions of dollars a year and entertain millions of fans, most of whom never make it to the stadium but follow their favorite teams on television, radio, newsprint, and more recently, over the internet.

The rise of spectator sports as an important form of entertainment began in the twentieth century. Like other forms of entertainment, the rapid rise in the twentieth century is closely related to rising income and decreasing average length of the workweek. Unlike those other forms of entertainment, spectator sports did not rely as much on technology changes for its development. That is not to say that these changes had no impact, however. Television, for example, while not changing the basic concept of spectator sports, changed the way most spectators consumed sports, and the vast amount of money produced by television changed the structure of organized sports leagues.

The automobile also had a significant impact on sports, in particular on the location of stadiums. As travelers to the ballpark changed from mass transit to private car, the need for parking, and hence the impracticality of inner-city locations for ballparks, moved them to the suburbs. Changing perceptions of the role of sports teams to a city have subsequently moved those stadiums back into the center city in the modern era of "retro" ballpark construction.

While professional sports, and spectator sports in general, flourished in the twentieth century, they originated earlier than that. The roots of professional team sports are the town and company competitions of the nineteenth century. The first professional team sport to formally organize was baseball. The first all-professional team, the Cincinnati Red Stockings, was founded in 1869. The first professional league, the National League, was formed in 1876. Professional hockey, basketball, and football did not debut for another half century, but those sports were already being played in front of cheering spectators in the nineteenth century. The first college football game, pitting Rutgers against Princeton, took place in November of 1869. It hardly resembled the game today, with Rutgers winning 6 to 4, but it is forever marked as the birth of one of the most popular sports in America.

Boxing is an example of an individual sport that attracted professionals at an early stage. Early boxing matches in America were popular as a means of wagering. These matches often pitted slaves against each other, with hefty wagers on the outcome. Because of its brutality, it was eventually outlawed and its popularity among spectators decreased when allegations of match fixing were reported.

Sports that have succeeded commercially are recognized as businesses in the entertainment industry. The supply of spectator sports has grown to match the demand. In the twentieth century, football, men and women's basketball, soccer, men and women's tennis, hockey, indoor (arena) football, men and women's golf, and (even for a short period) track spawned professional leagues and organizations, joining baseball, boxing, and horse racing as professional sports.

Municipally funded sports stadiums are an example of the commercialization of sports and the perceived economic benefits to a city of hosting big time sports. Most professional sports stadiums in the United States have been constructed primarily with public monies. Communities build these stadiums because they do not want to lose the team to another city. The professional sports leagues have closely controlled monopoly power of their leagues. Like any good monopolist, they restrict the supply of their product. In addition to maximizing profits in the traditional sense, this also ensures that more cities could serve as potential hosts of a professional team than there are teams in the league. That way, pressure can be exerted on municipalities for financial gains under the threat of the team moving to another city (Coates and Humphreys 1999, Johnson 1983, Johnson, Groothuis, and Whitehead 2001, Long 2005, Noll and Zimbalist 1997, Siegfried and Zimbalist 2000).

Television had an enormous impact on sports in the last half of the twentieth century. The financial success of sports is due to its exposure on television (Noll 1974). The most successful sports leagues, such as the National Football League (NFL), Major League Baseball (MLB), and the National Collegiate Athletic Association (NCAA), generate more money from television rights fees than they do from live attendance. Golf and tennis owe their large purses to the growth of television fees in the last two decades. The less successful professional team sports, such as hockey and basketball, have improved their status greatly with television packages but are still not on the same par as the aforementioned sports.

It is hard to imagine that sports teams once saw the media as a threat to the value of their franchises. But originally, they resisted putting their games on the radio for fear that customers would stay home and listen to the game for free rather than come to the park. They soon discovered that radio (and eventually television) was a source of income and free advertising, helping to attract even more fans as well as serving as an additional source of revenue.

Monopoly control of franchises is the backbone of any sports league. Sports leagues control schedules and maintain the quality of play on the field. But even more important, they serve to maximize profits for the teams. This is done in a number of ways, beginning with attempts to monopolize the market for playing talent, desirable markets, and television income. Leagues do this by signing the best available players and then tying up the next tier of talent at minor league levels. This prepares talent for the major leagues as well as keeps them away from potential competitor leagues.

Leagues also attempt to control the best markets. They locate teams in the largest markets in an effort to make it more difficult for a competitor to start up. At the same time, leagues limit the number of franchises to less than the market will bear. This ensures that they can exploit monopoly profits by limiting the output of their product. This is most obvious in the use of relocation of franchises as a threat to get stadiums built and season tickets sold (Gendzel 1995).

Beginning in the mid-1970s, teams lost the ability to suppress player wages. The right to bargain with other teams for their services caused seismic changes in the labor market. No longer are players shackled to one team forever, subject to the whims of the owner for their salary and status. Now they are free to bargain with any team. The impact on salaries has been incredible. The average salary of a professional athlete skyrocketed from $45,000 in 1975 ($182,000 in 2010 dollars) to more than $3 million by 2010. Not all of that increase is due to free agency. Revenues increased during this period due to the dramatic increase in television revenue caused by America's insatiable appetite for sports. The result is a much larger revenue pie to divide, with the players getting a larger piece of that pie (Kahn 2000, Rosen and Sanderson 2001, Scully 1974).

Americans love their sports. Despite the large amount of media attention, the passion fans display when rooting for the home team, and the importance our society seems to place on sports, the demand for them is still at its base described by the basic laws of supply and demand. The primary determinants of the demand for spectator sports are the same as the primary determinants for any good or service: income, the number of buyers, product quality (usually measured as team winning percentage), and the price and quality of related goods (in this case, other entertainment options) (Ahn and Lee 2003, Knowles, Sherony, and Haupert 1992, Schmidt and Berri 2006, Whitney 1988).

The impact of income and population on the demand for sports is straightforward. Higher incomes allow consumers to purchase more goods. A larger population means a greater potential audience from which to entice customers to the ballpark. It is no surprise, therefore, that teams located in larger and wealthier metropolitan areas will usually draw larger crowds at the ballpark as well as on television.

Since spectator sports are in the entertainment industry and are consumed for entertainment purposes, the demand for them is also subject to the quality and price of substitutes. Other spectator sports are an obvious example of a substitute. Large cities may have several other professional and college sports to choose from among for the sports fan. While sports seasons do not run at the same time, there is overlap between all of the seasons so that there is some head-to-head sports competition for every spectator sport.

It is not just sports that compete, however. All forms of entertainment must be considered as potential substitutes for spectator sports. Though they may not be perfect substitutes, they must be considered. The greater the number of potential substitutes, the higher their quality and the lower their price, the more difficult it will be for a sports team to draw an audience.

A live sporting event, like a movie or a stage show, is consumed at the same time as the last stage of production; thus it cannot be inventoried. This situation is ripe for an economic principle known as price discrimination. Price discrimination is the practice of selling the same good to different buyers for different prices. The airline industry practices this routinely. Passengers seated next to one another on a plane may be paying different prices for their tickets depending on when they bought them and what day they are returning. Since the earliest days of paid attendance, teams have discriminated based on seat location. Only recently have sports teams begun to exploit the full potential of price discrimination by varying ticket prices according to the expected quality, date, and time of the game.

Sports have a grip on the American public that is far greater than their economic importance. They are entertaining, the athletes are well paid, and the franchises are valuable, but in the end, it is all about entertainment. Sports will continue to be a financial success only as long as it is entertaining. When it ceases to be, then consumers will find entertainment elsewhere.

Conclusion

Before the twentieth century, most entertainment was provided in the home. It frequently took the form of games, storytelling, reading, and music making. There were forms of mass entertainment, but they were not common and tended to be consumed primarily by the urban upper class. Lower wages, longer work hours, less sophisticated technology, and a predominantly rural population were all contributing factors to the relatively primitive status of the entertainment industry. What little time was available for leisure was likely to be spent at home rather than used to travel to an entertainment venue.

If one wanted to go out to be entertained, the theater was the most likely destination. The choices included ballet, opera, symphony concerts, plays, or vaudeville—all of which might fall under the umbrella title of "stage shows." Opera, symphony, ballet, and plays (often referred to as "the legitimate stage," as opposed to vaudeville) were mostly consumed by a small percentage of households. They existed primarily in larger cities, tended to cost more to attend, and, as a result, attracted a disproportionate percentage of their audience from upper income Americans. Vaudeville alone was among the staged shows that were readily accessible to a wide range of Americans. Vaudeville theaters could be found in cities of virtually any size and were attended by a wide cross section of the American public.

Variety shows still exist but in a different format—the internet. While vaudeville is dead and television thrives on reality shows, sitcoms, and dramas, the internet is perhaps the ultimate example of the variety show. With the click of a mouse, one can move from sports to music to whatever else might be desired. The improvements in computer technology over the past decade have made video and audio streaming commonplace, making the computer a sophisticated and powerful entertainment medium.

The entertainment industry grew and matured during the twentieth century largely on the back of technological innovation. Even though the movie, radio, television, and computer industries did not even exist at the beginning of the century, all were common parts of our daily life by the end of it. While it is not the only factor contributing to the growth of the entertainment industry, technology has been the most obvious one.

Technology has blurred the distinction between entertainment media and caused upheavals in the industry along the way. Movie and television are good examples. The latter is an extension of the technology that created the former. When television first debuted, it was viewed as the eventual successor to the movie theater. Although it came after the movie industry, it is now difficult to tell the difference between the two industries. They share studio space and producers. Actors and directors frequently cross from one medium to the other in an industry that is composed of a shrinking number of companies that produce both television shows and movies.

Spectator sports, while initially wary of the growth of radio and television, learned to embrace them and evolve along with them. While technology is not necessary for the production of a sporting event, nor is it needed for it to be consumed, they are closely allied. Over time, spectator sports learned not to fear these other forms of entertainment but to exploit them, although it is not clear whether it is sports that exploits television or vice versa.

Today, technology has redefined all entertainment venues. The computer has altered the way we view movies and listen to music, and how we read books, newspapers, and magazines. It has changed how we follow our favorite sports team and will continue to impact the entertainment industry into the future. Will one of the current forms of entertainment become the twenty-first-century vaudeville? How will technology affect what we have now and what might evolve? In particular, how will the copyright and file sharing problems of today be answered and dealt with? None of these questions have an obvious solution as the twenty-first century begins.

References

Ahn, C. C. and Y. H. Lee, "Life-Cycle Demand for Major League Baseball," presented at the Western Economics Association International Conference, Denver, CO, 2003.

Aitken, Hugh, *Syntony and Spark: The Origins of Radio*, Princeton, NJ: Princeton University Press, 1985.

Allen, Jeanne Thomas, "Copyright and Early Theater, Vaudeville and Film Competition," *Journal of the University Film Association* 31, no. 2, Spring 1979, pp. 5–11.

Balio, Tino (Ed.), *Hollywood in the Age of Television*, Boston: Unwin Hyman, 1990.

Balio, Tino, *Grand Design: Hollywood as a Modern Business Enterprise: 1930–1939*, New York: Charles Scribner's Sons, 1993.

Barnouw, Eric, *The Golden Web: A History of Broadcasting from 1933 to 1953*, New York: Oxford University Press, 1968.

Batten, Frank, *The Weather Channel: The Improbable Rise of a Media Phenomenon*, Boston: Harvard Business School Press, 2002.

Baughman, James L., "Show Business in the Living Room: Management Expectations for American Television: 1947–56," *Business and Economic History* 26, no. 2, Winter 1997, pp. 718–26.

Berri, David J. and Martin B. Schmidt, "On the Road with the National Basketball Association's Superstar Externality," *Journal of Sports Economics* 7, no. 4, November 2006, pp. 347–58.

Berri, David J., Martin B. Schmidt, and Stacey L. Brook, "Stars at the Gate: The Impact of Star Power on NBA Gate Revenues," *Journal of Sports Economics* 5, no. 1, February 2004, pp. 33–50.

Bowden, Sue and Avner Offer, "Household Appliances and the Use of Time: The United States and Britain since the 1920s," *Economic History Review* 47, no. 4, November 1994, pp. 725–48.

Clevinger, Donna L. and George S. Vozikis, "A Historical Review of Early Entrepreneurial Theatrical Activity in a Growing Railroad Center," *International Entrepreneurship and Management Journal* 3, no. 2, June 2007, pp. 159–69.

Coates, Dennis and Brad Humphreys, "The Growth Effects of Sport Franchises, Stadia, and Arenas," *Journal of Policy Analysis and Management* 18, no. 4, 1999, pp. 601–24.

Comstock, George, *The Evolution of American Television*, Newbury Park, CA: Sage Publications, 1989.

Conway, Mike, *The Origins of Television News in America*, New York: Peter Lang Publishing, 2009.

Costa, Dora, "The Wage and the Length of the Work Day: From the 1890s to 1991," *Journal of Labor Economics* 18, no. 1, January 2000, pp. 156–81.

De Long, Thomas A., *The Mighty Music Box: The Golden Age of Musical Radio*, Los Angeles: Amber Crest Books, 1980.

De Vany, Arthur S. and W. David Walls, "Uncertainty in the Movie Industry: Does Star Power Reduce the Terror of the Box Office?" *Journal of Cultural Economics* 23, no. 4, November 1999, pp. 285–318.

Di Meglio, John E., *Vaudeville U.S.A.*, Bowling Green, OH: Bowling Green University Popular Press, 1973.

Douglas, George H., *The Early Days of Radio Broadcasting*, Jefferson, NC, and London: McFarland Publishing, 1987.

Eisemann, Thomas R., "The U.S. Cable Television Industry: 1948–1995: Managerial Capitalism in Eclipse," *Business History Review* 74, no. 1 Spring 2000, pp. 1–40.

Eliot, Marc, *Rockonomics: The Money Behind the Music*, New York: Franklin Watts, 1989.

Epstein, Edward Jay, *The Big Picture: Money and Power in Hollywood*, New York: Random House, 2005.

Erdman, Andrew L., *Blue Vaudeville: Sex, Morals and the Mass Marketing of Amusement: 1895–1915*, Jefferson, NC: McFarland and Co., Inc., 2004.

Eyman, Scott, *The Speed of Sound: Hollywood and the Talkie Revolution: 1926–1930*, Baltimore: Johns Hopkins University Press, 1997.

Fones-Wolf, Elizabeth, "Creating a Favorable Business Climate: Corporations and Radio Broadcasting: 1934–1954," *Business History Review* 73, no. 2, Summer 1999, pp. 221–55.

Frey, Bruno S., "Superstar Museums: An Economic Analysis," *Journal of Cultural Economics* 22, no. 2–3, 1998, pp. 113–25.

Gelatt, Roland, *The Fabulous Phonograph: 1877–1977*, New York: Macmillan, 1977.

Gendzel, Glen, "Competitive Boosterism: How Milwaukee Lost the Braves," *Business History Review* 69, no. 4, Winter 1995, pp. 530–66.

Gomery, Douglas, "Rethinking U.S. Film History: The Depression Decade and Monopoly Control," *Film and History* 10, no. 2, 1980, pp. 32–38.

Hanssen, F. Andrew, "Vertical Integration during the Hollywood Studio Era," *Journal of Law and Economics* 53, no. 3, August 2010, pp. 519–43.

Hausman, Jerry A. and Gregory K. Leonard, "Superstars in the National Basketball Association: Economic Value and Policy," *Journal of Labor Economics* 15, no. 4, October 1997, pp. 586–624.

Hull, Geoffrey P., *The Recording Industry*, Needham Heights, MA: Allyn & Bacon, 1998.

Hunnicutt, Benjamin, "Historical Attitudes toward the Increase of Free Time in the Twentieth Century: Time for Work, for Leisure, or as Unemployment," *Society and Leisure* 3, no. 2, November 1980, pp. 195–218.

Johnson, Arthur T., "Municipal Administration and the Sports Franchise Relocation Issue," *Public Administration Review* 43, no. 6, November–December 1983, pp. 519–28.

Johnson, B. K., P. A. Groothuis, and J. C. Whitehead, "The Value of Public Goods Generated by a Major League Sports Team: CVM," *Journal of Sports Economics* 2, no. 1, February 2001, pp. 6–21.

Jozefowicz, James J., Jason M. Kelley, and Stephanie M. Brewer, "New Release: An Empirical Analysis of VHS/DVD Rental Success," *Atlantic Economic Journal* 36, no. 2, June 2008, pp. 139–51.

Jung, Sang-Chul and Myeong Hwan Kim, "Does the Star Power Matter?" *Applied Economics Letters* 17, no. 11, July 2010, pp. 1037–41.

Kahn, Lawrence M., "The Sports Business as a Labor Market Laboratory," *Journal of Economic Perspectives* 14, no. 3, Summer 2000, pp. 75–94.

Knowles, Glenn, Keith Sherony, and Mike Haupert, "The Demand for Major League Baseball: A Test of the Uncertainty of Outcome Hypothesis," *American Economist* 36, no. 3, Fall 1992.

Kruse, Elizabeth, "From Free Privilege to Regulation: Wireless Firms and the Competition for Spectrum Rights before World War I," *Business History Review* 76, no. 4, Winter 2002, pp. 659–703.

Lewis, Tom, "A Godlike Presence: The Impact of Radio on the 1920s and 1930s," *OAH Magazine of History* 6, no. 4, Spring 1992, pp. 26–33.

Lewis, Tom, *Empire of the Air: The Men Who Made Radio*, New York: Harper Collins, 1991.

Liebowitz, Stan J., "File Sharing: Creative Destruction or Just Plain Destruction?" *Journal of Law and Economics* 49, no. 1, April 2006, pp. 1–28.

Lippmann, Stephen, "The Institutional Context of Industry Consolidation: Radio Broadcasting in the United States: 1920–1934," *Social Forces* 86, no. 2, December 2007, pp. 467–95.

Long, Judith Grant, "Full Count: The Real Cost of Public Funding for Major League Sports Facilities," *Journal of Sports Economics* 6, no. 2, May 2005, pp. 119–43.

Maoz, Yishay David, "Labor Hours in the United States and Europe: The Role of Different Leisure Preferences," *Macroeconomic Dynamics* 14, no. 2, April 2010, pp. 231–41.

McChesney, R. W., *Telecommunications, Mass Media, and Democracy: The Battle for the Control of U.S. Broadcasting: 1928–1935*, New York: Oxford University Press, 1993.

Millard, Andre, *America on Record: A History of Recorded Sound*, New York: Cambridge University Press, 1995.

Mol, Joeri M. and Nachoem M. Wijnberg, "Competition, Selection and Rock and Roll: The Economics of Payola and Authenticity," *Journal of Economic Issues* 41, no. 3 September 2007, pp. 701–14.

Noll, Roger and Andrew Zimbalist (Eds.), *Sports, Jobs and Taxes*, Washington, D.C.: Brookings Institution Press, 1997.

Noll, Roger (Ed.), *Government and the Sports Business*, Washington, D.C.: Brookings Institution Press, 1974.

Pokorny, Michael and John Sedgwick, "Profitability Trends in Hollywood: 1929–1999: Somebody Must Know Something," *Economic History Review* 63, no. 1, February 2010, pp. 56–84.

Pokorny, Michal and John Sedgwick, "Stardom and the Profitability of Film Making: Warner Bros. in the 1930s," *Journal of Cultural Economics* 25, no. 3, August 2001, pp. 157–84.

Rosen, Sherwin and Allen Sanderson, "Labour Markets in Professional Sports," *Economic Journal* 111, no. 469, February 2001, pp. F47–F68.

Rosen, Sherwin, "The Economics of Superstars," *American Economic Review* 71, no. 5, December 1981, pp. 845–58.

Sanjek, Russel, *Pennies from Heaven: The American Popular Music Business in the Twentieth Century*, New York: Da Capo Press, 1996.

Schmidt, Martin B. and David J. Berri, "Research Note: What Takes Them Out to the Ball Game?" *Journal of Sports Economics* 7, May 2006, pp. 222–33.

Scully, Gerald W., "Pay and Performance in Major League Baseball," *American Economic Review* 64, no. 6, December 1974, pp. 915–30.

Sedgwick, John and Michael Pokorny, "The Film Business in the United States and Britain during the 1930s," *Economic History Review* 58, no. 1, February 2005, pp. 79–112.

Shaw, Douglas V., "Making Leisure Pay: Street Railway Owned Amusement Parks in the United States: 1900–1925," *Journal of Cultural Economics* 10, no. 2, December 1986, pp. 67–79.

Siegfried, John and Andrew Zimbalist, "The Economics of Sports Facilities and Their Communities," *Journal of Economic Perspectives* 14, Summer 2000, pp. 95–114.

Snyder, Robert W., *The Voice of the City*, Chicago: Ivan R. Dee, 2000.

Taubman, Howard, *The Making of the American Theatre*, New York: Coward McCann, Inc., 1965.

Thomas, Jeanne, "The Decay of the Motion Picture Patents Company," *Cinema Journal* 10, no. 2, Spring 1971, pp. 34–40.

Toll, Robert, *On with the Show! The First Century of Show Business in America*, New York: Oxford University Press, 1976.

Vandenbroucke, Guillaume, "Trends in Hours: The U.S. from 1900 to 1950," *Journal of Economic Dynamics and Control* 33, no. 1, January 2009, pp. 237–49.

Walls, W. D., "Superstars and Heavy Tails in Recorded Entertainment: Empirical Analysis of the Market for DVDs," *Journal of Cultural Economics* 34, no. 4, November 2010, pp. 261–79.

Whitney, James D., "Winning Games versus Winning Championships: The Economics of Fan Interest and Team Performance," *Economic Inquiry*, October 1988, pp. 703–24.

2

Problems and Solutions

The History of Entertainment: A Brief Review

Americans have been entertaining themselves since the Colonists first arrived in the seventeenth century. Before the twentieth century, most of this entertainment was provided in the home. It frequently took the form of games, storytelling, reading, and music making. There were forms of mass entertainment, but they were not common and tended to be consumed primarily by the upper class. Lower wages, longer work hours, less sophisticated technology, and a predominantly rural population were all contributing factors to the relatively primitive status of the entertainment industry. Until 1920, most Americans lived in rural areas, which meant that venues for mass entertainment were scarce. What little time was available for leisure was likely to be spent at home rather than used to travel to an entertainment venue (Haupert 2006, Green and Laurie 1953, Matlaw 1979).

If one wanted to go out to be entertained, the theater was the most likely destination. The choices included ballet, opera, symphony concerts, plays or vaudeville—all of which might fall under the umbrella title of "stage shows." Ballet, opera, and symphony are considered to be more refined and "higher class," and vaudeville, as essentially a live variety show, was at the other end of the scale. Opera, symphony, ballet, and plays (often referred to as "the legitimate stage," as opposed to vaudeville) were mostly consumed by a small percentage of households.

They existed primarily in larger cities, tended to cost more to attend, and, as a result, attracted a disproportionate percentage of their audience from upper income Americans. Of the staged shows, vaudeville alone was readily accessible to a wide range of Americans. Vaudeville theaters could be found in cities of virtually every size and were attended by a wide cross-section of the American public.

Vaudeville served the same purpose that movies would later assume: true mass entertainment. While the movie industry would come to specialize in telling a single story in a 90-minute timespan, vaudeville was a variety show. This pattern of entertainment was repeated by early radio and then television pioneers, who transferred the old vaudeville variety shows to the small screen. Milton Berle's show, one of the pioneers of early television, was just such an example of a variety of acts pulled together for an hour or two of entertainment.

Variety shows still exist but in a different format—the internet. While vaudeville is dead and television thrives on reality shows, sitcoms, and dramas, the internet is perhaps the ultimate example of the variety show. With a click of the mouse, one can move from sports to music to whatever else might be desired. Improvements in technology over the past decade have made video and audio streaming commonplace, making not just the computer, but tablets and smartphones, sophisticated and powerful entertainment devices (Cairncross 1997).

Technology and Entertainment

The entertainment industry grew and matured during the twentieth century largely on the back of technological innovation. Even though the movie, radio, television, and computer industries did not even exist at the beginning of the century, all were common parts of our daily life by the end of it. One decade into the twenty-first century, nearly two-thirds of American adults attend the movies each year, and more than 8 in 10 households have a VCR or DVD player to view movies at home. More than 98 percent of households have at least one television, three quarters of which subscribe to cable or satellite. Over 99 percent of American households have at least one radio, and two-thirds of American homes have computers, over 90 percent of which have internet access.

While it is not the only factor contributing to the growth of the entertainment industry, technology has been the most obvious one. The printing press brought print to the door of anyone who could afford books. Newspapers and magazines became low cost means of reaching the masses and ultimately brought the world to the door of the average American. These changes took place over centuries. The technological changes impacting the entertainment industry took only decades.

Vaudeville, the movies, and sports brought the masses out to gather for their entertainment. Radios and television moved them back into their living rooms. The rise of the internet and the pervasiveness of the computer is currently driving Americans even further inside themselves. Technology has decreased the cost and increased the ease of being entertained. Wireless technology now gives us the possibility of being anywhere at any time.

While the twentieth century saw tremendous growth in the television and movie industries, as we move into the twenty-first century, the newspaper and popular magazine industries are withering. There are only three-quarters as many daily newspapers in circulation in the United States today as there were in 1900, and less than half of all American households even subscribe to a daily newspaper. Specialty magazines have proliferated, but the popular press magazines subscribed to by large percentages of the population, which contributed a common base of information, have largely disappeared. And, of course, vaudeville has disappeared entirely. The wave of the entertainment future is the internet, a concept which was unimaginable a mere generation ago.

Increasing wealth and innovations in technology led Americans to pursue a variety of different means of entertainment. Still, there are only 24 hours in a day, so inevitably one new means of leisure time pursuit came at the expense of another. Radio and phonographs substituted for live music performances, talking films replaced silent films and vaudeville, and television encroached on the movies. The automobile led to an increase in "going out" for entertainment, which in itself did not help the radio and phonograph industry. It was, however, a boon for places like taverns ("speakeasies" during Prohibition), ballparks, and miniature golf courses. Americans are very much into entertaining themselves but are not necessarily wedded to one way of doing so.

Technology has blurred the distinction between entertainment media and has caused upheavals in the industry along the way. Movie and television are good examples. The latter is an extension of the technology that created the former. When television first debuted, it was viewed as the eventual successor to the movie theater. Although it came after the movie industry, it is now difficult to tell the difference between the two. They share studio space and producers. Actors and directors frequently cross from one medium to the other in an industry that is composed of a shrinking number of companies that produce both television shows and movies. With the growing availability of cable movie channels and on-demand viewing capabilities along with improvements in television reception delivered by high definition (HD) and large flat screen televisions, the difference between watching a movie in a movie theater and at home is rapidly diminishing. It may be hard to imagine, but it was only a generation ago that a Hollywood movie first appeared on television, and then only after it had been out of theaters for several years. Now that same movie may appear on television just a few weeks after closing in theaters (Hilliard and Keith 2010, Stoeber 2004).

The same story can be told about the symbiotic relationships that have developed between radio, television, recorded music, and the movies. Indeed, at one time, each of these industries saw one or more of the others as a potential threat to its existence, but over time they grew to be close complements to one another.

Spectator sports, while initially wary of the growth of radio and television, learned to embrace them and evolve along with them. While technology is not necessary for the production of a sporting event, nor is it needed for it to be consumed, they are closely allied. Over time, spectator sports learned not to fear these other forms of entertainment but to exploit them, though it could be argued that it is actually television that exploits sports.

The Speed of Change

From its first radio station, licensed to broadcast in 1920 in Pittsburgh, the radio industry exploded across America. A decade later, there were over 600 radio stations, and by the conclusion of World War II, there were nearly 3,000. Not including satellite, low power, or booster stations, there were more than 14,000 radio stations in 2010, and radios went from being in less than half of American households in 1930 to more than 99 percent today.

For as quickly as radios exploded into the American home, the arrival of televisions was even more impressive. In 1950, only 8 percent of American homes had a television set. Within a decade, 79 percent had one. Today, less than 2 percent of American families do not own at least one television set. In fact, television is such a standard part of the American household that more than half of all homes have at least three sets, and 90 percent have some sort of recording device for their television. The number of cable and satellite channels is now in the hundreds, and the number of television broadcast stations has grown from the first one licensed in 1939 in New York City to over 100 a decade later and more than 1,700 today, to say nothing of the internet outlets available for watching television.

Not only has technology revolutionized the quality of the entertainment industry, it has led to substantial price decreases as well. Television sets, radios, and music players are all cheaper in actual dollars today than when they debuted, and when adjusted for inflation, the price differences are even more dramatic. In addition, the quality has made quantum leaps. Nobody would argue that the first record players can compete with today's pocket sized music devices or even a run-of-the-mill CD/radio player in terms of quality. And certainly the radios of the 1920s and televisions of the 1950s are no match for today's sets. But what is not as commonly known is how much cheaper these vastly superior pieces of equipment are now than they were originally.

The Cost of Leisure

The first Edison phonographs sold in 1880 for upwards of $150. Today, a portable CD/radio player is widely available for $50. It is a much better piece of equipment that reproduces music of a much higher quality and with infinitely more varieties to choose from. And consider that the $50 cost today is equivalent to about three hours of labor for the average American. In 1880, it would have taken the average American 10 weeks to earn enough to pay for that phonograph.

A standard tabletop radio sold for $99 in 1927. Today, a portable radio that also plays CDs and cassette tapes can easily be found for under $50. In 1929, that $99 radio represented 6 percent of the average household annual income. Today, the $50 radio, besides being far superior in quality, represents a fraction of a percent of that same average income. Adjusted for inflation, $99 in 1930 would buy an iPod and a portable satellite radio with a lifetime subscription today.

The price of television sets has dropped even more dramatically than radios. In 1950, an eight-inch black-and-white television with 12-channel capability (and no remote control!) sold for $190. By 2010, a 22-inch flat screen set with remote control and the capacity to receive an unlimited number of satellite- or cable-delivered channels in high definition can easily be found for less than $190. And keep in mind that those prices are not adjusted for inflation. When inflation is accounted for, that $190 set in 1950 would cost over $1,700 today.

Ticket prices have remained fairly steady when adjusted for inflation. The 50-cent movie tickets of the 1940s would be the inflation-adjusted equivalent of $8 today. The technical quality of movies today is much higher, though film historians may debate whether the quality of the stories has improved. Color, 70-mm film, special effects, 3D, and surround sound have all improved the technical quality of movies, even if the stories may have stagnated.

A theater ticket at a typical top tier New York vaudeville house in 1900 was $1.50 for the best seats. As a share of the average wage, that is the equivalent of $180 today, which is not much different than the price of a good seat at a Broadway show.

The average cost of a major league baseball game today ranges between $15 and $80 depending on the team. In 1910, bleacher seats sold for 25 to 75 cents, and reserved grandstand seats for about $1.50. That is the equivalent of $6 to $18 for a bleacher seat and about $36 for the reserved grandstand today.

In 2010, the average American household spent about $6,800 per year on entertainment and recreation, the largest share of it ($813) on video and audio products. In 1930, the first year for which such data are available, the average household spent $133 on recreation and entertainment ($2,170 adjusted for inflation). Most of it ($31.70) was spent on radios, records, and musical instrument repairs. The second biggest source of entertainment expenditures was movie tickets at $24.48. Spending on theater tickets and spectator sports was at $3.18 and $2.17 respectively. The biggest change in entertainment expenditures over the last half century has been in the category of gambling, which increased by a factor of more than 200, from less than 25 cents per household in 1930 to more than $50. Overall, American households spent 15 times more real dollars on their entertainment in 2010 than they did on the cusp of the Great Depression.

Developments in the Twenty-First Century

The Problem of Piracy

The wonders of the electronic age have brought our favorite movies and television shows into the palm of our hand—quite literally. This technological breakthrough is not without its costs, however. The same technology that can be used to bring us this entertainment can be used to steal it as well. One of the major problems facing the movie industry today is the theft of intellectual and creative property rights, that is, piracy (De Vany and Walls 2007, Liebowitz 2006, Waterman, Wook, and Rochet 2007).

One method of battling piracy while at the same time feeding the consumer desire to watch shows on a variety of devices, such as computers, phones, and tablets, is the development of the digital locker by Warner Brothers. It allows consumers who purchase a copy of a movie to obtain access to it on a variety of different devices. Disney is developing a similar project, which it calls Keychest.

The idea is not so much a new technology as a new response to technology by redefining the concept of ownership. Instead of buying a physical copy of a movie, such as a DVD or Blu-ray disc, consumers buy access to the movie on any of their devices. Using a concept similar to the computing "cloud," it would provide streaming access to movies purchased by consumers.

For one upfront price this technology would allow buyers to purchase a lifetime right to access content and view it on a variety of platforms and devices from the web. It could also facilitate other entertainment services, such as online movie subscriptions.

The concept addresses two big hurdles to widespread consumer adoption of movies downloads: difficulty of playing a movie back on mobile devices other than computers, and limited storage space on hard drives. It uses the same cloud system that web applications (such as Google Documents) uses, permitting users to store files on a remote server for access anytime and from any device rather than storing them on a specific device.

SNL Kagan estimates that industry revenue from video rentals and sales fell 10.5 percent to $18.5 billion from 2009 to 2010. The digital locker is one of the industry's attempts to stem the decline in home entertainment revenue that has been driven legitimately by Netflix and Redbox rentals and on the black market by piracy.

Antipiracy bills before Congress are not without controversy. On the one hand, the large entertainment conglomerates, such as Time Warner and movie studios, are concerned about piracy's impact on their bottom line. The Motion Picture Association of America (MPAA) estimated that piracy costs the U.S. economy about $60 billion a year, though they admit that figure includes tangentially related industry losses, such as trucking companies, which don't have as many deliveries to make to theaters if fewer people are attending, and would, therefore, lose income. It is this kind of analysis that leads others, particularly representatives of the internet companies that would bear the brunt of tough new antipiracy laws, to scoff at the overblown claims.

The piracy problem is one of both taking and access. The first person to illegally copy or download a movie, song, or television show commits the front-line act of piracy, but each time it is subsequently downloaded the intellectual property right is stolen again. Or is it? Some argue that many of the consumers who access technology in this way would not have purchased the product in the first place, and that by downloading it for free, they are doing the world a favor by further disseminating information. At least that is the angle the internet companies are more likely to take. Another way to look at it is advertising. If somebody sees a movie or hears a song on YouTube, they may be more likely to go out and buy another song, movie, or show from the artists, now that they have heard or seen that artist and liked what they saw.

Rapidly evolving technology has changed property rights issues on another front, that is, the way contracts are written and deals are made. With future uncertainty about delivery and reception methods, some contracts are taking a global approach. For its 2009 to 2010 season, *America's Got Talent* required contestants to sign contracts that allowed NBC the rights to the footage from their appearance so that it could be used in all possible media, throughout the universe, forever. That pretty much covers it all. Standard Hollywood language includes phrases like the ability to use content throughout the universe and/or to incorporate it in other works in any form, media or technology now known or hereafter developed. Another example of a contract covers rights "in any media, whether now known or hereafter devised, or in any form whether now known or hereafter devised, an unlimited number of times throughout the universe and forever" (Caves 2000).

Television

Technology is well in front of business organizations. The current method of producing and exhibiting television shows, for example, lags behind the technology to deliver and receive the programming. Originally, shows were produced and aired on networks, then cable channels. The only way to see them was on their original broadcast date or later in reruns. Now, however, many shows are available on line within 24 hours of their original airdate (Comstock 1989, Dupagne and Seel 1998, Hart 2004).

Television is still America's number one pastime, with the average American watching four and a half hours a day. But television is not always watched on a television set. Increasingly, especially among the younger generations, television shows are watched online. Television is competing with the internet, social network sites, and video games for the attention of Americans aged 12 to 34. This generation is still watching television shows, but they are streaming them on their computers, cellphones, and tablet devices. The long-term implications for the television industry are huge and could lead to a shift in advertising dollars away from the standard television market. The decrease in television watching among those under age 34 is recent and hence has not been occurring long enough to establish a trend. Nonetheless, it is likely to increase, as history shows us that adapting a technology increases its use over time, not decreases it—until it is replaced by something else.

DVRs (digital video recorders) have led to an increase in television watching among older Americans because the technology allows them to time shift their preferred shows. Of course, the ability to skip commercials when watching it later on creates a different problem for the industry. Nielsen does not count views of television shows on computer and mobile streams of shows in its ratings of television viewing. It counts them separately, making it difficult for the television industry to get a good handle on the changing viewing habits of Americans.

The television industry is anxious to make online and mobile viewing as measurable as traditional TV viewing in order to be able to better market commercial time to ad buyers. If the younger generation is getting their TV from different sources, then in the future they are likely to be getting it from these same sources. In other words, technology, not the business model, is likely to dictate the wave of the future.

Television has responded well to the rapid and expansive growth of the internet. While the internet has not affected the production of TV programming, it has affected its delivery. Over the first decade of the twenty-first century, television has seen an increase in viewers, advertising revenue, and subscriptions to cable and satellite. In terms of overall revenue, TV networks and video programming have been the only media (other than the internet itself) to grow since the advent of the internet. For consumers, there are more choices in more formats than at any time in the history of television.

One of the newest innovations has been the TV Everywhere concept, which allows a consumer to watch the television content they buy for their home on any of their television-capable devices, anywhere they are. Tablets, smartphones, and laptops can all be used to watch the cable, satellite, or over-the-air signals that come into the consumer's home. This has broadened the access consumers have to something they used to have to consume in their living room.

In a matter of a generation, TV has gone from an industry delivering a handful of channels over the air to cable, satellite, pay per view, video on demand, and now TV Everywhere. Furthermore, TV now captures revenue from both advertisers and consumers, who now consume most of their television not via free, over-the-air broadcasts, but via cable or satellite subscriptions. And branded cable stations such as ESPN, Nickelodeon, and Discovery, are better able to deliver a homogenous group of potential buyers to advertisers, increasing the value of a ratings point's worth of viewers (Batten 2002).

Cable is increasing its share of the television audience, meaning it is becoming ever more fractured. In some ways, this is good. Certain channels appeal to a homogenous group of viewers, such as Nickelodeon or ESPN; thus while there are fewer viewers, more of them appeal to certain advertisers. But watching TV online is not like watching it on TV. Recording shows and watching them online makes it harder for advertisers to reach their audience and be sure that the audience is even exposed to the message.

The dramatic increase of venues on which to watch TV shows and movies on the web threatens to undermine some of the most lucrative parts of the entertainment industry. Declining DVD sales and the questionable value of TV reruns (when they can be viewed online in so many places) are both examples of how the web has encroached upon the profitability of traditional revenue sources.

The cable and internet business is under siege from satellite, telephone, and internet companies pushing TV shows directly to consumers. The growing popularity of online video could prompt a new generation to cut off their cable connections, much as they have already done with their land telephone lines.

The relationship between cable television systems, like Warner and Comcast, and content providers, like ESPN and CNN, is symbiotic, but not always peaceful. Fights over content versus distribution have arisen many times as content providers threaten to withhold their programming from cable companies unless they get higher fees. On the other hand, cable companies threaten to drop the programming from their service if they do not get concessions. As a cable channel becomes more popular, such as the NFL network, it seeks to leverage that popularity into revenue by demanding fees from cable companies for the privilege of providing the channel to its subscribers. The cable network, on the other hand, faces the ire of the customer when it raises rates to cover these fees, so it fights back by threatening not to carry the channel, thus depriving it of an audience and threatening its ability to sell ads. The outcome depends on the relative bargaining strengths of the two sides.

As more content appears on the internet, and as more people go there to watch their programming, the bargaining position of the cable providers is eroded. It is no longer necessary to find a spot on a cable provider's network roster in order to reach an audience. While the traditional television audience is still the majority, there is no denying the impact that web based television will have on the industry in the future.

At the crux of the fight between providers and producers of TV content is the difference in the way networks such as Fox, ABC, CBS, and NBC are compensated for their content versus cable channels such as ESPN, Nickelodeon, and Discovery. The latter are paid per subscriber and sell ads. The former generate their income solely from ad revenue. Historically, that was the only source of revenue, since broadcasters had no way of capturing a subscription fee from a home that could freely receive the signal they broadcast. That historical relationship has been upheld, even though few households actually receive their television signals via broadcast anymore. It is unlikely that the status quo will survive though. Technological changes have altered the quality and quantity of television shows, and they are now impacting the business model of the industry as well.

The Movie Industry

With the growing market for on-demand movies on home sets, which are increasingly larger and have better quality picture, thanks to HD digital signals and Blu-ray technology, the traditional theater experience for the movies is increasingly in danger. In response, studios lengthened the window between theatrical release and video availability, making Netflix and Redbox consumers wait longer for the latest releases. They hope this will keep people coming to the theater. 3D is another innovation to keep people coming to the theater. While 3D television exists, the quantity of sets in homes is still small.

According to the National Association of Theatre Owners (NATO), by the end of 2011, an estimated 7,500 of 40,000 total U.S. movie screens were capable of screening 3D movies. The push to produce 3D movies is seen by some as a financial savior for the movie industry, which had been in a downward spiral going into the second decade of the twenty-first century.

Hollywood estimates are that blockbuster 3D films might increase profits by more than 25 percent even though they are more expensive to produce. 3D films usually charge a premium, averaging $3 per ticket in 2011. The tricky part of the equation, though, is the relative shortage of 3D screens. With more and more 3D films coming out but not enough screens to show them, the length of time any one of them remains on a screen is shortened (NATO, MPAA, Hollywood Box Office).

The current interest in 3D movies is similar to the rush to produce sound movies in the 1930s. In neither case was it clear the new technology was the wave of the future, and theaters did not hurry to install the expensive equipment necessary to project the new types of films. Of course, we know that the arrival of sound ultimately meant the end of silent pictures. The future is not yet written for 3D. It is expensive to convert a theater, and it is not a certainty that 3D will become the industry standard.

Movie theaters are also in a digital upgrade mode. Three of the nation's largest movie theater chains—AMC Entertainment, Cinemark Holdings, and Regal Entertainment Group—began to convert about 14,000 screens from traditional celluloid film exhibiting equipment to digital exhibition. This will not only reduce the need to ship, handle, and replace (when they wear out about every six weeks) bulky containers of film, it will also allow for enhanced digital effects, such as 3D movies, to be shown. Converting from celluloid to digital can run to about $70,000 per screen. But as the quality of the films increases, the cost of obtaining movies decreases. Instead of shipping films and producing them at a cost of $1,000 to $1,500 per copy, the film is produced on a hard drive. A consortium of theaters and studios have joined together in a venture known as DCIP (Digital Cinemark Implementation Partners). Under the plan, the celluloid copy cost would be replaced by a fee of about half that much, $850 per booking, to be paid to DCIP. When the new technology is in place, instead of receiving large film cases each week for their movies, theaters will instead use fiberoptic lines to transfer digital film files.

Alternative Markets for Movies

The foreign box office has become a bigger part of marketing plans for studios, meaning that films might need to have more global than purely American appeal in order to get studio funding. This is a recent phenomenon of the new century. In 2010, foreign box office receipts accounted for nearly 70 percent of the total box office, up from just under 60 percent at the turn of the century, and up from only about 25 percent in 1980. As a result, foreign actors are cast in more prominent roles and scripts are being written with global appeal in mind. In part, the foreign market's importance has replaced declining DVD sales, which used to account for the bulk of a movie's profits but fell off dramatically during the Great Recession. The changing habits of viewers and available technology suggest that DVD sales are unlikely to ever return to their prior level of importance. Other factors in the growing importance of foreign box office receipts are the decline of American attendance at movies and the growth of the number of screens in foreign markets (Hand 2002, Hanson and Xiang 2011, Jozefowicz, Kelley, and Brewer 2008).

It is not like the old days, when American films were just translated, or subtitled, and sent abroad to compete against inferior or nonexistent native markets. Increasingly, foreign markets in India, elsewhere in Asia, and in Europe are producing high quality fare that competes well with or even dominates American offerings. For example, in South Korea just a decade ago, locally made films accounted for less than 20 percent of the Korean box office. By 2010, that figure had risen to 50 percent.

One way to get ahead of this trend is what Fox did when it established Fox International Productions division in 2008. When the company noticed the increased competition for its films from local fare, it set up the new division so that it could start developing, producing, and distributing local-language movies in Asia.

The decrease in DVD sales, which has long been a lifeline for movie revenues, is due to online movie access. Now video on demand is being seen as a reasonable alternative market. It has the same drawbacks as the DVD did. Will it cause a reduction in theater attendance? With larger and higher quality sets and internet-compatible screens, it is likely that on the margin there will be more consumers who will substitute away from the theater and watch on the home screen instead. The real issue may not be the substitution of in-home streaming for DVD purchase or rental but rather the potential encroachment on the theatrical release window. If the window gets shorter and the movies become available online soon after, or even while they are still in the theater, there may be even more substitution. And then the theaters will object.

The theory behind the windowing system is to give each segment of the market a period of exclusivity. The problem is that the marketing costs for a movie's release are then lost. For example, when a new movie comes out, a significant amount is spent to market its theatrical release. For a major release, as much might be spent marketing the film as making it. Then, when the movie closes in the theater, instead of capitalizing on this momentum and marketing and releasing it immediately on video, a period averaging just over four months goes by in which the movie is not available at all (Chiou 2008).

Studios are pushing to shorten or even eliminate this window between theater and DVD, thus taking advantage of word of mouth advertising for the movie and the recent marketing blitz. Theater owners are against this because they fear the public will choose to watch the movie on DVD or on line instead of in the theater. Some studio executives even push for simultaneous release on DVD and theaters to let the public choose how they want to see the film. In 2010, the movie *Freakonomics* was actually released on video a month before it was in theaters.

One potential advantage of simultaneous release for studios is getting ahead of piracy. If the film is available on legitimate video from day one, the lower quality pirated versions will lose much of their market appeal.

Less controversial is the shrinking of other windows, for example, between video and video on demand. Shrinking this window also saves marketing costs but does not pit the studios against the theaters—a tension that is uncomfortable for the studios, given the large amount of money that is taken in from the box office.

Recently, studios have been reducing the window between video and video on demand. The results suggest that video rentals decrease slightly, but purchases of videos and video on demand actually increase, and these are the major moneymakers. With the increasing availability and quality of online video on demand, it is even more important to studios to get these dollars while interest in the movie is still high. Internet on-demand options are efficient and have higher profit margins for the studios, and they offer maximum convenience to customers. Since there is no physical product, production and inventory costs are eliminated. Theoretically, an internet service could have an unlimited supply of films available for streaming. The sooner these movies are available this way, the larger a source of income this will become, which is good for the studios, providers (Apple, Hulu, etc.), and consumers. It is not so good for retailers of rental movies. This release mechanism, which basically makes all venues available on the same day after the theatrical run is complete, is known as a "day and date" release strategy. Thus, it shrinks the windowing system by eliminating the window between video and pay per view to one date. There is no push to shrink the window between pay per view and television, and the window between theater and video will meet even more resistance. The National Association of Theatre Owners (NATO) alliance is tough, and alienating them is not in the studios' best interest. Another reason studios have been reluctant to encourage video on demand is their fear of offending major retailers of DVDs, such as Walmart.

Consumer expectations of instant gratification, made possible by wireless access on so many convenient, portable platforms, has made it difficult for the movie industry to maintain the old windows for movies, whereby they sold the same movie multiple times in different venues, starting with the theater and moving to pay cable, DVD, and commercial television. Now consumers expect to be able to see a movie on their personal electronic devices soon after it leaves the theater. These expectations are built in part on experiences with television shows. No longer is it necessary to carve out a set time to watch a favorite television program. Tivo or a digital video recorder DVR can record the show, which can then be watched at a more convenient time. Many shows can now be viewed online from a network site or a secondary provider such as Hulu as soon as 24 hours after its original airdate.

The second wave market of watching films has begun to change. Instead of buying and renting DVDs from retail outlets such as Hollywood Video or Blockbuster, customers are more likely to stream movies online or through on-demand cable services. Mail order services like Netflix and the convenience of Redbox outlets have also eaten into the traditional rental format. Blockbuster is an example of adaptation. They have been closing retail outlets and shifting their business to a mail order service like Netflix and kiosks like Redbox.

Live Entertainment

Technology is also impacting live entertainment. Consumers of technology are in the early stages of what may well prove to be a revolution in the way they experience live performance. They are already in a position to begin to take some of the control away from the performers and creators. Some of this input is indirect, such as tweeting reviews of performances as they are being performed. Some is unintentional, such as a cellphone ringing in the middle of a symphony performance, disturbing audiences members and performers alike. It is possible that in the future, the audience may be encouraged to participate, for example, via texting potential plot twists in live plays, and preferred songs to musicians.

The New York Philharmonic and the Indianapolis Symphony have invited audience members to use their cell phones to vote on the encore to be played at the end of a concert. On the downside of all this is, of course, the continued fracturing of our attention span. Just how many things can we do at once? And when is it appropriate to use or not use the technology? Live performances routinely warn patrons to turn off their electronic devices, but there is limited ability to enforce that.

And what happens when audiences decide that texting is okay during live events? If the audience is busy encouraging their friends to buy tickets to the amazing event they are witnessing, it could be great for producers,. On the other hand, they could be sending bad reviews, which might be why they are willing to divert their attention from the performance in the first place. Then the performers and producers will have to figure out how to harness this distraction and get the texters to become a part of the performance, not a distraction from it.

It is not just performance venues that are adjusting to new technology. Museums are another example of adopting technology to meet the demands of the customers. It is not uncommon for museums to make information about their exhibits available online and via texting. Some offer "interactive" tours in this way. Not only can I scan a barcode on an exhibit and be led to much more detail about it, I can also interact with the exhibit. Some museums, for example, are sent questions from patrons about the works they see on a tour, to which museum staff respond via text.

Live performances, including theaters, operas, and symphony orchestras, have begun to face serious financial difficulties at the dawn of the twenty-first century. The problem with live performances such as these is that it is difficult or impossible to benefit from productivity gains due to technological innovations. While technology can reduce costs in the television and movie industries (think of how technology can reduce editing time and labor hours) and expand the consumer base in sports (many more fans consume games on television than in person), it is difficult to do either with live theater. Watching a symphony orchestra, opera, or play on television is not considered a good substitute for the live event. The primary, and overwhelming, cost of these productions is the cost of labor, and the necessary quantity of workers has not changed much over time. It takes just as long and just as many performers to produce Beethoven's symphonies today as it did when they were written, and the same can be said for Verdi's operas and Shakespeare's works (Baumol and Bowen 1966, Heilbrun and Gray 2001, Kotler and Scheff 1997).

American symphony orchestras lose money on their operations. The cost of tickets does not cover the cost of performances. In fact, it almost never has. It used to be that fund raising and the sale of recordings could cover the rest. But recording income has decreased for most orchestras, forcing them to rely on charitable donations to balance the budget (Felton 1994).

And on the cost side it is difficult, if not impossible, to make any real budget cuts. Most of the costs are labor, and the size of the symphony cannot really be reduced. Only salaries can. Some management staff can be cut, but that is not a significant part of the budget. Some symphony orchestras have seen salary cuts, or two-tiered salary structures, whereby new hires are paid on a lower scale, as a way to survive. But layoffs and reductions in size are not likely to be the answer. One possibility is a variation on what the Cleveland Orchestra has done by establishing a residency in Florida, performing several concerts there each year. Joint ventures, say a Cleveland and Cincinnati Orchestra, which performs in both cities and replaces the orchestra in one, may be a solution. Virtual concerts in which tickets are sold to watch the performance on mobile devices are also possible, but they are not considered a good substitute for live performances.

Conglomerations in the entertainment industry allow for the diversification of risk and the potential for cross-marketing, though widening the scope risks increased management and coordination costs. The advantages, however, seem to outweigh the costs. In 2010, Disney's movie and sports divisions performed very well, which helped offset its struggling theme park division. By focusing its output on branded items, such as the Muppets or Mickey Mouse, Disney is able to exploit cross-marketing opportunities in theme parks, video games, and commercial products.

To capitalize on this ability, Disney purchased Marvel Entertainment in 2009. This move provided Disney with a stable of 5,000 comic book characters that can be used in movies, television, theme parks, video games, and commercial products.

Though Disney has produced many standalone movies, in recent years its focus has been on branded products that can more easily be marketed on other platforms to increase their revenues, for example, video games, theme parks, and commercial products. A one-off movie that performs poorly has little opportunity to raise money in another venue (Epstein 2005).

Recorded Music

Technology has had a huge impact on the recorded music industry. It has progressed from the old recording studio days when the studio sought out artists and controlled their recordings, tours, and even careers, to the short-lived but chaotic days of Napster when the market was turned upside down by a technology that skirted the sale of music. The old studio model is dead, but so too, in all likelihood, is its early replacement, the totally independent movement where a band does its own recording using affordable and sophisticated high quality equipment and markets itself on MySpace or YouTube. Now the move is once again toward some specialization, but without the oligopolization of the market at the studio level. The new structure will have room for managers, booking agents, and recording studios, but the center will be the artists who create the music. The survivors are likely to be lean organizations built to serve the musicians, not control the market (Barnet and Burriss 2001, Montoro-Pons and Cuadrado-Garcia 2011, Suisman 2009).

Lady Gaga embodies the new move in the music world. She has established a following with her outrageous costumes, catchy tunes, and talent, but more than that, she has figured out how to market herself in the twenty-first century music world. She has a traditional label behind her, but that is about all that is traditional about the way she has marketed her music.

The new music market is based on digital access. She still has the clout of a major record label to provide marketing muscle and touring influence, but she is a product of a new kind of recording contract. Beyond merely selling albums (or CDs or whatever physical copy of the music you want) her contract also involves touring and merchandising, sometimes in ways unheard of in the music industry. Lady Gaga, for example, has her own makeup deal. A natural tie if you have ever seen her in concert. Her act is heavy on visual appeal as well; the dance moves, the makeup and the costumes, which may also have some appeal to the fashion industry—thus leading to yet another potential tie-in.

The majority of Lady Gaga's music has been sold digitally. Digital downloads are the fastest growing segment of the music market, and it is one that Gaga has exploited. In fact, millions of her songs have been listened to free—legally, by her fans via You-Tube and MySpace and other online services. She is a leader in hits on these sites, proving that giving away your product does not mean that you cannot eventually profit from it.

Traditional record companies have slashed their workforce over the past decade in response to the revolution in the music industry. The Recording Industry Association of America reports that the workforce of the major record companies decreased by 60 percent in the first decade of the twenty-first century. With fewer employees, the record labels have cut down on the number of acts they represent and increased the intensity and scope they devote to those they feel are most likely to be the big hitmakers. They are now going after money in ways other than just producing CDs and records. This has given rise to what is referred to as the 360 deal, in which a label invests more up front to market an act in exchange for a percentage of the action in a wider variety of venues, such as merchandise sales, touring revenue, and other earnings.

For their part, while the artists get fewer of the dollars they generate from these venues, they have more marketing leverage behind them, making it more likely they can make money from these sources. In fact, marketing is even more important in the current environment in which anyone can launch a YouTube video. It is a crowded marketplace, and marketing helps an act stand out in that crowd.

The recorded music industry now centers on the computer. Digital sound has come to the forefront of the industry, and the greatest challenge facing it is how to retain control over the recorded product once it is produced. Computer file sharing systems like Napster and handheld devices like the iPod have revolutionized the industry. Listeners can share music files over the internet and download libraries of music onto their computers and handheld devices, bypassing the marketplace altogether. While this type of music sharing violates U.S. copyright laws, the laws are difficult to enforce and music sharing is expensive to monitor.

Despite changes in the types of music preferred by the listening public and the different means of delivering music, the industry looks remarkably like it did a century ago. The main issues are still the same. Manufacturers seek to push the envelope and deliver the highest quality sound possible. Performers still strive to express themselves through their art. Producers compete for the opportunity to promote and distribute the best-selling stars, and consumers clamor for the best equipment to listen to the best music. Despite all the advances in technology, or perhaps because of them, the same problem besets all the players in the industry: how to control the rights to the final product. The dawning of the computer age in the recorded sound industry is not likely to solve this problem, only to complicate it.

Government Regulation

The government will play a big part in the future evolution of entertainment. The U.S. Federal Communications Commission (FCC), which regulates the airwaves and grants access to them, is a key player. The FCC mandated the change from analog to digital TV signals as one way of freeing up space on the airwaves for other uses(Coase 1966). The airwaves are crowded and have to serve many masters, including TV, radio, cellphone, internet, emergency use, and GPS. Radio and television broadcasts are no longer the darlings, nor the biggest users of the airwaves. In fact, the broadcast of television signals is a dying use of the airwaves. Most customers receive their TV signals via cable. More of the bandwidth is being devoted to mobile broadband devices, such as smartphones and computers.

Bandwidth is at a premium for streaming video, and one of the most popular uses is to stream movies. This technology already exists in the form of Netflix and Hulu, but with the explosion of different platforms on which to watch movies, a method of streaming to any or all of them is what is under construction. Disney's Keychest is an example of how this might work. The value of a studio's library of previously released films and TV shows provides a perpetual source of income. Traditionally that income has been in the form of licensing fees from commercial and cable TV, DVD sales, and video rentals (think Netflix and Blockbuster). Even though DVD sales are falling off, the future revenues from the libraries are in no danger of going away, only of being earned in a different manner.

What to Expect in the Future

Laptops, tablets, and smartphones have started to transform the way we consume our entertainment. From watching movies and television shows anywhere and everywhere to texting reviews and blogging them during and after a show to posting reviews on Facebook and inviting our friends to socialize with us. The new uses of social media are affecting the way we market entertainment and think about it (Chingtagunta, Gopinath, and Venkataraman 2010).

Today, technology has redefined all entertainment venues. The computer has altered the way we view movies and listen to music as well as how we read books, newspapers, and magazines. It has changed how we follow our favorite sports team and will continue to impact the entertainment industry into the future. Will one of the current forms of entertainment become the twenty-first–century vaudeville? How will technology affect what we have now and what might evolve?

Technology has the potential to turn the television and movie industries on their heads. The ability to record programs and watch them without commercials later on has already sparked debate on the role of viewer ratings and what they mean. How should a show recorded and viewed later be counted by the ratings services? Advertisers are reluctant to use such figures because of viewers' ability to skip their commercials. The falling price of super-sized flat screen high definition television sets and surround sound has made it possible for more Americans to bring the experience of the movie theater into the home. The popularity of in-home movie systems has further blurred the distinction. This raises questions about the release strategy of movies. How long, if at all, should they play exclusively in a theater? The day when major motion picture releases are available for streaming in the home at the same time as they are on the big screen is in the not-too-distant future.

So what does the future hold for the entertainment industry? If we look back at the past century, technology has been the defining characteristic of its evolution. There does not seem to be any reason to think that will change. The advances in the first half of the twentieth century, which saw the electrification of the country and the dawning of recorded sound, movies, radio, and television, were dramatic. But the quantum leap in technology over the past generation has been at least as impressive thanks to the rise of portable electronic devices capable of providing access to entertainment. Technology has translated the television, record player, and radio, which each once held a conspicuous place in the living room, into a handheld phone, which can also be used to play games and surf the internet.

Television sets were once the size of ovens, with a screen eight inches on the diagonal. Today they are available with a 54-inch liquid crystal display (LCD) flat screen, and signals are transmitted in high definition over a cable. Early television was restricted to a handful of channels. The eventual arrival of cable and satellite television has increased the number of potential channels into the hundreds. Early television was broadcast in black and white. Now television shows are in color, and even 3D, and can be viewed on computers and cell phones, not just a television set.

The switch in the United States to digital television signals improved the quality of the product but not the content. The switch was not seemless however, adding to the complaints, in larger numbers from older viewers, about the forced transfer to digital. When the last major stations turned off their analog TV in June 2009 and began to broadcast entirely in digital, some of them moved their digital signals from the UHF frequency band (channels 14 through 69) to the VHF channels (2 through 13). To most viewers, these channels are just different numbers on their remote, but as signals in the airwaves, they are very different.

VHF had not been used much for digital signals, and there were fears that the switch would not go smoothly as a result of the lack of good quality antennas in consumer homes where cable was not present. Even though there were problems, it was not possible for all of the stations to remain on UHF or switch back because the FCC had sold off some of the UHF bandwidth to cell phone companies, leaving less available space for television broadcasts. Another reason for the switch to digital was to free up some UHF space to reserve for emergency services.

The movies and television have metamorphosed from substitutes to complements to the same industry. Mergers at the corporate level have turned television and movie studios into the same companies. Satellite technology has changed the landscape of the material shown on televisions and heard on radios. Since satellite transmissions are not broadcast into the public airwaves, but only to paying subscribers, they are not subject to FCC censorship regulations. This has led to a proliferation of material that would never be allowed over the public airwaves.

The technical quality of entertainment, if not the quality of the product itself, has increased along with the quantity of it consumed. The decadent salaries paid to top entertainers ensure that the best and most talented will continue to be attracted to the industry. Technology has improved the quality of the presentations as well. Today's digital movies are superior to the old silent reels, and even cinemascope seems primitive. Today's television offerings are being broadcast in high definition and on flat screen plasma televisions with screens measured in feet, not inches. Satellite radio has made static and fading signals a thing of the past, and the CD has turned the record into a relic. Now the iPod and computer threaten to eliminate the physical existence of recorded sound altogether, replacing it with digitally stored music in quantities too vast to number.

With almost every household owning a television, radio, and CD player, there is not much to be gained in the way of further market penetration. In terms of the other trends—shorter workweeks, urbanization, and increased incomes—there seem to be limits.

Average weekly manufacturing hours fell from 59 in 1900 to 38.1 on the eve of World War II. Since then, they have held steady. It does not appear that the trend is toward fewer work hours. That means if there is to be increased time for leisure, it will have to come from savings in time spent on household chores. There is certainly room to maneuver here, as technological advances could continue to allow for reductions in work time spent on domestic tasks. If technology does not help to reduce the amount of time spent on household chores, changes in other areas may. One that already has for many middle and upper income Americans is hired help. Rising incomes have allowed them to hire others to perform those chores. House cleaners, personal shoppers, yard workers, child care providers, and personal chefs have all played a part in reducing the amount of time spent on household jobs, thus freeing up leisure time, at least for those who can afford it (Vandenbroucke 2009).

The percentage of urban dwellers is already at 82 percent, having more than doubled since 1900, although most of that increase came in the first half of the twentieth century. By 1950, the total was up to 64 percent, and by 1970, it was over 73 percent. There is less land in America left to urbanize, and the rate of doing so has slowed dramatically.

Since 1960, the share of household expenditures devoted to housing, transportation, food, and clothing have all decreased. Spending on recreation, on the other hand, has increased by 60 percent. The biggest source of that increase has been expenditures on computer software and games, which have increased by 300 percent since 1990.

Increased income and education may lead to a greater diversification of the entertainment industry. As more people can afford to try more varieties of entertainment, the future holds the possibility of an even broader industry with more choices (Snowball 2010).

By the end of the twentieth century, Americans had fully endorsed the concept of entertainment and recreation. The American Time Use Survey conducted by the U.S. Bureau of Labor Statistics (BLS) shows that Americans age 15 and older spend five hours a day on leisure and recreation activities. Only work and sleep consume more time.

What does the future hold? The past would suggest we should expect more sophisticated forms of entertainment, more time to enjoy it, and bigger potential audiences as entertainment moves to the internet. It is likely that entertainment will continue to be defined by technology, particularly the personal computer, as it finds its way into more American homes and continues to improve in quality. In the end, watching the evolution of the industry in itself should be entertaining. Only time will tell.

References

Barnet, Richard D. and Larry L. Burriss, *Controversies of the Music Industry*, Westport, CT: Greenwood Press, 2001.

Batten, Frank, *The Weather Channel: The Improbable Rise of a Media Phenomenon*, Boston: Harvard Business School Press, 2002.

Baumol, William J. and William G. Bowen, *Performing Arts: The Economic Dilemma*, New York: Twentieth Century Fund, 1966.

Box Office Mojo, http://boxofficemojo.com/.

Bureau of Labor Statistics, Bureau of Labor Statistics, http://www.bls.gov/news.release/pdf/atus.pdf.

Cairncross, F., *The Death of Distance: How the Communications Revolution Will Change Our Lives*, Boston: Harvard Business School Press, 1997.

Caves, Richard E., *Creative Industries: Contracts between Art and Commerce*, Cambridge: Harvard University Press, 2000.

Chingtagunta, Praddep K., Shyam Gopinath, and Siriam Venkataraman, "The Effects of Online User Reviews on Movie Box Office Performance: Accounting for Sequential Rollout and Aggregation across Local Markets," *Marketing Science* 29, no. 5, September–October 2010, pp. 944–57.

Chiou, Lesley, "The Timing of Movie Releases: Evidence from the Home Video Industry," *International Journal of Industrial Organization* 26, no. 5, September 2008, pp. 1059–73.

Coase, Ronald, "The Economics of Broadcasting and Government Policy," *American Economic Review* 56, May 1966, pp. 440–47.

Comstock, George, *The Evolution of American Television*, Newbury Park, CA: Sage, 1989.

De Vany, Arthur S. and David W. Walls, "Estimating the Effects of Movie Piracy on Box-Office Revenue," *Review of Industrial Organization* 30, no. 4, June 2007, pp. 291–301.

Dupagne, M. and P. Seel, *High-Definition Television: A Global Perspective*, Ames: Iowa State University Press, 1998.

Epstein, Edward Jay, *The Big Picture: Money and Power in Hollywood*, New York: Random House, 2005.

Felton, Marianne Victorius, "Evidence of the Existence of the Cost Disease in the Performing Arts," *Journal of Cultural Economics* 18, no. 4, December 1994, pp. 301–12.

Green, Abel and Joe Laurie, Jr., *Show Biz: From Vaude to Video*, New York: Holt, 1951.

Hand, Chris, "What Makes a Blockbuster? Economic Analysis of Film Success in the United Kingdom," *Managerial and Decision Economics* 23, no. 6, September 2002, pp. 343–54.

Hanson, Gordon and Chong Xiang, "Trade Barriers and Trade Flows with Product Heterogeneity: An Application to US Motion Picture Exports," *Journal of International Economics* 83, no. 1, January 2011, pp. 14–26.

Hart, Jeffrey A., *Technology, Television and Competition: The Politics of Digital TV*, Cambridge: Cambridge University Press, 2004.

Haupert, Michael, *The Entertainment Industry*, Westport, CT: Greenwood Publishing, 2006.

Heilbrun, James and Charles M. Gray, *The Economics of Art and Culture*, New York: Cambridge University Press, 2001.

Hilliard, Robert L. and Michael C. Keith, *The Broadcast Century*, Burlington, MA: Elsevier, 2010.

Hollywood.com Box Office, http://www.hollywood.com/boxoffice/.

Jozefowicz, James J., Jason M. Kelley, and Stephanie M. Brewer, "New Release: An Empirical Analysis of VHS/DVD Rental Success," *Atlantic Economic Journal* 36, no. 2, June 2008, pp. 139–51.

Kotler, Philip, and Joanne Scheff. *Standing Room Only*. Boston: Harvard Business School Press, 1997.

Liebowitz, Stan J., "File Sharing: Creative Destruction or Just Plain Destruction?" *Journal of Law and Economics* 49, no. 1, symposium: Piracy and File Sharing, April 2006, pp. 1–28.

Matlaw, Myron (Ed.), *American Popular Entertainment: Papers and Proceedings of the Conference on the History of American Popular Entertainment*, Westport, CT: Praeger, 1979.

Montoro-Pons, Juan D., and Manuel Cuadrado-Garcia, "Live and Prerecorded Popular Music Consumption," *Journal of Cultural Economics* 35, no. 1, February 2011, pp. 19–48.

Motion Picture Association of America, http://mpaa.org/policy/industry.

National Association of Theater Owners, http://www.natoonline.org/

SNL Kagan, http://www.snl.com/Sectors/Media/FilmedEntertainment TVProgramming.aspx.

Snowball, Jeanette D., *Measuring the Value of Culture: Methods and Examples in Cultural Economics*, Berlin: Springer-Verlag, 2010.

Stoeber, Rudolf, "What Media Evolution Is: A Theoretical Approach to the History of New Media," *European Journal of Communication* 19, no. 4, December 2004, pp. 483–505.

Suisman, David, *Selling Sounds: The Commercial Revolution in American Music*, Cambridge: Harvard University Press, 2009.

Vandenbroucke, Guillaume, "Trends in Hours: The U.S. from 1900 to 1950," *Journal of Economic Dynamics and Control* 33, no. 1, January 2009, pp. 237–49.

Waterman, David, Sung Wook Ji, and Laura R. Rochet, "Enforcement and Control of Piracy, Copying, and Sharing in the Movie Industry," *Review of Industrial Organization* 30, no. 4, June 2007, pp. 255–89.

3

Entertainment around the World

Whether in America, Africa, Asia, or anywhere in between, entertainment has the same basic purpose, and it is affected by the same types of things. The more money and the more free time available, the more consumers will spend on entertainment. Thus, the most active entertainment industries in the world are in the wealthiest countries in the world. The concept of entertainment is not any different across countries, and neither, for the most part, are the most popular ways citizens of most any country have of entertaining themselves. Some of the details differ, but an American travelling abroad would not have much trouble identifying with the entertainment industry anywhere. And thanks to the internet, we can be exposed to worldwide entertainment right in our own living rooms.

Television

The television industry is largely the same across countries: networks act as the agents to bring viewers to advertisers. However, the technology has historically been different. Television has evolved in three main systems: PAL (phase alternating line), NTSC (National Television System Committee), and SECAM (sequential color with memory). These systems are different standards of transmitting an analog television signal. PAL is used in Europe, parts of Africa, the Middle East, Latin America, and Australia. NTSC is used primarily in North America, and SECAM is the dominant form in Asia and Eastern Europe. These are all technical means of transmitting an analog signal, but the bottom line to the consumer is that they are incompatible. For that reason, television sets will not work when moved from one region to another. Of more immediate impact on consumers, DVD and video copies of movies and television shows will not work on sets in other regions either (Hart 2004).

This problem is diminishing as digital transmission replaces analog. While the transmission technical details still differ in digital TV, sets are becoming more savvy and are more likely to be able to convert either signal. The latest technology for Blu-ray and DVD players likewise is capable of handling DVDs from multiple regions. The availability of an increasingly large body of material on the internet has begun to render the issue immaterial. However, over the last half of the twentieth century, as television grew to become one of the most popular leisure time activities in the world, these technical differences did produce some minor roadblocks to international connoisseurs of television who wished to import their favorite shows from one country to another (Dupgane and Seel 1998).

The global move to digital television signals frees up bandwidth for more valuable uses, including cell phones and wi-fi. It is also a higher quality signal and allows for more channels to be delivered in the same space. The digital transmission also offers the possibility of interactivity with the viewer, such as on-demand technology and internet. The United States, Japan, Canada, Arab countries, the United Kingdom, Australia, and some Latin American and Asian countries have all either eliminated, or are scheduled to eliminate, analog television signal transmissions in favor of digital transmission. Most countries have begun the transition process, though some still broadcast in both formats.

Besides technical differences, there are market differences between television industries around the world. European television is more centralized than in the United States. Television in the United States is based on local stations affiliating with networks, and a cable system of hundreds of channels, whereas European systems evolved as national and regional stations. Thus, there is less of a competitive market in Europe than the United States. The U.S. model has multiple stations in each local market, competing with one another for viewers. In European markets, television developed on a national scale, with state networks providing signals to the entire country and some regional stations added to the mix. Thus there is no real competition in the market. Because there are no networks in Europe, local stations, if they existed, would be on their own to provide programming. Other than local newscasts, local U.S. stations provide little if any of their own programming. Most of it is delivered by the network with which they are affiliated, though during nonprime hours they do purchase syndicated material. The lack of local ratings services in European markets makes it a challenge to sell advertising over the few local channels that do exist.

The Movie Industry

Hollywood is synonymous with movies the world over. But Hollywood is not the only source of films. In fact, it is neither the source of most films, nor the largest producer of them—at least not the total number of films. It still rules in worldwide box office revenues though, and in the all-important movie category of "buzz," Hollywood rules the world. But technology, changing tastes, and the migration of people across national borders have all combined to increase the global nature of the movie business and hint at its likely future.

Bollywood

Perhaps the most famous movie industry outside of Hollywood is the Indian movie industry, popularly referred to as Bollywood, which produces original films in Hindi. The industry is based in Mumbai. While Bollywood is the most famous, it is not the only location for the Indian film industry. There are other production centers in the country, which produce films in regional languages. Bollywood is the largest in the country, and one of the largest film production centers in the world.

The name Bollywood is derived, obviously, from Hollywood, with the *B* standing for Bombay, the former name of Mumbai. Unlike Hollywood, there is no actual place called Bollywood. The name is actually not even original, as it was taken from the nickname Tollywood, given in the 1930s to the Bengali film industry, which was centered in Tollygunge, the center of the Indian film industry at the time.

While Bollywood actually produces more films than Hollywood studios, they are not on the same scale. The most expensive

Bollywood productions tend to be in the area of about $20 million. The most expensive Bollywood film of all time, *Ra.One*, produced in 2011, cost $27 million, which is about what Johnny Depp was paid to reprise his role as Captain Jack Sparrow in a *Pirates of the Caribbean* sequel. Hollywood blockbusters routinely cost in the hundreds of millions of dollars to produce, not to mention marketing costs. Indians tend to buy more movie tickets than do Americans, but the American film industry takes in much more money, both from higher average ticket prices and wider and deeper ancillary revenue sources.

Prior to the mid-1990s, special effects, costumes, and sets of the average Bollywood movie paled in comparison to their American counterparts. However, the wider availability of American movies and television programs in India led to increased expectations on the part of Indians, putting pressure on Bollywood to improve its offerings, which it has done.

Bollywood faces problems similar to those of Hollywood related to pirated films. DVD copies of movies are often available even before the official release of the movie. The Indian film industry estimates that piracy costs more than $100 million a year in lost revenue. On the positive side, though, the only way that Pakistanis can see Bollywood movies is by purchasing DVD copies on the black market, since the Pakistani government has banned the sale, distribution, and exhibition of Indian films in the country.

Like Hollywood, there are several available outlets for a Bollywood movie to earn revenue. Legitimate DVD sales, television broadcasts, and foreign box office are all possibilities. Producers often recoup their costs by selling these ancillary rights to their films. The growing population of Indians in western countries has helped the foreign box office for Bollywood films grow.

The Indian film market has made major gains toward respectability in the twenty-first century. Reliance Entertainment, part of an Indian conglomerate, was in serious talks in 2008 to finance Steven Spielberg and David Geffen ventures. The company had already signed production deals with big names in Hollywood, for example, director Chris Columbus and stars Brad Pitt and George Clooney. Reliance is interested in Hollywood so that it can diversify its portfolio and create a new genre of Indian American film. As the global market grows, the opportunities grow with it.

Though Bollywood is still much smaller than Hollywood as measured by total revenue, it is growing at a faster rate. By the end of the first decade of the twenty-first century, Bollywood was growing at double-digit rates, while Hollywood was barely growing at 3 percent.

The Indian film industry is actually ahead of Hollywood in terms of discovering and embracing new types of distribution for its films. For example, Bollywood embraced the internet as an outlet for its films much more quickly than has Hollywood. In part, this is because of the large population of Indians living outside of the country, whose only real access to Bollywood films is over the internet. Bollywood films are often released online, for a nominal download fee of about $10, at the same time as their theatrical release. While it may seem like they are cannibalizing their own theater revenues, the theater and internet versions of a film are not perfect substitutes. While the story is the same, the experience certainly is not. Those who download the film, especially expatriates living in western countries, would not likely have purchased a ticket to see the film in a theater anyway, so instead of losing those customers to the download, they are selling a product they likely would not have, gaining revenue otherwise unavailable.

Eros International, India's largest integrated film studio, is aggressive about moving into the new digital age. To take advantage of the interest in films on the internet and other mobile devices, Eros began digitizing its entire library of films in 2009 to ensure that their library would be available for sale on the variety of platforms consumers are now viewing films, such as tablets and smartphones.

Eros also helped produce two Hollywood films in 2009: *Tron Legacy* and *Moby Dick*. Eros ended fiscal year 2011 with total income increasing by 24 percent to $1.2 billion, less than a third of what an average Hollywood studio earned.

Importance of Foreign Box Office

Technology has played a major role in increasing the importance of the foreign box office for films produced anywhere. A more mobile population has spread people around the globe in locales far from their country of origin, but this movement has not diminished their interest in their own culture, which includes home-grown films. This is as true for Americans in Europe as it is for

Indians in the United Kingdom and Chinese in North America. The internet, digital films, satellite transmission, and wide variety of platforms on which to see films means the box office is only one choice. As a result, the global box office and ancillary sources of revenue are increasingly important as a source of revenue for films, regardless of where they are made (Bakker 2003a, Bakker 2005, Bakker 2008).

As exposure to foreign cultures increases, so does interest in their cultural products, including movies. Hollywood has seen its dependence on the foreign box office nearly triple in the last quarter century. One result of this globalization of the movies has been an increase in the number of foreign stars and coproduced ventures with foreign studios. The lower cost of distributing digital films and the growth in importance of online sources of movie revenue have only increased the importance of global markets in the revenue stream of any film, whether produced in Hollywood, Bollywood, or anywhere in between (Hand 2002, Hanson and Xiang 2011, Jozefowicz, Kelley, and Brewer 2008).

European Cinema

The British film market comprises about 7 percent of the global box office, and only about twice that percentage of the U.K. box office. The dominant share of the box office, as in most of the world, is captured by Hollywood films. The British film industry relies heavily on its American counterpart. Many British films are coproduced with American studios, using British and American actors and behind the screen personnel. U.K. production facilities, such as Pinewood Studios, feature cutting-edge technology that is often used by foreign companies producing all or part of their film in the United Kingdom. The common language, frequent collaboration, and cultural similarities sometimes make it difficult to tell British from American influence in the two countries' films (Macmillan and Smith 2001, Miksell 2006, Miksell 2009, Sedgwick and Pokorny 2005).

In the 1970s, British studios established a reputation for their leading work in special effects. While Hollywood has since caught up, Aardman Animations, a British company located in Bristol, is still world-renowned for its stop-motion animation films.

The internet and the move to digital film have allowed the two countries' studios to work even more closely on globally distributed productions. As the technology develops, the future is likely to result in digital distribution and production of films as a common means of release.

Asian Film

The Asian film industry is associated with films produced in Japan, China, and Korea. The Japanese anime style of filmmaking has grown in popularity this century in the United States and Europe. The rising popularity of anime and the growing number of independent filmmakers helped buoy the flagging Japanese film industry. The opening up and rapid growth of the Chinese economy has further bolstered the Asian film industry. Not only are Asian films recapturing some of their domestic markets, they are increasingly exported. The appearance of Asian films in American theaters is still not common, but their popularity among American viewers online and via DVD is growing (Sunada 2010).

South Korea is one of the few countries outside of the United States to watch more domestically produced films than foreign films. In large part this is due to a Korean law limiting the number of foreign films that can be shown per year. Another law requires that Korean films play for a minimum of 73 days per year in each theater. The Korean television industry is similarly protective, requiring that 25 percent of films shown must be of domestic origin, though that ratio is set to decrease. The popularity of Korean films in the domestic market is increasing. For example, in South Korea just a decade ago, locally made films accounted for less than 20 percent of the Korean box office. By 2010, that figure had risen to 50 percent despite the loosening of restrictions on the exhibition of foreign films.

A less complimentary association with Asia and the movie industry is their link in the video piracy problem. In particular, the Chinese market is cited as a main source of bootlegged films.

Piracy Issues

Some countries, including Canada, Spain, and Panama, allow individuals to download copyrighted music for personal use. Copyright enforcement in these cases extends only to the distribution and sale of the material. In Russia, copyrighted music and films may be copied for personal use. The holders of creative copyrights are reimbursed through a tax on goods associated with the copying of film and music, such as computers, blank CD-RW disks, and recording devices. These differences in copyright laws make for some strained relations between American film and recording studios and foreign governments when copyright infringement issues arise.

The protection of intellectual property rights in China has been granted only since 1979. Within China, it is illegal to infringe on domestic or foreign copyrights. Chinese law protects these copyrights, and China has accepted the major international conventions in regard to protecting copyrights. All of this has occurred in the last generation, yet instances of copyright violations stemming from China are still common.

The incidence of music copyright infringement in China is among the highest in the world. The International Federation of the Phonographic Industry (IFPI) claims that as much as 95 percent of all music sales in China are unauthorized, originating from bootleg copies of music. Illegal file sharing, of the sort for which Napster was infamous, is common on a large scale according to IFPI. The problems in China stem from a lack of enforcement, varying degrees of which exist in different areas of the country, and unclear copyright laws, some of which have undergone major alterations in the recent past in an attempt to clarify and strengthen them. Much of the increase in Chinese attention to piracy has come since the United States filed an action against China with the World Trade Organization (WTO) in 2007 for violating intellectual property rights (De Vany and Walls 2007, Liebowitz 2006, Waterman, Wook and Rochet 2007).

Spectator Sports

The professional sports industry is worldwide. The concept is the same the world over; only the sports differ. While American football is the undisputed king in the United States, followed by baseball, basketball, and then hockey, that pecking order changes in other parts of the world. Football is popular the world over, but not the American version. What the rest of the world calls football, we call soccer, and soccer is the sport of choice in Europe, the Middle East, and Latin America.

Baseball is popular in Asia and Latin America, there is professional basketball in China and Europe, and tennis and golf are played professionally on five continents. But the granddaddy of them all are the Olympic Games, held every four years in each of two venues: winter and summer, in different locations. The popularity of the Olympics, and the attention and economic impact they bring, lead to competitive bidding among nations to host the quadrennial extravaganza. The Olympics have their roots in ancient Greece, but the current iteration of the games, referred to as the Modern Olympic Games, dates from 1896.

The Olympic Games were originally a five-day festival with religious connections. The ancient Olympics ended in 391 CE when a decree issued by the Roman emperor Theodosius I prohibited all pagan worship, which included the Olympic Games. The games were reborn under the guidance of Baron Pierre de Coubertin in Athens, Greece, in 1896.

Sports that have succeeded commercially are widely recognized as being businesses in the entertainment industry. The growth of professional sports in an economy is a function of economic development. As wealth and leisure time grow, so does the demand for sports as a consumption good. This helps explain why professional sports are a much larger part of the entertainment landscape in developed countries (Drever and MacDonald 1981, Garcia and Rodriguez 2002).

Television had the greatest impact on sports in the last half of the twentieth century. The financial success of sports is due to its exposure on television. The most successful professional team sports in the world (soccer, American football, and the Olympics) generate more money from television rights fees than they do from live attendance. Golf and tennis owe their large purses to the growth of television fees in the last two decades. The less successful professional team sports, such as hockey and basketball, have improved their status greatly with television packages, but they are still not on the same par as the aforementioned sports (Feddersen and Rott 2011).

The tradition that is Hockey Night in Canada began on radio in 1935. The Canadian Broadcasting Company began doing weekly television broadcasts in the 1950s. For years, either the Montreal or Toronto team would be televised every Saturday night during the season. When the two teams met in the 1959 Stanley Cup, the TV ratings set an all-time high in Canada.

The single most popular sporting event in the world is the World Cup soccer tournament, an international soccer championship held every four years, and like the Olympics, staged each time in a different country. More people watch the World Cup than any other sporting event. It was inaugurated in Uruguay in 1930 in response to the professionalization of soccer. As more of the world's best players became professionals, it became apparent that a true championship match could not be played in the Olympics anymore, where the international championship had been staged (Falter, Perignon, and Vercruysse 2008).

Professional sports leagues have all evolved in a monopoly framework, seeking to control the competition, the consumer base, and the labor pool, to varying degrees of success. In team sports, the owners formed cartels. Organizers of individual sports like tennis and golf attempted to control the tournaments. Without fail, the most financially successful sports leagues have been cartels that grew and thrived on the back of exploited labor and monopolized geographic areas for teams. In the United States, competing leagues arose to cash in on the monopoly profits in football, hockey, basketball, and baseball, and in every case they were either bankrupted or merged into the established league. As a result, despite a century of monopoly profits, each of these sports still enjoys monopoly status.

In other parts of the world, though sports are at least as popular, this format has not been as apparent. In Europe, football leagues are divided into divisions, with the worst teams in each division dropping down a rung and the best moving up to the next division at the end of each season. These divisions are primarily organized on a scale of city size, hence by revenue generating ability. The top division teams are in major metropolitan areas, while the bottom division teams are located in smaller towns in older stadiums. The lower division teams generate less revenue and hence pay lower salaries and attract lesser talent. For the most part, teams in the lower leagues survive by developing players and selling them to teams in the higher leagues, where the players can generate greater marginal revenues (Cain and Haddock 2005, Forrest and Simmons 2006).

The same formula works in every country and sport: the highest salaries are paid to the best athletes, attracting them to the teams that can then sell tickets to a public demanding the best in athletic entertainment. Regardless of the sport or the country, that fundamental relationship holds. Whether it is Spanish basketball, German soccer, Pakistani cricket, or Japanese baseball, the business of sports as an entertainment venue is universal.

Live Performance

The cost disease, a situation in which labor costs increase but labor productivity does not, affects live performance around the world. The way it is addressed varies somewhat in different countries. In Europe, because government support of the arts is the norm, cost disease is not an issue. Governments simply pick up the cost, which, of course, is passed on to taxpayers. Europeans pay more in taxes than Americans, and when it comes to the arts, the benefits are noticeable. Germany, for example, with its public funding of the arts, has more than 20 times as many full-time symphony and opera companies per capita as the United States does (Baumol and Bowen 1966, Sullivan and Pry 1991).

Some of the best theater in the world can be found in Europe. The opera houses of Germany, Italy, and France are regarded as among the premier venues in the world, and London's West End is the European equivalent of Broadway for theatergoers.

In Asia, theater is also a popular form of entertainment, though it is not as universally recognized as it is in the western hemisphere. South Korea established the National Theater of Korea in 1950. It serves as one of the premier theaters in Asia, hosting the National Drama Company of Korea, which performs both international and traditional Korean material. The National Changgeuk Company specializes in changgeuk, a traditional Korean opera.

Traditional Japanese theater is performed around the world. There are many forms, but the most famous are the kabuki (famous for its spectacular costumes and elaborate swordfights) and the puppet theater known as bunraku. As the country opened to western influence in the twentieth century, it opened also to western theater influences. The modern Japanese drama reflects these influences, but it has not replaced the more traditional formats, thus offering the Japanese theatergoer a wide range of possibilities.

Conclusion

The world of entertainment is shrinking as technology improves. Technology knows no boundaries, and that is certainly true in the global entertainment industry. One way in which technology has had an interesting impact is outsourcing. Outsourcing is typically thought of as something a large corporation does to save on unskilled labor costs. However, the ability to share files and send them over the airwaves has expanded the outsourcing market to include previously unexportable creative endeavors. For example, YouTube has allowed anyone in the world to publicize their music to anyone else in the world. It has also allowed for global collaboration. Indian choreographers and dancers record videos to the music of an American musician, and Eastern European orchestras record the soundtrack for a British movie. As the quality of technology continues to improve, this will become more common.

References

Bakker, Gerben, "Entertainment Industrialized: The Emergence of the International Film Industry: 1890–1940," *Enterprise and Society* 4, no. 4, December 2003, pp. 579–85.

Bakker, Gerben, "The Decline and Fall of the European Film Industry: Sunk Costs, Market Size, and Market Structure: 1890–1927," *Economic History Review*, New Series, 58, no. 2, May 2005, pp. 310–51.

Bakker, Gerben, *Entertainment Industrialized: The Emergence of the International Film Industry: 1890–1940*, New York: Cambridge University Press, 2008.

Baumol, William J. and William G. Bowen, *Performing Arts: The Economic Dilemma*, New York: Twentieth Century Fund, 1966.

Cain, Louis P. and David D. Haddock, "Similar Economic Histories, Different Industrial Structures: Transatlantic Contrasts in the Evolution of Professional Sports Leagues," *Journal of Economic History* 65, no. 4, December 2005, pp. 1116–47.

De Vany, Arthur S. and David W. Walls, "Estimating the Effects of Movie Piracy on Box-Office Revenue," *Review of Industrial Organization* 30, no. 4, June 2007, pp. 291–301.

Drever, P. and J. MacDonald, "Attendances of South Australian Football Games," *International Review of Sports Sociology* 16, no. 2, 1981, pp. 103–13.

Dupagne, M. and P. Seel. *High-Definition Television: A Global Perspective*, Ames: Iowa State University Press, 1998.

Falter, Jean-Marc, Christophe Perignon, and Olivier Vercruysse, "Impact of Overwhelming Joy on Consumer Demand: The Case of a Soccer World

Cup Victory," *Journal of Sports Economics* 9, no. 1, February 2008, pp. 20–42.

Feddersen, Arne and Armin Rott, "Determinants of Demand for Televised Live Football: Features of the German National Football Team," *Journal of Sports Economics* 12, no. 3, June 2011, pp. 352–69.

Forest, David and Rob Simmons, "New Issues in Attendance Demand: The Case of the English Football League," *Journal of Sports Economics* 7, no. 3, August 2006, pp. 247–66.

Garcia, Jaume and Placido Rodriguez, "The Determinants of Football Match Attendance Revisited: Empirical Evidence From the Spanish Football League," *Journal of Sports Economics* 3, no. 1, February 2002, pp. 18–38.

Hand, Chris, "What Makes a Blockbuster? Economic Analysis of Film Success in the United Kingdom," *Managerial and Decision Economics* 23, no. 6, September 2002, pp. 343–54.

Hanson, Gordon, and Chong Xiang, "Trade Barriers and Trade Flows with Product Heterogeneity: An Application to US Motion Picture Exports," *Journal of International Economics* 83, no. 1, January 2011, pp. 14–26.

Hart, Jeffrey A., *Technology, Television and Competition: The Politics of Digital TV*, Cambridge: Cambridge University Press, 2004.

Jozefowicz, James J., Jason M. Kelley, and Stephanie M. Brewer, "New Release: An Empirical Analysis of VHS/DVD Rental Success," *Atlantic Economic Journal* 36, no. 2, June 2008, pp. 139–51.

Liebowitz, Stan J., "File Sharing: Creative Destruction or Just Plain Destruction?" *Journal of Law and Economics* 49, no. 1, symposium: Piracy and File Sharing, April 2006, pp. 1–28.

Macmillan, Peter and Ian Smith, "Explaining Post-War Cinema Attendance in Great Britain," *Journal of Cultural Economics* 25, no. 2, May 2001, pp. 91–108.

Miksell, Peter, "'Selling America to the World?' The Rise and Fall of an International Film Distributor in Its Largest Foreign Market: United Artists in Britain: 1927–1947," *Enterprise and Society* 7, no. 4, December 2006, pp. 740–76.

Miksell, Peter, "Resolving the Global Efficiency versus Local Adaptability Dilemma: US Film Multinationals in Their Largest Foreign Market in the 1930s and 1940s," *Business History* 51, no. 3, May 2009, pp. 426–44.

Sedgwick, John and Michael Pokorny, "The Film Business in the United States and Britain during the 1930s," *Economic History Review* 58, no. 1, February 2005, pp. 79–112.

Sullivan, Edward J. and Kevin B. Pry, "Eighteenth Century London Theater and the Capture Theory of Regulation," *Journal of Cultural Economics* 15, no. 2, December 1991, pp. 41–52.

Sunada, Mitsuru, "Vertical Integration in the Japanese Movie Industry," *Journal of Industry, Competition and Trade* 10, no. 2, June 2010, pp. 135–50.

Waterman, David, Sung Wook Ji, and Laura R. Rochet, "Enforcement and Control of Piracy, Copying, and Sharing in the Movie Industry," *Review of Industrial Organization* 30, no. 4, June 2007, pp. 255–89.

4

Chronology

1810	Phineas T. Barnum is born in Bethel, Connecticut, on July 5.
1837	Tony Pastor is born in New York City on May 28.
1846	Benjamin F. Keith, the "father of vaudeville" is born in Hillsboro Bridge, New Hampshire, on January 26.
1847	Thomas Edison is born on February 11 in Milan, Ohio.
1861	Helen Louise Leonard is born on December 4 in Clinton, Iowa. As Lillian Russell, she will go on to dominate the American stage, becoming one of America's greatest actors in the early twentieth century.
1863	Pierre de Coubertin, founder of the modern Olympic Games, is born in Paris on New Year's Day.
1868	The All England Lawn Tennis and Croquet Club is founded. In 1877 it will host the first Lawn Tennis Championship.
1867	Inventor Eldridge Johnson is born on February 18. He and Thomas Edison are credited with the invention of the phonograph.

1869	The first college football game, pitting Rutgers against Princeton, takes place on November 6.
1869	The first all-professional baseball team, the Cincinnati Red Stockings, is formed.
1871	P. T. Barnum debuts his first circus.
1871	The first professional sports league, the National Association of Professional Baseball Clubs, charged a $10 franchise fee.
1873	Radio pioneer Lee de Forest is born in Council Bluffs, Iowa.
1873	Enrico Caruso is born on February 25 in Naples, Italy.
1874	Harry Houdini is born as Ehrich Weisz on March 24 in Budapest, Hungary.
1876	National League of Professional Baseball Teams is organized.
1877	The Wimbledon tennis championships are held for the first time. In its inaugural year, only a men's singles championship is held. Wimbledon will go on to become the oldest, and arguably, most prestigious tennis championship in the sport.
1878	On April 24, the Edison Speaking Phonograph Company is organized in Connecticut.
1881	Tony Pastor opens what is considered to be the first true vaudeville theater, in New York City.
1879	William Hays is born on November 5 in Sullivan, Indiana.
1879	William Fox is born Wilhelm Fried in Tolcsva, Hungary, on January 1.

1880	William Claude Dukenfield, better known as W. C. Fields, is born in Darby, Pennsylvania, on January 29.
1883	Benjamin F. Keith stages his variety show in a Boston storefront.
1885	Benjamin F. Keith and Edward F. Albee become partners, launching the Keith-Albee vaudeville circuit.
1888	Al Jolson is born on May 26 in Lithuania. He was the first person to speak in the movies.
1889	Louis Glass invents the "jukebox," though it would not be known by that name for another generation.
1890	Howard Armstrong, inventor of FM radio, is born in New York City on December 18.
1891	P. T. Barnum dies in Bridgeport, Connecticut, on April 7.
1891	David Sarnoff, one of the leading figures in the development of the U.S. entertainment industry as head of RCA for more than three decades, is born in Minsk, Belarus.
1891	The game of basketball is invented in Springfield, Massachusetts, by Dr. James Naismith.
1892	Mary Pickford, America's first female screen superstar, is born in Canada on April 9.
1894	The first kinetoscope parlor, the precursor to the modern movie theater, opens in New York city on April 14.
1895	George Halas, one of the founders of the National Football League (NFL), is born on February 2 in Chicago.
1895	Enrico Caruso makes his professional opera debut in Naples, Italy.

1896	The theater syndicate is formed by six theater owners; Marc Klaw and A. L. Erlanger are the most prominent. They establish a booking monopoly and by 1904 control the booking in over 500 theaters, including all but a few of the first-class theaters in New York City.
1896	On April 23, Thomas Edison makes the first public display of his motion picture projector, which he calls the Vitascope.
1896	The first modern Olympic Games are held in Athens from April 6 to 15. Two hundred forty-one athletes from 14 countries participated in 43 events.
1896	Eldridge Johnson develops a spring driven motor for the gramophone. The invention will be one of the critical components in the commercial success of the modern record player.
1897	The first broadcast rights to a professional sporting event are sold. Each team in the National League of Professional Baseball Teams received $300 in free telegrams as part of a league-wide contract to transmit game play-by-play over the telegraph wire.
1899	Guglielmo Marconi immigrates to the United States from Italy. Later that year, he is granted the first patent related to wireless communication.
1899	Nipper the dog first appears as a trademark for the Gramophone Company. Nipper became famous when the American rights to the trademark were purchased by the Victor Talking Machine Company. He will go on to become one of America's most enduring and recognizable trademarks.
1900	The Association of Vaudeville Managers of the United States is formed.
1901	On February 22, the White Rats of America, the vaudeville actors union, stages a successful protest

against the new booking system established by the-ater owners, walking out of theaters on the east coast and in the Midwest. Within two weeks, theater own-ers cave in to their demands to end the system.

1901   Eldridge Johnson founds the Victor Talking Machine Company.

1901   William S. Paley, founder of CBS, is born in Chicago on Sept 28.

1901   Walt Disney is born in Chicago on December 5.

1902   Enrico Caruso makes his first recording for Victor on their prestigious Red Seal label.

1902   Harry and Herbert Miles establish the first distribu-tion company for motion pictures.

1903   *The Great Train Robbery* is released. It is the first motion picture that truly resembles what we would recognize today as a movie.

1903   European nations sign the first international treaty governing the use of airwaves for wireless transmis-sions. The United States refuses to sign.

1903   Enrico Caruso appears for the first of 863 times on the stage of the New York Metropolitan Opera.

1904   Enrico Caruso records the first million-selling record, *Vesti la guibba*.

1905   Harry and John Davis open the first permanent movie theater in Pittsburgh.

1905   Harry Houdini returns from his European tour an international celebrity.

1906   The Victor Talking Machine company introduces the Victrola model, which will go on to become the industry standard.

1906	On Christmas Eve, inventor Reginald Fessenden broadcasts the first recognized radio signal.
1906	Lee de Forest is granted a patent for the audion tube, the invention on which the radio industry would eventually be founded.
1906	Philo T. Farnsworth is born in Utah on August 19.
1906	The United Booking Office is incorporated by Benjamin Keith and Edward Albee.
1907	The United States Amusement Company is formed by Marc Klaw, A. L. Erlanger, and the Schubert brothers.
1907	Florenz Ziegfeld, Jr. creates the Ziegfeld Follies.
1908	The Motion Picture Patents Corporation (MPPC) is formed by merging the 10 major companies holding the important motion picture industry patents, including Edison, Vitagraph, and Biograph, the three largest holders of patents for cameras, film, and projectors.
1908	The term "television" is coined by *Scientific American* in an article speculating about future technological innovations.
1908	Milton Berle, "Mr. Television," is born on July 12 in New York City.
1908	Ethel Merman is born Ethel Zimmermann on January 16.
1908	Tony Pastor dies on August 26.
1909	The Copyright Act is revised, creating new protection for music publishers, authors, composers, and songwriters.
1909	The Theater Owners Booking Association, the vaudeville circuit for African American performers, is formed.

1909   The National Hockey Association, the first profes-
        sional hockey league, was formed with teams in
        Ontario and Quebec. It would dissolve during World
        War I and be replaced by the National Hockey
        League (NHL).

1910   The General Film Company, a cartel of distribution
        and production companies in the movie industry, is
        formed.

1910   On June 24, the United States passes the Wireless Ship
        Act, requiring that any ship carrying more than 50
        passengers or sailing more than 200 miles between
        ports be equipped with radio communication
        equipment.

1911   Babe Didrikson is born on June 26 in Port Arthur,
        Texas.

1911   Lucille Ball is born on August 6 in Jamestown,
        New York.

1912   The federal government nationalizes the broad-
        cast spectrum with passage of the Radio Act,
        requiring that all operators of radio equipment be
        licensed and allocated a wavelength on which to
        broadcast.

1912   The International Olympic Committee sanctions the
        participation of female athletes in the Olympic
        Games for the first time.

1912   The *Titanic* sinks on April 11. David Sarnoff relays the
        tragedy to a spellbound America from his post in a
        New York City wireless station. Sarnoff will go on to
        become chief executive officer (CEO) of Radio Corpo-
        ration of America (RCA), one of the most important
        corporations in the history of the American entertain-
        ment industry.

1913   Actors Equity, the stage performers' union, is
        formed.

1913	Martin Beck opens the Palace Theater in Times Square. It was considered the grandest vaudeville theater of its day and represented the peak of achievement for any vaudeville act until it closed in 1932.
1913	Harry Houdini's mother dies, sending him on a search for a way to communicate with the dead. This will ultimately become part of his act, as he exposes the fraudulent world of mediums.
1914	Lee de Forest and Howard Armstrong meet in court for the first time in what will become a lifetime battle between the two inventors over radio patents.
1914	"Doc" Herold begins the first regular radio broadcast by illegally tapping into the Santa Fe Railway streetcar lines to broadcast to an audience in San Jose, California.
1914	Benjamin F. Keith dies of heart failure on March 26.
1915	Fox Film Corporation is formed after William Fox successfully wins a legal battle that ends the film trust.
1916	On November 25, Lee de Forest broadcast the first sporting event on the radio when he broadcast the Harvard–Yale football game.
1916	The White Rats strike vaudeville theaters in December for more than a month. Both sides lose money, but management breaks the union.
1916	In November, Lee de Forrest earns the dubious distinction of being the first person to incorrectly predict the outcome of a presidential election over the airwaves when he signs off at 11 p.m. on election night by declaring Charles Evans Hughes the winner over Woodrow Wilson.

1917   The National Hockey League (NHL) is organized in
            on November 22 in Montreal. It replaces the National
            Hockey Association, which suspended operations
            during World War I.

1918   U.S. antitrust legislation dissolves the General Film
            Company and Motion Picture Patent Corporation
            trusts, changing the landscape of the motion picture
            industry.

1919   On January 16, the 18thAmendment was ratified,
            prohibiting the sale of alcohol. This meant that base-
            ball teams could no longer profit from selling beer,
            one of their most popular concessions, at the ballpark.

1919   The Ringling Brothers and Barnum and Bailey
            circuses merge.

1919   The White Rats merge with Actors Equity, the stage
            performers' union.

1919   Paramount merges with Famous Players and Lasky,
            becoming the first fully integrated movie company,
            producing, distributing, and exhibiting motion
            pictures.

1919   United Artists is created by Charlie Chaplin, Mary
            Pickford, Douglas Fairbanks Sr., D. W. Griffith, and
            William Hart.

1919   In Des Moines, Iowa, on September 6, President
            Woodrow Wilson becomes the first president to
            broadcast a speech on the radio.

1919   Jackie Robinson is born in Cairo, Georgia, on January 31.

1919   On October 17, the Radio Corporation of America
            (RCA) is incorporated. Born out of the merger of
            General Electric and Marconi Wireless, it would go
            on to dominate the radio and television industries
            for the next half century.

1920	In July, *Variety* begins a best-seller chart for phonograph recordings. This would ultimately become the "Top 40."
1920	On November 2, the first licensed commercial radio broadcasting station, KDKA, begins operation in Pittsburgh.
1920	The American Professional Football Association is formed with 11 teams. Two years later, it will change its name to the National Football League (NFL).
1921	Enrico Caruso dies on August 2.
1922	On August 28, the first commercial airs on a licensed radio station. The Queensboro Corporation pays station WEAF in New York $50 to advertise a new apartment complex it is leasing.
1922	Lillian Russell dies on June 6. She is buried with full military honors.
1922	William Hays is named first president of the Motion Picture Producers and Distributors of America (eventually renamed Motion Picture Association of America).
1922	In *Federal Baseball Club of Baltimore v the National League*, the Supreme Court rules that baseball is not interstate commerce and therefore is exempt from antitrust laws.
1923	Congress divides radio stations into high, medium, and low power classifications. This division would go on to ensure that ownership and operation of the largest and most profitable stations is controlled by large corporations.
1924	Will Hays establishes the Production Code Administration, essentially a censorship board for the movie industry.

1925   Charles Jenkins is granted the first patent for a television system. His mechanical system will prove to be unworkable, however.

1926   AT&T sells its radio assets to RCA, abandoning the radio business to concentrate on telephones.

1926   Harry Houdini dies on October 31 from complications resulting from a burst appendix that occurred during one of his tricks.

1927   Keith-Albee merges with the Orpheum circuit, creating a nationwide monopoly of vaudeville theaters.

1927   Columbia Record Company purchases United Independent Broadcasters and renames the company the Columbia Phonograph Broadcasting System, later changed to Columbia Broadcasting System, or CBS.

1927   On October 6, *The Jazz Singer*, the first talking picture, is released. Within five years, silent films will disappear from the market.

1927   Philo T. Farnsworth receives the first patent for electronic television. He will go on to be recognized as the father of television.

1928   The first Academy Awards are presented. *Wings* is named best picture, Emil Jennings wins the best actor award, and Janet Gaynor wins the best actress award.

1928   Mickey Mouse stars in his first film, when he was known as Steamboat Willie.

1928   Philo Farnsworth makes the first successful public demonstration of television on September 1, showing a clip of a Mary Pickford movie.

1928   Columbia Broadcasting System (CBS) is formed on October 1 by William S. Paley.

1929   Berry Gordy is born on November 28 in Detroit.

1929   Thomas Edison ceases production of his cylinder phono-
            graph, ceding the market to the disk recording system.

1929   Grace Kelly, the future Princess of Monaco, is born in
            Philadelphia.

1930   The National Association of Performing Artists
            (NAPA) is formed for the purpose of eliminating the
            free use of recordings by radio stations. Ironically,
            the recording industry will be sued in years to come
            for paying radio stations to play their music.

1930   The government initiates its first antitrust legislation
            against RCA, forcing it to unravel its monopoly agree-
            ments with General Electric (GE) and Westinghouse.

1930   In bankruptcy proceedings, William Fox sells the
            company that continues to bear his name.

1931   *Cimmaron* becomes the first western to win the Acad-
            emy Award for best picture. It would be 60years
            before another western won the honor.

1931   The car radio debuts. RCA and General Motors enter
            into an agreement for RCA to manufacture radios
            that will be installed in GM cars.

1931   Thomas Edison dies on October 18.

1931   Roone Arledge is born on July 8.

1932   Walt Disney releases *Flowers and Trees*, the first color
            cartoon, which wins him his first of a record 22 Acad-
            emy Awards.

1932   Babe Didrikson wins five events, setting four world
            records, and ties for first in a fifth event at the
            National Amateur Athletic Union track and field
            championships. Two weeks later, she captures two
            gold and a silver medal at the Olympic Games. She is
            voted Woman Athlete of the Year by the Associated
            Press for the first of six times.

1933	Prohibition is repealed with passage of the 21st Amendment on December 5. Once again, beer becomes a staple at American sporting events.
1933	In June, the National Industrial Recovery Act (NIRA) is signed into law, legalizing the oligopolistic structure of the movie industry and solidifying the "studio era" of production in which a small number of companies would control the industry from production through exhibition.
1933	The Screen Actors Guild (SAG) is formed as a union for movie actors.
1933	Mary Pickford makes her last screen appearance, starring in *Secrets*, distributed by United Artists.
1934	Hollywood studios grant Will Hays, president of the Motion Picture Producers and Distributors of America, the authority to enforce the Production Code, an internal form of movie censorship, on all studios.
1935	Elvis Presley is born on January 8 in Tupelo, Mississippi.
1935	Philo Farnsworth scores a legal victory over RCA in a patent infringement suit. The victory will ultimately lead to RCA license patent rights from Farnsworth—the first time the corporation was ever on the buying end of a licensing agreement.
1937	Pierre de Coubertin dies in Geneva, Switzerland, on September 2.
1937	On December 21, *Snow White and the Seven Dwarfs* opens.
1938	RCA Victor debuts the record club.
1938	Howard Armstrong begins experimental FM broadcasts. FM would not become commercially successful until long after his death.

1938	Ted Turner is born in Cincinnati, Ohio, on November 19.
1939	The first commercial television broadcast is made at the World's Fair in New York City.
1940	The U.S. Federal Communications Commission (FCC) standardizes television broadcasts. Broadcasters will be assigned specific frequencies at which they may broadcast. They also have to agree on a standard image quality for their broadcasts.
1941	The American Broadcasting Corporation is born when the FCC forces RCA to divest itself of one of its two broadcast networks. RCA keeps NBC. The network would actually assume the ABC moniker two years later.
1941	Both NBC and CBS begin regularly scheduled commercial television broadcasts on July 1.
1941	Capitol Records is founded.
1942	In August, the American Federation of Musicians (AFM) goes on strike for nearly a year, winning wage and working condition concessions for artists from the recording industry.
1942	Cassius Clay, who would later change his name to Muhammad Ali, is born in Louisville, Kentucky, on January 17.
1942	The federal government suspends most television broadcasting as a result of World War II.
1943	Olivia de Havilland challenges the movie industry "renewal clause" of her contract in court. She would eventually win, bringing about the end of the studio era.
1945	The DuMont television network is born, joining CBS and NBC as one of the three major networks.

1945	Eldridge Johnson dies on November 14.
1946	The National Basketball Association (NBA) is founded as the Basketball Association of America on June 6 in New York City. In 1949, it will merge with its rival, the National Basketball League, and change its name to the National Basketball Association.
1946	W. C. Fields dies on Christmas Day in Pasadena, California.
1946	The New York Yankees become the first professional sports team to sign a local television contract deal to sell the broadcast rights to their games.
1947	Columbia purchases time on 537 radio stations to introduce its new songs, ushering in an era of publishers paying stations to air their music; this is a significant change from a decade earlier when publishers were suing radio stations to keep them from playing their music without paying for it.
1947	Jackie Robinson breaks the color line in Major League Baseball when he appears in a game for the Brooklyn Dodgers on April 15.
1947	On December 23, the last vaudeville show plays when the State Theater, opened in 1919 by Marcus Loew, closes its doors.
1948	The *Texaco Star Theater Vaudeville Show,* hosted by Milton Berle, debuts on television on June 8.
1948	Columbia introduces the 331/3 rpm LP (long-playing) record.
1948	On January 1, the American Federation of Musicians goes on strike for the second time. They will stay out for one year.

1948   For the second time, the movie industry is found to be in violation of antitrust laws and studios are forced to divest. This marked the formal end of the studio system.

1948   The Ladies Professional Golf Association (LPGA) is formed.

1948   The FCC puts a moratorium on the issuance of new television broadcasting licenses, essentially freezing the supply of television stations at 108 (the 50 in existence plus the 58 under construction). No further stations were granted a license for four years.

1949   The sitcom (situation comedy) is born. *Mama* airs for the first time in what will become an eight-year run.

1949   The first regular newscast is aired. *The Camel News Caravan*, anchored by John Cameron Swayze, broadcast 15 minutes of news each night from New York City.

1949   Victor introduces the 45 rpm rapid changer, which automatically drops a 45 rpm record from a stack onto the phonograph turntable, removing the necessity of the listener from constantly changing records.

1949   The charity telethon debuts. Milton Berle hosts the fundraiser on behalf of the Damon Runyon Cancer Research Foundation.

1950   Al Jolson, stage and screen star, dies on October 23.

1950   Desilu Productions is formed by Lucille Ball and Desi Arnaz. It produced many hit television series, including the *I Love Lucy Show*, and innovated the now common method of filming television shows rather than broadcasting them live. Lucille Ball was the first woman to head a television production studio when she bought out Arnaz after their 1960 divorce.

1951   American Bandstand, hosted by Dick Clark, debuts, marrying television and the recorded music industries.

1951   The first live coverage of a congressional hearing takes place. Senator Estes Kefauver chairs the committee investigating organized crime.

1951   Milton Berle signs an exclusive 30-year contract with NBC TV.

1952   William Fox, owner of one of the Big Eight movie studios during the Hollywood studio era, dies on May 8. No movie industry executives attended his funeral.

1953   Bill Haley releases *Shake, Rattle and Roll*, regarded by many as the first true rock and roll hit, with independent label Essex.

1953   Elvis Presley records his first two songs as a birthday present for his mother.

1953   Howard Armstrong makes his final contribution to radio with his discovery of the concept of multiplexing, which would eventually lead to stereo broadcasting. Armstrong would not live to see his concept carried to its conclusion.

1953   The FCC chooses the RCA system of color television broadcasting as the industry standard.

1954   The Major League Baseball Players Association (MLBPA) is formed.

1954   William Hays dies in Sullivan, Indiana, on March 7.

1954   Oprah Winfrey is born on January 29 in Tennessee.

1954   Howard Armstrong commits suicide on January 31, distraught over his legal difficulties.

1955	RKO becomes the first studio to sell one of its movies to a television network. General Teleradio uses the films to fill time on its television schedule.
1955	The DuMont television network ceases to operate, leaving in place the three networks (ABC, CBS, NBC) that will dominate the television landscape for the next generation.
1955	William Henry "Bill" Gates is born on October 28.
1955	Disneyland Park opens.
1956	Babe Didrikson Zaharias dies in Galveston, Texas, on September 27.
1956	President Eisenhower holds the first live presidential press conference, originating from San Francisco.
1956	Grace Kelly weds Rainier III, Prince of Monaco, on April 18, to become Princess Grace.
1957	Elvis Presley performs for the only time outside of the United States, performing five shows in Canada.
1957	Elvis Presley performs on the Ed Sullivan show. His gyrating hips are censored, and he is allowed to be filmed only from the waist up.
1960	Motown Record Corporation is formed by Berry Gordy.
1961	Lee de Forest, inventor of the audio tube, dies on June 30.
1963	The Beatles release their first album, *Please Please Me*.
1964	The Beatles "invade" America for the first time.
1964	The 8-track cassette is introduced by Lear.
1964	The cassette tape is introduced by the Phillips Company.

1964	The FCC mandates that all television sets constructed must be able to receive both UHF and VHF signals.
1964	Cassius Clay changes his name to Muhammad Ali and wins the heavyweight boxing title for the first of a record three times.
1966	The Telecommunications Act is passed, limiting the number of radio and television stations that a single entity may own and the maximum size of the audience they can reach.
1966	Walt Disney dies on December 15.
1967	The National Football League (NFL) merges with the American Football League (AFL), ending six years of rivalry and forming the NFL that exists to this day.
1967	Muhammad Ali is stripped of his boxing title and boxing license, and arrested for draft evasion. While he was never imprisoned, he could not box for three years.
1968	The All England Club in Wimbledon allows professional tennis players to enter the tournament for the first time.
1968	The Motion Picture Association of America (MPAA) creates the film rating system, a voluntary system for movie studios to rate their own films using a letter system. Today, that system includes ratings of G, PG, PG-13, R, and NC 17.
1970	On September 21, the Cleveland Browns and New York Jets play the first Monday Night Football (MNF) game. MNF aired on ABC until 2005, making it one of the longest running prime time commercial network television series of all time.
1970	The first cable superstation is born when Ted Turner launches station WTBS in Atlanta (originally called WTCG).

1971	Elvis Presley is awarded a Grammy Award for lifetime achievement at the age of 36.

1971	Disney World opens on October 1.

1971	On March 11, Philo Farnsworth, age 64, acknowledged inventor of television, dies. On December 12, David Sarnoff, longtime executive of RCA and a bitter rival of Farnsworth in the race to commercialize television, dies at the age of 80.

1972	Jackie Robinson dies on October 24.

1975	The first satellite transmission of a cable television signal takes place on September 30 when the Muhammad Ali v Joe Frazier heavyweight boxing championship is broadcast from Manila.

1975	Arbitrator Peter Seitz strikes down Major League Baseball's reserve clause, paving the way for free agency for professional athletes.

1975	Eldrick "Tiger" Woods is born on December 30.

1976	The Copyright Act's First Sale Doctrine is passed. The doctrine states that the first purchaser of any copyrighted work can use it any way they see fit as long as it is not duplicated and sold for commercial gain. This paves the way for the home video and audio recording markets.

1976	The sale of satellite receivers to private households is allowed, opening up the market for satellite television.

1977	The Supreme Court rules that the FCC does not have the authority to bar pay channels from cable systems.

1977	Elvis Presley dies on August 16 at his home in Memphis, Tennessee.

1979	Screen legend Mary Pickford dies a virtual recluse on May 27.

1980   The Sony Walkman, the original personal audio headset device, debuts.

1980   Cable News Network makes its first broadcast. It will revolutionize television news.

1980   Shawn Fanning is born in Brockton, Massachusettson November 22.

1981   MTV broadcasts for the first time, launching the music video industry.

1981   The International Olympic Committee (IOC) ratifies the participation of professionals in the Olympic Games.

1982   The first compact disk (CD) hits the market. CDs will virtually wipe out records and tapes in the music industry.

1982   Princess Grace (nee Grace Kelly) dies in an automobile accident in Monaco on September 14.

1983   Football legend George Halas dies on October 31.

1984   The Cable Communications Policy Act is passed, deregulating the cable industry.

1984   Oprah Winfrey hosts her first talk show on a local Chicago station.

1984   Broadway dims its lights in tribute to Ethel Merman, who died on February 15.

1985   RCA comes full circle when it is sold to GE, the company from which it was spawned half a century earlier.

1986   The *Oprah Winfrey Show* begins national syndication, and Winfrey forms her own production company, Harpo Productions.

1987   Sixty-six years after his death, Enrico Caruso is awarded a posthumous Grammy Award for lifetime achievement.

1989   Lucille Ball dies on April 26.

1990   William S. Paley, longtime executive of CBS, dies on October 26.

1992   Cable television is once again regulated by the FCC. The re-regulation of the industry is mostly in the area of pricing.

1994   The Home Audio Recording Act is passed, putting a surcharge of 2 percent on the price of audio tape recorders and 3 percent on blank cassette tapes to be placed in a fund for distribution to record companies, artists, music publishers, and songwriters.

1995   The FCC repeals its ban on network ownership of television programs.

1995   The first computer animated movie, *Toy Story*, is released on November 22.

1996   The Telecommunications Act is passed, loosening restrictions on ownership of television and radio stations.

1997   Tiger Woods becomes the fastest Professional Golf Association (PGA) member to attain the number one ranking in the world on June 15, after less than one year as a professional.

1999   Muhammad Ali is named Sportsman of the Century by *Sports Illustrated* magazine and Sports Personality of the Century by the BBC.

1999   Napster begins operating, forever changing the way music is purchased.

2001   Napster ceases operation after losing a copyright infringement case.

2001   Apple introduces the iPod on October. It is released for sale on November 10.

2002   Milton Berle dies in Los Angeles on March 27.

2002   Twenty-five years after his death, Elvis Presley earns his eighteenth number one hit on the U.K. charts.

2002   Roone Arledge dies on December 5.

2011   *The Oprah Winfrey Show* ends its 24-year run.

5

Biographical Sketches

Muhammad Ali (1942–)

Muhammad Ali was born Cassius Marcellus Clay, Jr. on January 17, 1942, in Louisville, Kentucky. Clay was a boxer, winning the gold medal in the light heavyweight division at the 1960 Rome Olympic Games before turning professional. By the time he retired, he was widely considered to be the greatest boxer of all time. In 1999, he was named Sportsman of the Century by *Sports Illustrated* and Sports Personality of the Century by the British Broadcasting Corporation (BBC).

Clay won his first professional fight on October 29, 1960. His first title fight was on February 25, 1964. He defeated defending champ Sonny Liston to become the youngest boxer ever to dethrone a heavyweight champion.

Clay changed his name to Muhammad Ali after joining the Nation of Islam in 1964. Three years later, he refused to be drafted into the U.S. military, citing religious beliefs. He was arrested and found guilty of draft evasion. His boxing license was suspended and he was stripped of his boxing title, but he did not get sent to prison. However, he was unable to box for nearly four years while he appealed the charges all the way to the Supreme Court, where he proved victorious.

He went on to win the heavyweight title a record three different times before retiring from boxing in 1981.

Ali was famous for his braggadocio and predicting the round in which he would knock out his opponent. This helped to win him a huge public following. A 1993 Associated Press (AP) poll found that 97 percent of Americans over the age of 12 could identify Ali. In 2002, he received a star on the Hollywood Walk of Fame for his contributions to the entertainment industry.

Roone Arledge (1931–2002)

Roone Arledge Jr. was born and died in New York City, where he spent almost his entire life. He was born on July 8, 1931; graduated from Columbia University in 1952; and except for his military service, spent his entire adult life working in New York City. He died there on December 5, 2002.

Arledge was an American broadcasting pioneer. Among his innovations were *Monday Night Football, Wide World of Sports*, and the news programs *20/20, Nightline*, and *This Week*. These innovations led to his election to the Television Academy Hall of Fame in 1990.

His first job was with the DuMont Television Network in 1952. He took a leave for military service, but by the time he returned, the network had folded. He took a position as a stage manager across town at the NBC affiliate. From there, he moved to ABC, at the time still a fledgling network, as an assistant producer. One of his first assignments was to produce a children's puppet show, which won an Emmy in 1958, his first of 37.

Arledge began working on sports programming and was named president of Sports for ABC in 1968. In 1977, he added the title of president of News. At the time, ABC News was the lowest rated news program. By the time he retired in 1998, it had risen to the top. While president of sports, he produced 10 Olympics Games broadcasts and developed *Monday Night Football*. He relinquished his title as president of Sports in 1986.

Howard Armstrong (1890–1954)

Edwin Howard Armstrong was born in New York City on December 18, 1890, and died on January 31, 1954. He invented three of the electronic components that are fundamental to radio, television, and radar. The first, the regenerative circuit, he invented while a student at Columbia University, where he would later hold a position on the faculty for 40 years. The second invention was the superheterodyne, which increased the amplitude of the broadcasts and turned AM broadcasts into a national industry. Armstrong's most famous invention was FM radio, although he never lived to see its commercial success.

Armstrong was one of the last of the breed of independent inventors. He never worked for a corporate employer; rather, he did most of his inventing while on the faculty at Columbia. He owned his own patents, which he freely donated to the U.S. government for use during both world wars. During World War I, he was stationed in Paris with the U.S. Army Signal Corps, where he helped set up and maintain a wireless communication system for the Allied forces. The French government awarded him the Legion of Honor for his contributions.

Howard Armstrong and Lee de Forest were contemporaries and antagonists. While both of their inventions were necessary for the development of wireless communication, and radio in particular, neither man liked the other. They spent most of their lives and much of their fortunes in court fighting over patents. The patent battle between de Forest and Armstrong over who had actually discovered regeneration would become one of the longest-lasting and most bitter patent fights in history. By the time the Supreme Court finally found in favor of de Forest, much to the incredulity of the scientific community, the patents had long expired, de Forest was ruined financially, and Armstrong was ruined emotionally.

Armstrong committed suicide in 1954 after losing another patent case, this one to RCA. The two cases were unrelated except for the intensity displayed by Armstrong. That intensity served him well in the laboratory but led to his downfall in the courts. He was unable to make a business decision separate from his emotional attachment to the inventions he felt were being stolen from him.

Lucille Ball (1911–1989)

Lucille Ball was born on August 6, 1911, in Jamestown, New York, and died on April 26, 1989, in Los Angeles. She appeared in 91 movies and was a juggernaut in the television industry, starring in several shows and heading up the influential Desilu production studio, the first woman to hold such a position.

Ball began her film career with a bit part in 1933. Her early career was dominated by small roles in feature films and leading roles in B pictures, which earned her the nickname Queen of the B's. Ball gained her fame in television, which she entered in 1951. She was nominated for 13 Emmy Awards and won four. In 2002, *TV Guide* named her the greatest television star of all time.

In 1951, she helped create the *I Love Lucy* show, costarring her then-husband Desi Arnaz. The show ran until 1957 and has been popular in syndication ever since. Ball and Arnaz negotiated to film their show in Hollywood at a time when most television shows were aired live from New York City studios. As part of the negotiation, they kept the rights to the show, which turned out to be a very profitable deal for Desilu. *I Love Lucy* became the primer for how to make money by syndicating a show.

Desilu pioneered the now common method of filming television shows before a live studio audience with multiple cameras. Desilu, under the direction of Ball, who became sole owner when she bought out Desi Arnaz after their 1960 divorce, produced many successful television series.

P. T. Barnum (1810–1891)

Phineas Taylor Barnum was born July 5, 1810, in Bethel, Connecticut. He died April 7, 1891, in Bridgeport, Connecticut. He was an author, publisher, and politician, but primarily a showman. Above all, he was America's first great marketing genius.

He ran a newspaper in 1829 and used it to editorialize against church elders. This eventually led to a libel suit that landed him in jail for two months.

Barnum made and lost more than one fortune. Among his great successes were General Tom Thumb, "the smallest person to walk on his own," the singer Jenny Lind, America's first aquarium, and the Siamese Twins, Chang and Eng.

He moved to New York City in 1834 and began his show business career. First he staged a variety troupe, and later he purchased a museum and used it to promote exhibitions of all kinds, from sideshows to beauty pageants and stage shows. His museum grew to three buildings and nearly one million exhibits before it burned to the ground in 1865. A replacement burned three years later, after which Barnum abandoned the museum.

In 1871, he entered the circus business. In 1881, he merged with James Bailey and James Hutchinson to form what would eventually be known as Barnum & Bailey's Circus. Barnum introduced the concept of the three-ring circus, making Barnum & Bailey the world's largest. In 1919, it would merge with Ringling Brothers to form the Ringling Brothers and Barnum & Bailey circus, which tours to this day.

Milton Berle (1908–2002)

Milton Berle was born Milton Berlinger in New York City on July 12, 1908. He died on March 27, 2002, in Los Angeles. Berle is the personification of the evolution of the American entertainment industry. He began his career in silent films and vaudeville, and ended it in Las Vegas and on television. He hosted the NBC *Texaco Star Theater* from 1948 to 1955, becoming one of the first stars of the new medium and earning the sobriquet Mr. Television. Berle is credited for popularizing television. After his show began, sales of sets more than doubled to two million in 1949.

Texaco Star Theater began as a radio show in September 1948. The television version of the show was one of the most popular in the burgeoning medium, reaching number one in the Nielson ratings on a regular basis. Berle and the show each won Emmy Awards for the first season.

In 1951, NBC signed Berle to an exclusive 30-year television contract. It turned out to be a huge mistake. His television popularity had already peaked. Two years later, Texaco pulled out as sponsor of his show. Buick picked it up but dropped out after two years. He appeared in various shows for NBC over the years but was never able to regain his earlier success.

Berle served as an inspiration for a legion of comedians, though he had the reputation of being difficult to work with and unwilling to share the stage. He was, however, generous with his time, regularly giving charity concerts. He was the first person to host a charity telethon, for the Damon Runyon Cancer Research Foundation in 1949. He helped to raise millions of dollars for charities over more than half a century.

Enrico Caruso (1873–1921)

Enrico Caruso was born on February 25, 1873 in Naples, Italy. He was the first international recording star, making nearly 300 records (beginning in 1902). He recorded the world's first million-selling record with his recording of *Vesti la guibba* in 1904.

Caruso was a talented musician and a shrewd businessman who profited by embracing the new technology of recorded sound. Despite its inferior sound quality, Caruso recognized the profit potential of early recordings and exploited it to his advantage. He made more than 250 recordings for the Victor Talking Machine Company between 1904 and 1920, earning millions of dollars in royalties along with worldwide fame.

He made his professional opera debut in Naples in 1895. He would eventually appear on every major opera stage in the world. He made his American debut at the New York Metropolitan Opera in 1903 for the first of 863 times, the last of which was in December 1920, shortly before his death.

He toured widely and often, giving recitals and operatic performances in cities around the world, commanding the unheard of fee of $10,000 per night for a series of concerts in Havana, Cuba, in 1920. During World War I, he gave numerous benefit concerts to raise money for the war effort.

Caruso was ill most of the last year of his life. While recuperating in Italy, he fell gravely ill and died on August 2, 1921. His funeral was attended by thousands.

In 1932, Victor began re-releasing his early recordings. Remastering and digitizing of Caruso's recordings has continued as technology has evolved, and they are now available as digital downloads. In 1987, he was posthumously awarded a Grammy for lifetime achievement.

Pierre de Coubertin (1863–1937)

Pierre de Coubertin, a French educator, was born in Paris on January 1, 1863. He was the founder of the modern Olympic Games, serving as president of the International Olympic Committee from 1896 until 1925 and honorary president until his death.

He was born into an aristocratic Parisian family and raised in a highly cultured environment, traveling the world and dallying in sports throughout his young adult life. He was noble and idealistic. He refused comfortable positions in the military and politics and instead devoted his life to improving the French educational system, which he believed should include sports as a fundamental part of the curriculum.

It was his interest in sports, combined with the recent archeological finds in Olympia, which aroused his interest in the ancient Olympic Games in the early 1890s. It led to a conviction on his part to resurrect the games.

The first modern games, held in Athens in 1896, were a success, but Coubertin disappointed the Greeks when he announced that they would not host the next games, scheduled for 1900. He stressed the importance of changing host cities in an effort to involve more nations in what he saw as a noble effort to unite the world through sports.

Coubertin had a much higher standard for the Olympics than a mere sporting spectacle. He defined the purpose of the Olympic Games on four principles: the pursuit of perfection, chivalry, egalitarianism and truce among nations.

He died of a heart attack in Geneva, Switzerland, on September 2, 1937, and was laid to rest in Lausanne, though his heart was interred in a monument near the ruins of ancient Olympia.

Lee de Forest (1873–1961)

Lee de Forest was born in Council Bluffs, Iowa, on August 26, 1873, the son of a Yale-educated preacher. When he was a young boy, his family relocated to Alabama. With few friends, de Forest turned toward tinkering to keep himself occupied. He designed and invented from an early age, showing an aptitude for mechanical engineering. De Forest's first job after graduation was with the Western Electric Company in Chicago.

Expanding upon ideas he read about in scientific journals, de Forest patented an improved method of receiving telegraph signals. It became his first in a long line of patents. As talented a scientist as de Forest was, he would never duplicate that success in business. Throughout his career, he continuously found himself short of cash and involved in lawsuits over patents.

De Forest would be accused many times in his career of liberally borrowing for his inventions from the work of others. This was one reason he spent so much time and money fighting in patent courts. His most famous patent, the one that the radio industry was founded upon, was granted in the fall of 1906. The audion tube allowed wireless signals to be received from greater distances and with greater clarity than ever before. It was directly responsible for the evolution of radio.

In the midst of the Depression, de Forest and fellow inventor Howard Armstrong were recognized as the inventors who made the radio industry possible. It was generating revenues of nearly $2 billion annually and featured some of the most prominent companies in America: RCA, Zenith, Motorola, and Magnavox. Yet the inventors were largely broke. They had spent most of their money suing one another.

De Forest spent the waning years of his life seeking fame and fortune. He lobbied intensely, though unsuccessfully, for the Nobel Prize in Physics in the mid-1950s. De Forest died on June 30, 1961, leaving behind an estate valued at $1,200. The industry his invention was responsible for was worth billions.

Walt Disney (1901–1966)

Walt Disney was born on December 5, 1901, in Chicago. His life-long interest in art and nature eventually led him into the production of animated films. His early efforts met with mixed success. He formed a company that went bankrupt, created an animated series that showed promise, and moved to California at the age of 21.

In 1932, *Flowers and Trees*, the first color cartoon, won Disney his first Academy Award. He would go on to be nominated a total of 59 times and would win 22. Both totals are records. He also won seven Emmy Awards for his television work.

On December 21, 1937, *Snow White and the Seven Dwarfs* opened. It was the first full-length animated movie, and the first in what would become a string of successful full-length animated movies by Disney. The film won him the second of his four honorary Oscars; the first was for the creation of Mickey Mouse.

Disney branched out in the 1950s. He began television programming in 1954 and opened Disneyland Park in 1955. In 1961, he was one of the first to produce full-color programming in his new show, *Wonderful World of Color*.

In 1964, he announced plans for Disney World in Florida. It would feature the Magic Kingdom, hotels, golf courses, and his concept of the ideal future city, EPCOT. But Disney would not live to see its completion. He died of lung cancer on December 15, 1966. His brother Roy oversaw the planning for Disney World, which opened with great fanfare on October 1, 1971.

Thomas Edison (1847–1931)

Thomas Edison was Born February 11, 1847, in Milan, Ohio. He died on October 18, 1931, in West Orange, New Jersey. He was an inventor and businessman, known as the Wizard of Menlo Park.

During his lifetime, he was awarded 1,093 U.S. patents, yet he had only three weeks of formal schooling. From the age of seven, he was homeschooled, tutored, or self-taught.

At the age of 14, he took a job selling candy on passenger trains and began publishing a paper, the *Weekly Herald*. It became the first such publication ever to be typeset, printed, and sold on a train. By age 15, he had a job as a telegraph operator. His first invention, which he never patented, was the automatic repeater, which transmitted telegraph signals between unmanned stations.

In 1868, he moved to Boston, worked as a telegrapher, invented in his free time, and received his first patent, for an electronic vote counting machine, in 1869. It did not sell, however, which steeled his resolve to never invent anything again that could not make him money.

He is credited with numerous patents for inventions that defined the entertainment industry, including the phonograph in 1878, the kinetoscope in 1891, and the Vitascope, the precursor to the modern movie projector, in 1896. Edison also developed the first sound pictures. The kinetophone, also patented by Edison, combined his phonograph with his kinetoscope. However, this early combination of sound and moving pictures was too expensive to be successfully marketed. It would be more than a generation before the commercial viability of sound and picture would be achieved.

Shawn Fanning (1980–)

Shawn Fanning was born in Brockton, Massachusetts on November 22, 1980. He is a computer programmer most famous for developing Napster, a pioneering use of the peer-to-peer (P2P) file sharing platforms, which began operating in 1999. Its life was short lived, but its impact was permanent. From a fraction of total revenues in 1998, digital sales of music grew to comprise nearly one-third of all revenues for the music industry by 2010.

Copyright infringement lawsuits were filed almost as soon as Napster began operating. The first to file was the Recording Industry Association of America, on December 7, 1999. They were eventually joined by bands and recording studios in a series of lawsuits filed over the next two years. Napster was shut down in July 2001 after just two years of operation.

After losing the copyright infringement case, Napster was ordered to monitor the activities of its network and block access to infringing material when notified. Napster was unable to do this. It declared bankruptcy and sold its assets. The site was ultimately obtained by Best Buy and now exists as a subscription service for digital music downloads. After Napster, Fanning moved on to a succession of other digital media companies.

Philo Farnsworth (1906–1971)

Philo Farnsworth may be the most famous obscure inventor in American history. Like Thomas Edison and Henry Ford, his invention is so commonplace that it seldom receives a second thought. Unlike Edison and Ford, though, Farnsworth is hardly a household name, despite being credited with inventing the television.

Farnsworth was born August 19, 1906, in Utah but grew up on a farm in Idaho after the family moved there when he was young. When he first revealed his idea for television, his father urged him to keep it secret—not so that his idea would not be stolen, but because he thought it so preposterous that people would think Philo was crazy.

On January 7, 1927, Farnsworth filed his first patent application for a television system. It would take two decades, a world war, and a monumental court battle before television would become the commercial success we know today.

While Farnsworth won the court battles that acknowledged him as the inventor of television, by the time he won, his patents were on the verge of expiring, and he lost the financial windfall they entailed.

Farnsworth saw his financial fortunes evaporate in 1947 with the expiration of his original television patents. Farnsworth turned his interests to an attempt to harness a cheap, safe source of power: nuclear fusion. His efforts would absorb the rest of his life but never prove successful. He died on March 11, 1971, at which time there were more homes in the world with television sets than indoor plumbing.

W. C. Fields (1880–1946)

William Claude Dukenfield was born January 29, 1880, in Darby, Pennsylvania, and died on December 25, 1946, in California from alcohol-related complications. Fields, who changed his name for the stage, was also an accomplished juggler and writer.

He began his entertainment career at age 15, juggling at local theaters. He entered vaudeville as a juggler, gaining international fame. After touring Europe, he returned to the United States and began to add comedy bits to his routine. Eventually, the ratio of juggling to comedy dwindled and he became a headline comedian, again gaining international fame.

In 1906, he made his debut on Broadway in the musical comedy *The Ham Tree*, but his first real starring role was with the Ziegfeld Follies. His signature act there was a comedy billiards skit involving trick shots and bizarre pool cues.

He appeared in his first movie in 1915, but his vaudeville touring prevented him from seriously pursuing the medium for another decade. Once he did, however, he became a major star and contributed to the writing of many of his shows, usually under a pseudonym. He ultimately appeared in 46 films.

Fields's health began to flag in the final few years of his life, and his film career stagnated. His last starring role was in 1941. Thereafter, he was able to make only brief appearances in films. He was a patient at the Las Encinas Sanatorium in Pasadena for the last two years of his life, though he continued to make guest appearances in movies and on the radio until shortly before his death.

William Fox (1879–1952)

William Fox was born Vilmos (Wilhelm) Fried in Tolcsva, Hungary, on January 1, 1879. His family emigrated to America before his first birthday, and his name was Anglicized to William Fox. Despite never finishing grade school, he went on to become one of the Big Eight movie moguls during the "studio era." He got into the movie business in 1904 when he bought a nickelodeon, an early version of a movie parlor, in Brooklyn. Fox won the legal battle that resulted in the divestiture of the Motion Pictures Patent Company, ending the film trust that controlled the industry in the first part of the twentieth century.

He founded Fox Film Corporation in 1915, consisting of Hollywood studios and a chain of theaters that would eventually top 1,000. He was forced out of his own company in 1930 after a federal antitrust investigation and the stock market crash pushed him into bankruptcy. He later served a year in prison for attempting to bribe the judge during his bankruptcy proceedings. He died on May 8, 1952, a Hollywood pariah. No movie industry producers attended his funeral.

Bill Gates (1955–)

William Henry Gates, chairman and chief software architect of Microsoft, oversees a company that generates tens of billions of dollars of revenue annually and employs over 61,000 workers in plants located in more than 100 countries.

Gates is also well known as a philanthropist. He and his wife established the Bill and Melinda Gates Foundation, the largest charity in the world. Its goal is to help fight poverty and improve health care around the world. He has also established a scholarship fund for minority students.

Bill Gates was born in Seattle, Washington, on October 28, 1955. He showed an early aptitude for computers, writing his first program code at the age of 13. He left Harvard after his junior year to found Microsoft with his boyhood friend Paul Allen. The firm's initial focus was on operating systems, the set of instructions telling the computer how to run its programs. They soon developed their own operating system, which became the highly successful Windows system that now runs 80 percent of the world's computers.

Gates proved to be correct in his belief that the desktop computer was the wave of the future. He started Microsoft in the belief that it would become a common business tool, and that there was a future in the business of developing software for those computers.

In 1998, the federal government filed an antitrust lawsuit against Microsoft. The company was accused of exercising monopoly control over personal computer (PC) operating systems and using its power to the detriment of consumers. Microsoft settled with the Justice Department in 2001.

Berry Gordy (1929–)

Berry Gordy was born on November 28, 1929 in Detroit, Michigan. He was the founder of Motown Records, a songwriter, and sometime movie producer. He might be best known, however, for his ability to recognize and cultivate musical talent. Among his more famous discoveries were The Supremes, Marvin Gaye, The Temptations, Gladys Knight, Stevie Wonder, and The Jackson 5.

Gordy got his start in the recording industry by opening a record store and writing songs. His first success was a song written for Jackie Wilson that was recorded in 1957. It was a hit in the United Kingdom, reaching the Top 10 list, and the success led to future recordings.

He invested his earnings from songwriting into producing. His first label, Tamla Records, was founded in 1959 and specialized in R&B. He soon started to release under his Motown label, beginning with "Bad Girl" by The Miracles in 1959. In 1960, he produced his first number one hit, "Shop Around," and put Motown on the map as a serious independent production company. In 1960, he merged his Tamla and Motown labels and formed Motown Record Corporation.

In 1972, he produced his first movie, *Lady Sings the Blues*, which earned its star, Diana Ross, an Academy Award nomination. He would go on to produce three more films and contribute music to more than 100 soundtracks.

Gordy sold his interest in Motown to MCA and Boston Ventures in 1988, the same year he was inducted into the Rock and Roll Hall of Fame.

George Halas (1895–1983)

George Stanley "Papa Bear" Halas, one of the original franchise owners and a founder of the National Football League (NFL), was born February 2, 1895, in Chicago. Before he became involved with the NFL, he played professional baseball, earning a brief tour with the New York Yankees in 1919. An injury and the arrival of a new outfielder by the name of Babe Ruth ended the baseball career of Halas, much to the benefit of professional football.

After his abridged professional baseball career ended, Halas accepted a position with a starch manufacturing company in Decatur, Illinois. He filled multiple roles, including sales representative, player on the company baseball team, and player-coach of the company football team. It was in this latter position that he represented the company's owner, A. E. Staley, at the 1920 meeting in Canton, Ohio, that formed the NFL. Halas was awarded one of the inaugural franchises, the Decatur Staley's, which were moved to Chicago and renamed the Bears after one financially unsuccessful season in Decatur.

Halas was the first owner to broadcast NFL games on radio and television, and it was his idea to share television revenues equally among all league teams, arguing that the league would only be as strong as its weakest member. His foresight in the sharing of league revenues is widely regarded as among the wisest business decisions in all professional sports.

Halas succumbed to cancer on October 31, 1983, at the age of 88. He remained active in the operation of the Bears from their inauguration as the Staley's in 1920 until his death.

William H. Hays, Sr. (1879–1954)

Will Hays, the forty-sixth postmaster general of the United States, is better known for his role in establishing the motion picture rating system. He was born on November 5, 1879, in Sullivan, Indiana, and died there on March 7, 1954.

Hays began his career in politics, rising to chairman of the Republican National Committee in 1918. He was appointed postmaster general in 1921 after successfully managing Warren G. Harding's campaign for the presidency. He resigned from the position after one year to become the first president of the Motion Picture Producers and Distributors of America (eventually renamed the Motion Picture Association of America). He retained that position until he retired in 1945.

Hays was hired at a time when the there was a growing outcry for federal oversight of the movie industry. He was hired as a public relations move to "clean up" the industry. In addition to being a conservative Republican, he was a Presbyterian deacon.

In 1934, facing widespread threats of Catholic boycotts of immoral movies and reduced funding from Catholic financiers, the studios granted Hays the authority to enforce a production code on all studios. The first item in the production code was "no picture shall be produced that will lower the moral standards of those who see it." From there, the items became more specific, such as no nudity, no ridiculing religion, no depiction of illegal drug use, and no use of certain words. The result was a strict regime of self-censorship that endured until the 1960s, when the industry established the age-based rating system in use to this day.

Harry Houdini (1874–1926)

Harry Houdini was born on March 24, 1874, in Budapest, Hungary, as Ehrich Weisz. His family emigrated to the United States when he was a small child. He changed his name to Houdini after his idol, French magician Robert-Houdin, when he became a magician.

One of Houdini's signature tricks was to arrive in a new town before a scheduled performance and challenge the local police to handcuff him. He offered $100 to anyone who could proffer handcuffs from which he could not escape. He never had to pay.

He was a headliner on the vaudeville circuit, and in 1900 he took his act to Europe. He returned to the United States in 1905 an international celebrity.

He was a premier magician but was best known for his fantastic escape tricks. Among his more notable stunts were escaping from a straitjacket while hanging upside down from the top of a building, breaking out of the jail cell that held the assassin of President Garfield, and extricating himself from a sealed container of water despite being shackled.

The death of his mother in 1913 led to his fascination with spiritualism. After her death, he spent the rest of his life in search of a true medium, while exposing charlatans. He offered $10,000 to anyone who could produce a psychic effect that he could not duplicate, but the reward went unclaimed.

He died on October 31, 1926, of peritonitis, a complication resulting from a burst appendix that occurred during one of his tricks.

Eldridge Johnson (1867–1945)

Eldridge R. Johnson was born in Wilmington, Delaware, on February 18, 1867. Along with Thomas Edison, he is credited with the rise of the phonograph and recorded sound industry.

In 1896, Johnson developed a spring-driven motor for a gramophone. After perfecting the motor, he set about perfecting other parts of the machine. He also developed a new method of making recording masters using electroplated wax pressings. The recordings were superior to any disk on the market and became the foundation upon which his company would grow in the next century.

Since he was the victor in various legal battles over patents, Johnson renamed his company the Victor Talking Machine Company, and his gramophones were renamed Victrolas. The Victor Talking Machine Company was wildly successful. The Victorla became the most influential phonograph in the country. Its outstanding physical feature was the absence of the horn that protruded from the top of other talking machines. The Victrola was totally enclosed, resembling a fine piece of furniture as much as a technological innovation and the state-of-the-art home entertainment unit.

Johnson recognized that the ultimate demand for the talking machines would be a function of the availability and quality of recordings to play on the machines, and he set out to perfect a process of mass-producing quality recordings. Having accomplished that, he signed the greatest singing talent to exclusive contracts and dominated the phonograph industry through control of the recordings. His Victrola was technically inferior to Edison's machine in many ways, but while Edison focused on perfecting the sound quality of the phonograph, Johnson secured a lock on the quality of the recordings to be played on it. This ultimately proved to be the undoing of Edison. While Edison is credited with the greatest technological breakthroughs, Johnson is credited with popularizing the invention. When he died on November 14, 1945, he was one of the richest men in the United States.

Al Jolson (1888–1950)

Al Jolson was born Asa Yoelson on May 26, 1888, in Lithuania. His popularity extended from the vaudeville stage to the radio airwaves to the silver screen. Today he is perhaps best known for his groundbreaking and prophetic phrase "You ain't heard nothin' yet," the first spoken words in movie history. That line, from *The Jazz Singer* (1927), was Jolson's motion picture debut. It vaulted him to the top of the movie star system of the day, which he dominated much as he had the vaudeville circuit for the previous two decades.

The son of a rabbi, Jolson planned to become a cantor but instead turned to the stage. After his New York City debut in 1899, he worked in circuses, minstrel shows, and vaudeville. He first appeared on stage in black face, an entertainment style in which white actors imitated African Americans by coloring their faces with burnt cork, in 1909. The style brought him fame and fortune, though it is regarded today as a derogatory form of entertainment.

Jolson's career was typical of many famous entertainers in the early twentieth century. He honed his craft by working his way up the ladder, from the small-time circuit to the big-time circuit, and then to Broadway, where he first appeared in 1911; the radio; and eventually the movies. He was preparing to conquer the new entertainment frontier of television, mulling competing offers to star in his own show, when he died of a heart attack on October 23, 1950.

Benjamin Franklin Keith (1846–1914)

Benjamin Franklin Keith was born in Hillsboro Bridge, New Hampshire, on January 26, 1846, as one of eight children. He was known as the father of vaudeville, though he never performed on its stage. Keith assembled the most impressive string of theaters and monopolized the booking of the performing talent, establishing near total control over the industry before his death of heart failure on March 26, 1914.

Keith staged his first variety show in a Boston storefront in 1883. It was a financial success, and soon his variety shows became a regular offering. In 1885, he took on Edward F. Albee as a partner. Together they built up the premier theater chain in the nation, monopolizing the best theaters in the biggest cities in the east. Through the United Booking Office, they also monopolized the acts that appeared on the stage.

Keith also made a name for himself by providing a wholesome atmosphere in his theaters. While others before him pioneered the concept of family friendly acts, it was Keith who brought decorum to the audience. Prior to his efforts, the audience at a vaudeville show was often raucous and offensive. Attendance was bolstered after he received the support of church groups who lauded his high standards in the audience and his staunch refusal to allow questionable material on the stage. Thus, vaudeville emerged as family entertainment, suitable for ladies and children.

Together Keith and Albee created a centrally run, scientifically managed industry that would forever alter the field of American leisure consumption. At the time of his death, the Keith-Albee empire was considered by many in the industry to be the greatest consolidation of money and power in the entertainment world.

Princess Grace of Monaco (Grace Kelly) (1929–1982)

Her Serene Highness The Princess of Monaco, born Grace Patricia Kelly in Philadelphia on November 29, 1929, lived the fairy tale dream of every little girl. First she became a famous Hollywood star and then a real life princess when she married Rainier III, Prince of Monaco, in April 1956. The civil ceremony took place on April 18 and the religious ceremony, attended by the glitterati of Hollywood and royalty, took place the following day. Her life ended tragically on September 14, 1982, when the car she was driving went out of control after she suffered a stroke.

Kelly began her acting career on the American stage at the age of 20, moved into television in its nascent days of live broadcasts in the 1950s, and became a star of the big screen when she won the 1955 Academy Award for best actress for her role in *Country Girl*.

Kelly abandoned her acting career after filming the musical comedy *High Society*, released in the summer of 1956, just three months after she became a princess. The film displayed her tremendous acting range, from musical comedy to drama, mystery, and westerns.

Though she married into the royal family of Monaco, she never gave up her American citizenship, maintaining dual American and Monegasque citizenships. She bore three children, and was active in promoting the arts and charitable aid to children.

Ethel Merman (1908–1984)

Born Ethel Zimmermann on January 16, 1908, in Queens, Ethel Merman became the queen of Broadway's musical theater. When she died on February 15, 1984, Broadway dimmed its lights in her honor. Merman was a self-taught singer who never received formal training.

She is regarded as one of the greatest stars of musical comedies in Broadway history. At the height of her career, she was in such demand by producers, composers, and writers that she was able to command 10 percent of the box office gross in addition to her weekly salary.

She debuted with a bang in 1930 in *Girl Crazy* when, according to Merman herself, she held a high C for 16 bars in her solo, bringing down the house and launching her career. Throughout her prime, she was lauded for her ability to hit and hold notes, and praised for her comic timing.

She was nominated three times for Tony Awards, winning for her lead role in *Call Me Madam* in 1951. She has two stars on the Hollywood Walk of Fame and received a Tony Special Award in 1972.

Her stage career lasted more than half a century, culminating with her final public performance in 1982 during a benefit concert at Carnegie Hall. Merman also recorded albums, appeared in 14 movies, and hosted a radio show and television specials. Her last major Broadway role was in *Gypsy* in 1959. This was her thirteenth musical, nearly all of them hits. She returned for a reprisal of her role in *Annie Get Your Gun* in 1966 and a brief run in *Hello Dolly!* in 1970, a role she had turned down when it was first offered to her in 1964.

Arthur C. Nielsen (1897–1980)

Arthur C. Nielsen, Sr. was born in Chicago on September 5, 1897. He worked as an electrical engineer before starting his own market research company, the A.C. Nielsen company, in 1923. He advanced the field of market research and ultimately devised the method by which television audiences are measured.

The initial purpose of his company was to provide retailers with reliable information on their sales and marketing programs. He test-marketed new products and perfected the technique of using random sampling to measure product sales. These techniques were especially important before technology decreased the cost of gathering and analyzing large quantities of data.

Nielsen was a pioneer in developing methods of measuring the size of radio and television audiences. He first developed a National Radio index for broadcasters and advertisers in 1942. In 1950, he added a television ratings service. The ratings service is now the currency by which television advertising is sold. The ratings, which are determined four times each year in what is known as the "sweeps" period, are used to determine ad rates for various television shows. The ratings often determine which shows are renewed and cancelled from season to season.

Arthur Nielsen, Jr. took over the company when his father died on June 1, 1980. By the time of his death in 2011, the company, which was acquired by the Dutch conglomerate VNU in 1999 and eventually renamed the Nielsen Company in 2007, not only provided ratings for television but also digital media audiences, consumer-generated media, and consumer shopping patterns.

William S. Paley (1901–1990)

William S. Paley was born in Chicago on September 28, 1901. He was the first president of Columbia Broadcasting System and the creator of the network system of affiliated television and radio stations that defines the industry to this day. The affiliate system, as it was first created by NBC, was a subscription system in which local stations paid a fee to the network and received programming in return. Paley turned that system on its head. He paid local stations, which then agreed to air the network programming. Paley correctly figured that the he could reap more advertising revenue with the promise of the larger nationwide audiences his system garnered.

Samuel Paley, Bill's father, bought the struggling Columbia Phonographic Broadcasting System in 1927 to use as an advertising medium for the family cigar business. The next year, it was reorganized as the Columbia Broadcasting System (CBS) and Bill took over as president. He had no radio experience but possessed a gift for recognizing entertainment that appealed to the average listener.

Another innovation of Paley's was the network newscast. He created the CBS news division in the waning years of the 1930s as war built in Europe. He anticipated the public's desire for information about the war and profited from an outstanding news department that carried over to television.

Paley remained president of CBS until 1947, when he was elevated to chairman of the board, a position he held until his death on October 26, 1990.

Tony Pastor (1837–1908)

The first true American vaudeville hall was built by Tony Pastor, a saloon owner who opened a separate theater for entertainment in New York in 1881. Pastor's theater was novel because it provided entertainment that was appropriate for women and children as well as appealing to men. By 1885, the concept had spread to other cities along the eastern seaboard.

Pastor was born in New York City on May 28, 1837. He began singing for money at the age of 12 in P. T. Barnum's museum. He fashioned a successful career as a songwriter and singer, appearing regularly on the stage in local saloon theaters by his early twenties.

In 1865, he began staging and starring in his own shows. He soon recognized the potential profit to be earned from an audience that would include women if the shows could be tamed down. By the early 1870s, he instituted "ladies night," when women would be granted free admission to see an entertainment program without the raciness usually seen in the saloon.

Tony Pastor ran his New Fourteenth Street Theater until his death on August 26, 1908. His shows caught on with the public because he provided a variety of good family entertainment that was free of alcohol, profanity, and lewd behavior. The shows he sponsored were forbears of vaudeville, although they lacked their polish. The evolution of vaudeville would improve upon Pastor's offering but continue to follow his recipe: a venue for family-oriented entertainment, free from alcohol, vulgarity, and raucous behavior.

Mary Pickford (1892–1979)

Mary Pickford (born Gladys Mary Smith) was the first true movie star and the first female executive in the industry. Pickford was born in Canada on April 9, 1892. Her magnetic screen presence won her legions of fans. In 1919, at the height of her screen fame, she co-founded United Artists with Hollywood stars Charlie Chaplin and Douglas Fairbanks, and director D. W. Griffith.

Pickford appeared in more than 180 films from 1909 until her final screen credit in 1933. Most of her movies were made during the silent picture era. She made only four screen appearances after the arrival of talking pictures in 1927, though one of them, *Coquette* (1929), won her the Academy Award for best actress.

Pickford was instrumental in the creation of the star system that is commonplace today. She suggested that Biograph, the studio she worked for in 1908, use her name to market its films (of course she would have profited as well). When Biograph failed to act on her suggestion, she signed a contract with Carl Laemmle, who was only too happy to follow her advice and who reaped millions by exploiting the name of Mary Pickford to promote his movies. Pickford herself did well by this arrangement. In 1916, at the height of her popularity and drawing power, she was earning more than $500,000 per year as both an actress and head of her own production company. She was the first woman producer in the business.

When she married actor Douglas Fairbanks in 1920, Mary Pickford may have been the most famous woman in the world. After exiting from the acting business, she began to fade from the public eye. She died in her sleep on May 27, 1979.

Elvis Presley (1935–1977)

Elvis Presley was born on January 8, 1935, in Tupelo, Mississippi. He died on August 16, 1977, at his home in Memphis, Tennessee. He began his singing career in 1954 for the Sun Records label. The next year, his contract was sold to RCA Victor, and by 1956 he was an international superstar. His musical influences were country, gospel, and rhythm and blues, all of which lent to his unique musical sound and style.

Elvis sold over one billion records worldwide, more than any other recording artist. More than 150 of his U.S. releases have gone gold or platinum. He had 18 singles and 10 albums that reached the top of the Billboard pop charts. He also had number one hits on the country, gospel, and R&B charts, as well as foreign charts. Despite his worldwide fame and success, Elvis never performed outside of the United States except for five shows in Canada in 1957.

He won three Grammy Awards, plus the Grammy for lifetime achievement, which he received at the age of 36.

He starred in 31 feature films as an actor and made three network television specials as well as numerous guest appearances. He made his television debut in 1956. In January 1957, on his third appearance on the Ed Sullivan show, his hips were famously censored. He was shown only from the waist up.

In 2002, a remix of an earlier recording reached the top of the U.K. charts, giving him his eighteenth number one hit in the United Kingdom—a quarter century after his death.

Jackie Robinson (1919–1972)

Jackie Robinson was the first African American to play in Major League Baseball (MLB) in the twentieth century when he joined the Brooklyn Dodgers for the 1947 season. Robinson was not only a great player, which was validated by his election to the Baseball Hall of Fame in 1962, but a civil rights pioneer as well.

Robinson was born on January 31, 1919, in Cairo, Georgia, but moved to California as a boy. He became the first athlete to letter in four varsity sports at University of California–Los Angeles (UCLA). He was variously described during his college career as the greatest football player, basketball player, and runner in the country. He also won collegiate titles in swimming and tennis, and played professional football in Hawaii.

Robinson enjoyed an outstanding MLB career, winning the Rookie of the Year award in 1947 and the Most Valuable Player award two years later. He led the Dodgers to the World Series championship in 1955, all after starting his career as a 28-year-old rookie. He had played for several years before that in the Negro Leagues.

During his rookie season, Robinson was subjected to merciless taunting and derisive comments, but he never fought back or responded in public. During his second season, however, with the silence restriction removed, Robinson began to speak out and achieved renown far beyond baseball as a civil rights spokesman.

After baseball, Robinson accepted a position as vice-president for the Chock Full O' Nuts corporation and served on the board of the National Association for the Advancement of

Colored People (NAACP). He devoted much of his postretirement time to making public appearances for civil rights causes. Robinson died on October 24, 1972. In 2003, he was posthumously awarded the Congressional Gold Medal, the highest award bestowed by Congress.

Lillian Russell (1861–1922)

Lillian Russell, one of America's first entertainer celebrities, was actually buried with full military honors when she died on June 6, 1922. She had spent the last decade heavily immersed in politics, and immediately prior to her death, she had completed a fact-finding mission in Europe for President Warren Harding, who approved the military funeral. While politics consumed the last part of her life, it was the stage that made her famous.

Born Helen Louise Leonard on December 4, 1861, in Clinton, Iowa, Russell grew up in Chicago and moved with her mother to New York City in 1879 to pursue her musical studies more seriously. While performing in the chorus of a New York production of Gilbert and Sullivan's operetta *H.M.S. Pinafore*, she caught the attention of Tony Pastor, an early vaudeville pioneer. She assumed the stage name Lillian Russell and began performing in Pastor's theater that year.

For three decades, Russell remained one of the foremost singers in the United States, starring frequently in operettas and on vaudeville. She performed with a variety of touring companies, including one that she headed. In 1888, she was earning upwards of $20,000 a year headlining for the Casino Theater in New York. It was at the Casino that she performed her most famous role, Gabrielle Dalmont in *An American Beauty*, a title that became her soubriquet. At the turn of the twentieth century, she was able to command over $3,000 a week to appear on the vaudeville stage.

She began to wind down her career after marrying her fourth husband, prominent politician Alexander P. Moore, in 1912. She devoted more of her time to furthering his political career and causes, including the sale of Liberty Bonds during World War I, and successfully campaigning for Warren Harding during the 1920 presidential election.

Russell turned her attention to politics and seldom entertained in her later years, yet she never fell out of favor with her adoring public. She was America's first true entertainment superstar.

David Sarnoff (1891–1971)

David Sarnoff is the personification of the classic American success story. He was born February 27, 1891, in Minsk, Belarus. His family came to America in 1900, and he worked his way up from a poor immigrant unable to speak a word of English to the president and chief executive officer (CEO) of one of the largest corporations in America. At the time of his death, he was a highly decorated war hero, recipient of numerous awards and honors, and widely recognized as one of the greatest business minds in American history.

He began his career as a messenger boy for the Commercial Cable Company in 1906. He ended it as chief executive officer and chairman of the board of Radio Corporation of America (RCA).

Besides its pioneering work in the radio and television fields, RCA launched the National Broadcasting Corporation (NBC) to oversee the production and distribution of over-the-air entertainment. In addition, RCA pioneered car radios, striking a deal with General Motors in 1931 to manufacture radios for their cars. Sarnoff also merged with the Victor phonograph company, giving RCA control of the largest manufacturer in that industry. One of the outcomes of this merger was the combination radio-phonograph.

Sarnoff engaged in one of his bitterest battles over television, fighting Philo Farnsworth for the title of Father of Television and the rights to valuable patents that controlled the industry. For the only time in his career, Sarnoff had to agree to purchase the licensing rights to a patent from someone else. He licensed Farnsworth's patents for RCA's use.

Color television was the last accomplishment for David Sarnoff, who died on December 12, 1971. At the time of his death, he was lauded as one of the greatest executives in American business history. He was an acknowledged visionary without equal in his pioneering of the electronic entertainment industry. The man who never formally attended high school or college had collected more than two dozen honorary degrees by the time of his death.

Ted Turner (1938–)

Robert Edward "Ted" Turner III is one of the pioneers of cable television. He began with one local station in Atlanta in 1970 and built it into one of the largest and most powerful media empires in the world. He also purchased two professional sports teams, became the largest private landholder in the country, and opened a chain of restaurants specializing in fresh bison meat.

Turner was born on November 19, 1938, in Cincinnati, Ohio. His family moved to Savannah, Georgia, when he was nine. He graduated from Brown University, where he was a mediocre student but an excellent yachtsman, competing in the Olympic trials in 1964 and skippering the winning yacht in the America's Cup championship in 1977.

Turner got his start in business at age 24 when he took over the family billboard company after his father's death. He added the Atlanta television station a few years later and began to move into electronic media.

CNN, which is now a television staple, was a radical idea when Turner debuted it in 1980. Prior to that, he pioneered the concept of the "superstation" in 1970 when he convinced distant cable companies with excess capacity to carry his Atlanta station. The real interest in his station was that it had the television rights to Atlanta Braves baseball games.

Turner's broadcasting grew to include several television stations and the MGM film library. In 1995, Turner merged his cable empire with Time Warner, becoming vice chairman of the media conglomerate. Five years later, America Online (AOL) was added to the stable. Turner resigned his position with the company in 2003.

Oprah Winfrey (1954–)

Oprah Winfrey was born in Kosciusko, Mississippi, on January 29, 1954.

At age 17, she won the Miss Black Tennessee beauty pageant. Two years later, she began her broadcasting career began with WVOL a radio station in Nashville. From there she moved into television, taking a position as a reporter and anchor with a local Nashville station. In 1976, she moved to Baltimore as a co-anchor and hosted her first talk show.

In 1984, she moved to Chicago and took over a low-rated morning talk show that she renamed *The Oprah Winfrey Show*. In 1986, her show moved from local to national broadcast and quickly became the top-rated talk show in syndication. In 1987, it received three Daytime Emmy Awards, including Outstanding Host for Winfrey. Her show dominated daytime television until she cancelled it in 2011.

In 1998, she received a Lifetime Achievement Award from the National Academy of Television Arts and Sciences and became the youngest recipient of the Broadcaster of the Year award. She was nominated for both an Academy Award and a Golden Globe Award for best supporting actress in *The Color Purple*.

She formed her own production company, Harpo Productions, in 1986. By 2010, her company was producing television shows, movies, and plays, and it was also publishing magazines and web domains. In 1988, Harpo Productions purchased the rights to *The Oprah Winfrey Show* from ABC, making Oprah Winfrey the first woman to own and produce her own talk show.

Winfrey has authored five books. Her Oprah Book Club became so popular that its selections became instant best sellers. In 1999, she received the National Book Foundation's fiftieth anniversary gold medal for service to the industry.

In 2003, she became the first African American woman to be named to the *Forbes* list of billionaires.

Tiger Woods (1975–)

Eldrick "Tiger" Woods become the fastest golfer ever to achieve the number one world ranking on June 15, 1997, after less than a year as a professional. He quickly became the greatest drawing card in the history of golf, if not all of professional sports, before suffering an inglorious meltdown due to a personal scandal.

Woods was born on December 30, 1975, and began golfing at the age of two. He was a child prodigy, winning the Junior World Championships six times, including four in a row from 1988 to 1991. In 1994. he won the first of three consecutive U.S. Amateur Championships, the only player ever to accomplish the feat. He attended Stanford on a golf scholarship starting in the fall of 1994 and left to turn professional in August 1996.

He is widely considered the best golfer in the history of the game and one of the greatest athletes of all time. He has won more than 100 professional tournaments worldwide, including 71 on the Professional Golfers Association (PGA) tour (third all time) and 38 on the European tour (also third all time), and 14 major championships, second only to Jack Nicklaus. He was voted PGA Rookie of the Year in 1996 and PGA Player of the Year a record 10 times, including five years in a row from 1999 to 2003.

Woods won the 2000 U.S. Open, British Open, and PGA Championships along with the 2001 Masters Tournament, becoming the first person ever to hold all four titles at once. The achievement quickly became known as the Tiger Slam.

On November 27, 2009, Woods was involved in a one-car automobile accident that quickly morphed into a career-threatening scandal involving serial infidelity. He would eventually divorce his wife of six years, take a leave of absence from golf, fire his swing coach and caddy, and change professional agencies, all in an effort to refocus his career. As part of the fallout, Woods was dropped as a spokesman by several of his sponsors, costing him millions of dollars in endorsement income.

Before the scandal, he was highly sought after as a spokesman for his talent, his congeniality, and his multiracial background. Woods is half Asian, one-quarter African American, and one-eighth each Native American and Dutch, making him a veritable one-man United Nations.

Babe Didrikson Zaharias (1911–1956)

Mildred Didrikson was born in Port Arthur, Texas, on June 26, 1911. She is widely regarded as the greatest female athlete of all time. Her nickname, Babe, allegedly stemmed from her prodigious baseball skills. Her greatest fame, however, was achieved in track and golf.

She caught the attention of the world in 1932 at the National Amateur Athletic Union track and field championships, where she won five events outright, setting world records in four of them, and tied for first in another. A mere two weeks later, she posted record performances in capturing two gold and one silver medal at the Olympic Games. To cap off the year, she was voted Woman Athlete of the Year by the Associated Press. She would go on to earn that distinction five more times.

In 1938, she married professional wrestler George Zaharias and changed her surname name to Didrikson Zaharias. Soon after, she took up golf.

Didrikson Zaharias mastered golf as thoroughly as she had track and field, winning more than 80 tournaments. Beginning in 1946, she won 17 consecutive tournaments—a mark never equaled by any golfer, male or female. In 1948, she became a founding member of the Ladies Professional Golf Association.

In 1953, Didrikson Zaharias was diagnosed with cancer. She underwent radical surgery in April and amazed the sporting world by entering a professional golf tournament three months later. She did not win the tournament but did win her third and final U.S. Open the following year. In 1955, doctors discovered that her cancer had returned. She died in Galveston, Texas, on September 27, 1956.

6

Data and Documents

Data

Television and Radio in the United States

The growth of new technology steers the direction of the entertainment industry. As radios became more affordable and common, their use as sources of news, entertainment, and commerce grew. The same can be said for television, and ultimately, the internet.

TABLE 6.1

Quantity of Selected Media in the United States 1890–2010

Year	Number of Radio Stations	Number of TV Broadcast Stations	Cable TV Subscribers (thousands)	Households with Radio (thousands)	Households with TV (thousands)	% Households with VCR	% Households with DVD	% Households Subscribe to Cable	% of Population Using Internet
1890									
1900									
1910									
1920	1								
1930	618			13,750					
1940	850			28,500					
1950	2,897	104		40,700	5,030				
1960	4,389	626	650	50,193	45,750			1.1	
1970	6,830	881	4500	62,000	59,550			6.5	
1980	7,871	1,011	16,000	78,600	76,300	2.0		20.0	
1990	9,379	1,442	50,000	92,800	92,100	63.1	0.0	53.7	1.7%
2000	10,577	1,663	66,500	101,823	100,800	84.6	12.5	74.4	43.1%
2010	14,420	1,774	58,300	107,276	110,335	72.0	88.0	51.1	74.0%

Consumer Expenditures on Consumption

As consumer incomes and leisure time have increased, so has the amount spent on entertainment and recreation. How Americans have spent their time and money on entertainment has changed over time.

TABLE 6.2
Expenditures on Entertainment in the United States 1890–2010

Year	% Personal Consumption Expenditures Spent on Recreation	Total	Video, Audio, Musical Instruments	Movies	Theater	Spectator Sports	Commercial Participant Amusements
1890							
1900			69				
1910	3.0	860	108	167			22
1920	3.7	2,055	260	301	81	30	128
1930	5.7	3,990	900	732	95	65	203
1940	5.3	3,761	500	735	71	98	197
1950	5.8	11,147	2,400	1,376	183	222	448
1960	5.6	18,295	3,000	951	365	290	1,161
1970	6.5	39,049	8,500	1,162	735	516	1,819
1980	7.1	128,137	20,400	2,578	1,520	2292	9,100
1990	7.6	290,200	43,900	5,100	5,200	4800	25,200
2000	8.7	585,700	67,300	8,600	10,300	11,500	75,800
2010	9.0	897,100	107,100	10,400	14,500	20,700	74,500

The column header "Personal Consumption Expenditures for Recreation (millions)" spans Total, Video/Audio/Musical Instruments, Movies, Theater, Spectator Sports, and Commercial Participant Amusements.

The Movie Windows

The typical release pattern and timing of a Hollywood movie. Historically this pattern has maximized total revenue for the film. Recent changes in technology, particularly the number of consumers with access to the internet, has created some tension between movie theaters and studios, who believe an earlier online release of movies would be more profitable for them, but at the expense of movie theaters.

TABLE 6.3
Typical Release Patterns for Major Motion Pictures

Theater	16–18 Weeks	Home Video and Video Rental	16–18 Weeks	Video on Demand, Pay per View, Hotels and Airlines	8–16 Weeks	Pay Cable	2 Years	Cable and Network TV

Variables Affecting Leisure Time

Leisure time is a function of income, length of workweek, and cost of consuming leisure goods, such as recreation and entertainment. All of these variables have moved in the direction of increasing leisure time and expenditures on entertainment over the past century.

TABLE 6.4
Variables Affecting the Quantity of Leisure Time in the United States 1890–2010

Year	Gross Domestic Product (GDP) (billions)	Total Population (thousands)	% Urban Population	Disposable Income (billions)	Average Weekly Hours Worked (Nonagriculture)
1890	14.7	62,947	35.1		60
1900	20.2	75,995	39.7	14.1	59
1910	33.4	91,972	45.7	26.4	56.6
1920	88.4	105,711	51.2	71.5	51
1930	91.2	122,775	56.2	74.5	44.7
1940	101.4	131,670	56.5	75.7	38.1
1950	293.8	150,698	64.0	206.9	40.5
1960	526.4	179,323	69.9	350	39.7
1970	1,038.5	203,212	73.5	691.7	39.8
1980	2,789.5	226,542	73.7	2,133.7	38.1
1990	5,803.1	248,710	78.0	4,285.8	39.2
2000	9,817	281,422	79.0	7,194	39.6
2010	14,755	308,745	82.0	11,377.3	38.1

Broadway Theaters

Broadway is the pinnacle of the American theater industry, and along with London's West End, is considered the highest level of theatre in the English-speaking world. Broadway refers to theatrical performances in one of the 40 professional theatres with 500 or more seats located in the Theatre District of Manhattan.

TABLE 6.5
Broadway Theater Current Seating and Year of Opening

Theater	Year Opened	Capacity
Al Hirschfeld Theatre	1924	1,437
Ambassador Theatre	1921	1,088
American Airlines Theatre	1918	740

(continued)

TABLE 6.5 (Continued)

Theater	Year Opened	Capacity
August Wilson Theatre	1925	1,222
Belasco Theatre	1907	1,016
Bernard B. Jabcos Theatre	1927	1,078
Booth Theatre	1913	766
Broadhurst Theatre	1917	1,156
Brooks Atkinson Theatre	1926	1,109
Circle in the Square Theatre	1972	776
Cort Theatre	1912	1,082
Ethel Barrymore Theatre	1928	1,058
Eugene O'Neill Theatre	1925	1,108
Foxwoods Theatre	1998	1,829
Gerald Schoenfeld Theatre	1917	1,079
Gershwin Theatre	1972	1,935
Helen Hayes Theatre	1912	597
Imperial Theatre	1923	1,443
John Golden Theatre	1927	804
Longacre Theatre	1913	1,091
Lunt-Fontanne Theatre	1910	1,509
Lyceum Theatre	1903	922
Majestic Theatre	1927	1,645
Marquis Theatre	1986	1,615
Minskoff Theatre	1973	1,710
Music Box Theatre	1921	1,009
Nederlander Theatre	1921	1,232
Neil Simon Theatre	1927	1,445
New Amsterdam Theatre	1903	1,801
Palace Theatre	1913	1,743
Richard Rodgers Theatre	1925	1,380
Samuel J. Frieman Theatre	1925	650
Shubert Theatre	1913	1,460
St. James Theatre	1927	1,710
Stephen Sondheim Theatre	1918	1,055
Studio 54	1927	922
The Broadway Theatre	1924	1,761
Vivian Beuamont Theatre	1965	1,105
Walter Kerr Theatre	1921	947
Winter Garden Theatre	1911	1,526

Top-Rated Television Shows

Television was for a long time a national source of entertainment in the sense that the three major networks provided entertainment and news that millions of American households would simultaneously consume. With the growth of satellite and cable television access and their increased number of channels, and with the proliferation of internet news and entertainment sites, the number of viewers of any single televised episode has been splintered. The television broadcasts with the greatest number of viewers tend to be from before the days of large cable television access, or major sporting events, like the Super Bowl and Olympic Games.

TABLE 6.6
All-Time Top Rated Television Shows in United States

Rank	Show or Episode	Number of Households (millions)	% Households	% Share	Date	Network
1	Super Bowl XLIV (New Orleans Saints vs. Indianapolis Colts)	106.5		68	February 7, 2010	CBS
2	M*A*S*H series finale: "Goodbye, Farewell, and Amen"	50.15	60.20	77	February 28, 1983	CBS
3	Dallas episode: "Who Done It?" aka "Who Shot J. R.?"	41.47	53.30	76	November 21, 1980	CBS
4	O. J. Simpson murder case	39.21	52.10	71	June 20, 1994	CNN
5	Roots Part VIII (finale)	36.38	51.10	71	January 30, 1977	ABC
6	Super Bowl XVI (San Francisco 49ers vs. Cincinnati Bengals)	40.02	49.10	73	January 24, 1982	CBS
7	Super Bowl XVII (Washington Redskins vs. Miami Dolphins)	40.48	48.60	69	January 30, 1986	NBC
8	XVII Winter Olympics: Ladies' figure skating, short program featuring Nancy Kerrigan and Tonya Harding	45.69	48.50	64	February 23, 1994	CBS

(continued)

TABLE 6.6 (Continued)

Rank	Show or Episode	Number of Households (millions)	% Households	% Share	Date	Network
9	Super Bowl XX (Chicago Bears vs. New England Patriots)	41.49	48.30	70	January 26, 1986	NBC
10	The Oprah Winfrey Show (guest: Michael Jackson)	36.5	47.90	67	February 10, 1993	NBC

Longest Running Television Shows

Some television shows have entertained viewers across generations. The longest running have been news programs. The two notable exceptions on this list are the daytime drama *Guiding Light*, which has seen numerous cast turnovers in its half century of production, and *The Tonight Show*, which has been piloted by five different regular hosts since its debut in 1954.

TABLE 6.7
Longest Running Television Shows in United States

Length (years)	Seasons	Series	Network	Number of Episodes
62	62	Meet the Press (NBC News)	NBC	4,843+
59	61	CBS Evening News (CBS News)	CBS	16,400+
61	61	Music and the Spoken Word	Syndicated	
58	58	Today (NBC News)	NBC	20,700+
57	59	Hallmark Hall of Fame	NBC, CBS, PBS, CBS, ABC, CBS	236
57	57	Guiding Light (CBS Daytime)	CBS	15,762
56	56	World News (ABC News)	ABC	15,722+
54	55	The Tonight Show	NBC	10,452+
54	55	Face the Nation (CBS News)	CBS	
53	54	It Is Written	Syndicated	

All-Time Domestic Box Office Champions

The all-time box office leaders by total domestic ticket sales. This list does not take into account foreign markets, which are becoming a more important source of revenue in the twenty-first century. These figures are nominal, meaning they do not take inflation into account.

TABLE 6.8
Highest Grossing Films in United States Movie Industry

Rank	Title	U.S. Box Office ($)
1	Avatar	760,462,559
2	Titanic	600,779,824
3	The Dark Knight	533,316,061
4	Star Wars: Episode IV: A New Hope	460,935,665
5	Shrek 2	436,471,036
6	E.T.: The Extra Terrestrial	434,949,459
7	Star Wars: Episode I: The Phantom Menace	431,065,444
8	Pirates of the Caribbean: Dead Man's Chest	423,032,628
9	Toy Story 3	414,317,223
10	Spider Man	403,706,375
11	Transformers: Revenge of the Fallen	402,076,689
12	Star Wars: Episode III: Revenge of the Sith	380,262,555
13	The Lord of the Rings: The Return of the King	377,019,252
14	Spider Man 2	373,377,893
15	The Passion of the Christ	370,270,943

Longest Running Broadway Shows

A successful Broadway show has to run long enough to recoup its startup costs in order to remain profitable. In the case of the shows in this list, those costs were easily recovered, and these shows went on to become the most profitable in history. During runs of this length, the cast will turn over numerous times, often launching the careers of several actors in the process.

TABLE 6.9
All-Time Longest Running Shows on Broadway

Rank	Title	Genre	Opening Date	Closing Date	Performances
1	The Phantom of the Opera	Musical	January 26, 1988	—	10,091+
2	Cats	Musical	October 7, 1982	September 10, 2000	7,485
3	Les Miserables	Musical	March 12, 1987	May 18, 2003	6,680
4	A Chorus Line	Musical	July 25, 1975	April 28, 1990	6,137
5	Oh! Calcutta!	Revue	September 24, 1976	August 6, 1989	5,959
6	Chicago	Musical	November 14, 1996	—	6,441+
7	Beauty and the Beast	Musical	April 18, 1994	July 29, 2007	5,461

(continued)

TABLE 6.9 (Continued)

Rank	Title	Genre	Opening Date	Closing Date	Performances
8	The Lion King	Musical	November 13, 1997	—	6,036+
9	Rent	Musical	April 29, 1996	September 7, 2008	5,123
10	Miss Saigon	Musical	April 11, 1991	January 28, 2001	4,097
11	Mamma Mia!	Musical	October 18, 2001	—	4,380+
12	42nd Street	Musical	August 25, 1980	January 8, 1989	3,486
13	Grease	Musical	February 14, 1972	April 13, 1980	3,388
14	Fiddler on the Roof	Musical	September 22, 1964	July 2, 1972	3,242
15	Life with Father	Play	November 8, 1933	May 31, 1941	3,224

Best-Selling Albums Worldwide

Though the technology of producing music and selling it has changed over time, the basic concept is still the same: discover talent and market it to the public. This list includes the sale of physical units, not electronic downloads.

TABLE 6.10
Best-Selling Albums World Wide

Artist	Album	Released	Genre	Sales (millions)
Michael Jackson	Thriller	1982	Pop/R&B	110
AC/DC	Back in Black	1980	Hard Rock/Heavy Metal	49
Pink Floyd	The Dark Side of the Moon	1973	Progressive Rock	45
Whitney Houston/ Various Artists	The Bodyguard	1992	Soundtrack	44
Meat Loaf	Bat out of Hell	1977	Rock	43
Eagles	Their Greatest Hits (1971–1975)	1976	Rock	42
Various Artists	Dirty Dancing	1987	Dance/Pop	42
Backstreet Boys	Millennium	1999	Pop	40
Bee Gees/Various Artists	Saturday Night Fever	1977	Disco	40
Fleetwood Mac	Rumours	1977	Rock	40

(*continued*)

TABLE 6.10 (Continued)

Artist	Album	Released	Genre	Sales (millions)
Shania Twain	Come On Over	1997	Country/Pop	39
Led Zeppelin	Led Zeppelin IV	1971	Hard Rock/Heavy Metal	37
Alanis Morissette	Jagged Little Pill	1995	Rock	33
The Beatles	Sgt. Pepper's Lonely Hearts Club Band	1967	Rock	32
Celine Dion	Falling into You	1996	Pop	32

Best-Selling Singles Worldwide

This list of best-selling singles includes physical copies, not electronic downloads.

TABLE 6.11
Best-Selling Singles Worldwide

Artist	Single	Released	Genre	Sales (millions)
Bill Haley & His Comets	Rock Around the Clock	1954	Rock and Roll	25
Bing Crosby	White Christmas	1942	Pop	50
Bing Crosby	Silent Night	1935	Traditional Pop	30
Elton John	Candle in the Wind 1997/Something About the Way You Look Tonight	1997	Pop	33
USA for Africa	We Are the World	1985	Pop	20
The Ink Spots	If I Didn't Care	1936	Doo Wop	19
Baccara	Yes Sir, I Can Boogie	1977	Pop	18
Scorpions	Wind of Change	1991	Hard Rock	14
The Beatles	I Want to Hold Your Hand	1964	Rock	12
Village People	YMCA	1978	Pop, Disco	12

Highest Paid Actors: 2011

The best Hollywood actors are rewarded handsomely for their ability to attract fans to the box office. Note the disparity between genders when it comes to box office draw.

TABLE 6.12
Highest Total Earnings for Actors in 2011

	Actor		Actress	
Rank	Name	Pay (Past Year millions of $)	Name	Pay (Past Year millions of $)
1	Leonardo DiCaprio	77	Angelina Jolie	30
2	Johnny Depp	50	Sarah Jessica Parker	30
3	Adam Sandler	40	Jennifer Aniston	28
4	Will Smith	36	Reese Witherspoon	28
5	Tom Hanks	35	Julia Roberts	20
6	Ben Stiller	34	Kristen Stewart	20
7	Robert Downey, Jr.	31	Katherine Heigl	19
8	Mark Wahlberg	28	Cameron Diaz	18
9	Tim Allen	22	Sandra Bullock	15
10	Tom Cruise	22	Meryl Streep	10

Highest Paid Athletes: 2011

Forbes magazine estimates the earnings of athletes from all sources, including salary, winnings (in the case of golfers and tennis players), as well as endorsements.

TABLE 6.13
Highest Salaries/Winnings for Athletes in 2011

Rank	Athlete	Sport	Earnings (millions of $)
1	Tiger Woods	Golf	62.3
2	Phil Mickelson	Golf	61.2
3	LeBron James	Basketball	44.5
4	Peyton Manning	Football	38.1
5	Alex Rodriguez	Baseball	36
6	Kobe Bryant	Basketball	34.8
7	Kevin Garnett	Basketball	32.8
8	Matt Ryan	Football	32.7
9	Tom Brady	Football	30
10	Dwight Howard	Basketball	28.6

Largest Season Attendance at Spectator Sports

Spectator sports are popular around the world. These figures are for full season attendance. They are driven by the popularity of the sport as well as the number of teams in the league and the length of the season.

TABLE 6.14
All-Time Largest Seasonal Attendance at Spectator Sporting Events Worldwide

League	Sport	Location	Season	Total Attendance	Average attendance per game
MLB	Baseball	North America	2011	73,451,522	30,352
NCAA Division 1 Football	American football	United States	2011	37,411,795	46,074
Nippon Professional Baseball	Baseball	Japan	2010	21,679,596	25,626
NBA	Basketball	North America	2010–2011	21,302,573	17,319
NHL	Hockey	North America	2010–2011	20,928,036	17,126
NFL	American football	United States	2010	17,141,859	66,960
Premier League	European football (soccer)	England	2010–2011	13,407,540	35,283
Bundesliga	European football (soccer)	Germany	2010–2011	13,057,899	42,673
La Liga	European football (soccer)	Spain	2010–2011	11,039,808	29,128
Football League Championship	European football (soccer)	England and Wales	2010–2011	9,598,336	17,388

American Professional Sports Stadiums

Sports stadiums in the United States have become big business in recent years, not just for the architects who design them and the firms that build them, but for the governments that usually pay for them. To help finance the high cost, the naming rights of these stadiums are often sold. Most of the professional stadiums in these four team sports have been built in the last quarter century.

TABLE 6.15
Professional Sports Stadiums in the United States

NFL Stadiums			
Stadium Name	Team	Year Built	Capacity
University of Phoenix Stadium	Arizona Cardinals	2006	63,000
Georgia Dome	Atlanta Falcons	1992	71,149

(continued)

TABLE 6.15 (Continued)

NFL Stadiums

Stadium Name	Team	Year Built	Capacity
M&T Bank Stadium	Baltimore Ravens	1998	69,084
Ralph Wilson Stadium	Buffalo Bills	1973	75,339
Bank of America Stadium	Carolina Panthers	1996	73,250
Soldier Field II	Chicago Bears	2003	63,000
Paul Brown Stadium	Cincinnati Bengals	2000	65,600
Cleveland Stadium	Cleveland Browns	1999	72,300
Cowboys Stadium	Dallas Cowboys	2009	80,000
Sports Authority Field	Denver Broncos	2001	76,125
Ford Field	Detroit Lions	2002	65,000
Lambeau Field	Green Bay Packers	1957	72,515
Reliant Stadium	Houston Texans	2002	69,500
Lucas Oil Stadium	Indianapolis Colts	2008	63,000
EverBank Stadium	Jacksonville Jaguars	1995	73,000
Arrowhead Stadium	Kansas City Chiefs	1972	79,409
Sun Life Stadium	Miami Dolphins	1987	75,000
Metrodome	Minnesota Vikings	1982	64,035
Gillette Stadium	New England Patriots	2002	68,000
Superdome	New Orleans Saints	1975	69,082
MetLife Stadium	New York Giants/Jets	2010	82,566
O.com Coliseum	Oakland Raiders	1966	63,146
Lincoln Financial Field	Philadelphia Eagles	2003	68,500
Heinz Field	Pittsburgh Steelers	2001	64,500
Qualcomm Stadium	San Diego Chargers	1967	71,294
Candlestick Park	San Francisco 49ers	1971	64,450
CenturyLink Field	Seattle Seahawks	2002	68,000
Edward Jones Dome	St. Louis Rams	1995	66,000
Raymond James Stadium	Tampa Bay Buccaneers	1998	65,657
LP Field	Tennessee Titans	1999	67,000
FedEx Field	Washington Redskins	1996	80,000

MLB Stadiums

Stadium Name	Team	Year Built	Capacity
Chase Field	Arizona Diamondbacks	1998	49,033
Turner Field	Atlanta Braves	1996	49,381
Camden Yards	Baltimore Orioles	1992	48,876
Fenway Park	Boston Red Sox	1912	39,928
Wrigley Field	Chicago Cubs	1914	41,118
U.S. Cellular Field	Chicago White Sox	1991	40,615
Great American Ball Park	Cincinnati Reds	2003	42,271
Progressive Field	Cleveland Indians	1994	43,405
Coors Field	Colorado Rockies	1995	50,381

(continued)

TABLE 6.15 (Continued)

MLB Stadiums

Stadium Name	Team	Year Built	Capacity
Comerica Park	Detroit Tigers	2000	40,120
Sun Life Stadium	Florida Marlins	1993	36,331
Minute Maid Park	Houston Astros	2000	42,000
Kauffman Stadium	Kansas City Royals	1973	38,177
Angel Stadium	Los Angeles Angels of Anaheim	1966	45,050
Dodger Stadium	Los Angeles Dodgers	1962	56,000
Miller Park	Milwaukee Brewers	2001	41,900
Target Field	Minnesota Twins	2010	42,000
Citi Field	New York Mets	2009	45,000
Yankee Stadium	New York Yankees	2009	52,355
O.co Coliseum	Oakland A's	1968	37,077
Citizens Bank Park	Philadelphia Phillies	2004	43,647
PNC Park	Pittsburgh Pirates	2001	38,496
Petco Park	San Diego Padres	2004	42,500
AT&T Park	San Francisco Giants	2000	41,600
Safeco Field	Seattle Mariners	1999	47,116
Busch Stadium	St. Louis Cardinals	2006	46,000
Tropicana Field	Tampa Bay Devil Rays	1998	43,772
Rangers Ballpark in Arlington	Texas Rangers	1995	48,911
Rogers Centre	Toronto Blue Jays	1989	50,516
Nationals Park	Washington Nationals	2008	41,222

NBA Stadiums

Stadium Name	Team	Year Built	Capacity
Philips Arena	Atlanta Hawks	1999	18,729
TD Garden	Boston Celtics	1995	18,854
Time Warner Cable Arena	Charlotte Bobcats	2005	19,026
United Center	Chicago Bulls	1994	22,220
Quicken Loans Arena	Cleveland Cavaliers	1994	20,562
American Airlines Center	Dallas Mavericks	2001	19,200
Pepsi Center	Denver Nuggets	1999	19,099
Palace at Auburn Hills	Detroit Pistons	1905	22,076
Oracle Arena	Golden State Warriors	1966	19,596
Toyota Center	Houston Rockets	2003	18,300
Bankers Life Fieldhouse	Indiana Pacers	1999	18,345
Staples Center	Los Angeles Lakers/Clippers	1999	18,997
FedEx Forum	Memphis Grizzlies	1994	18,165
American Airlines Arena	Miami Heat	2000	19,600
Bradley Center	Milwaukee Bucks	1988	18,717
Target Center	Minnesota Timberwolves	1990	20,500
Prudential Center*	New Jersey Nets	2007	18,500

(continued)

TABLE 6.15 (Continued)

NBA Stadiums

Stadium Name	Team	Year Built	Capacity
New Orleans Arena	New Orleans Hornets	2002	18,000
Madison Square Garden	New York Knicks	1968	19,763
Ford Center	Oklahoma City Thunder	2008	19,599
Amway Center	Orlando Magic	2010	18,500
Wells Fargo Center	Philadelphia 76ers	1996	21,600
US Airways Center	Phoenix Suns	1992	19,023
Rose Garden Arena	Portland Trailblazers	1995	19,980
Power Balance Pavilion	Sacramento Kings	1988	17,317
AT&T Center	San Antonio Spurs	2002	18,500
Air Canada Centre	Toronto Raptors	1999	19,800
Energy Solutions Arena	Utah Jazz	1991	19,911
Verizon Center	Washington Wizards	1997	20,173

NHL Arenas

Stadium Name	Team	Year Built	Capacity
Honda Center	Anaheim Ducks	1993	17,174
TD Garden	Boston Bruins	1995	17,565
First Niagara Center	Buffalo Sabres	1996	18,690
Scotiabank Saddledome	Calgary Flames	1983	19,289
RBC Center	Carolina Hurricanes	1999	18,680
United Center	Chicago Blackhawks	1994	19,717
Pepsi Center	Colorado Avalanche	1999	18,007
Nationwide Arena	Columbus Blue Jackets	2000	18,144
American Airlines Center	Dallas Stars	2001	18,532
Joe Louis Arena	Detroit Red Wings	1979	20,066
Rexall Place	Edmonton Oilers	1974	16,839
BankAtlantic Center	Florida Panthers	1998	19,250
Staples Center	Los Angeles Kings	1999	18,118
Xcel Energy Center	Minnesota Wild	2000	18,064
Bell Centre	Montreal Canadiens	1996	21,273
Bridgestone Arena	Nashville Predators	1996	17,113
Prudential Center	New Jersey Devils	2007	17,625
Nassau Veterans Memorial Coliseum	New York Islanders	1972	16,250
Madison Square Garden	New York Rangers	1968	18,200
Scotiabank Place	Ottawa Senators	1996	19,153
Wells Fargo Center	Philadelphia Flyers	1996	19,537
Jobing.com Arena	Phoenix Coyotes	2003	17,125
Consol Energy Center	Pittsburgh Penguins	2010	18,387
HP Pavilion at San Jose	San Jose Sharks	1993	17,562
Scottrade Center	St. Louis Blues	1994	19,150
Tampa Bay Times Forum	Tampa Bay Lightning	1996	19,204

(*continued*)

TABLE 6.15 (Continued)

NHL Arenas

Stadium Name	Team	Year Built	Capacity
Air Canada Centre	Toronto Maple Leafs	1999	18,819
Rogers Arena	Vancouver Canucks	1995	18,890
Verizon Center	Washington Capitals	1997	18,506
MTS Centre	Winnipeg Jets	2004	15,004

*Temporary Home. Primarily an NHL arena.

Sites of the Olympic Games

The Olympics have their roots in ancient Greece. The modern Olympics were established by Baron Pierre de Coubertin and are now the largest sporting event in the world, held every fourth year in a different location. The winter Olympic games were established in 1924. They were held in the same year as the summer games up through 1992, when the decision was made to move them to an alternating schedule with the summer games.

TABLE 6.16

Olympic Games Host Cities

Year	Summer Games	Winter Games
1896	Athens, Greece	
1900	Paris, France	
1904	St. Louis, United States	
1906	Athens, Greece (unofficial)	
1908	London, United Kingdom	
1912	Stockholm, Sweden	
1916	None	
1920	Antwerp, Belgium	
1924	Paris, France	Chamonix, France
1928	Amsterdam, Holland	St. Moritz, Switzerland
1932	Los Angeles, United States	Lake Placid, United States
1936	Berlin, Germany	Garmisch-Partenkirchen, Germany
1940	None	None
1944	None	None
1948	London, United Kingdom	St. Moritz, Switzerland
1952	Helsinki, Finland	Oslo, Norway
1956	Melbourne, Australia	Cortina d' Ampezzo, Italy

(continued)

TABLE 6.16 (Continued)

Year	Summer Games	Winter Games
1960	Rome, Italy	Squaw Valley, United States
1964	Tokyo, Japan	Innsbruck, Austria
1968	Mexico City, Mexico	Grenoble, France
1972	Munich, Germany	Sapparo, Japan
1976	Montreal, Canada	Innsbruck, Austria
1980	Moscow, Russia	Lake Placid, United States
1984	Los Angeles, United States	Sarajevo, Yugoslavia
1988	Seoul, South Korea	Calgary, Canada
1992	Barcelona, Spain	Alberville, France
1994		Lillehammer, Norway
1996	Atlanta, United States	
1998		Nagano, Japan
2000	Sydney, Australia	
2002		Salt Lake City, United States
2004	Athens, Greece	
2006		Turin, Italy
2008	Beijing, China	
2010		Vancouver, Canada
2012	London, United Kingdom	

The World Cup

The World Cup represents the grand championship of European football, or soccer. The official name of the tournament is the FIFA World Cup, which is an international association of football (soccer) competition. Like the Olympics, it is held every four years in a different location. A competition for women was added in 1991.

TABLE 6.17
World Cup Host Cities and Champions

Year	Site	Men's Champion	Women's Champion
1930	Uruguay	Uruguay	
1934	Italy	Italy	
1938	France	Italy	
1942	None		
1946	None		
1950	Brazil	Uruguay	
1954	Switzerland	West Germany	
1958	Sweden	Brazil	

(continued)

TABLE 6.17 (Continued)

Year	Site	Men's Champion	Women's Champion
1962	Chile	Brazil	
1966	England	England	
1970	Mexico	Brazil	
1974	West Germany	West Germany	
1978	Argentina	Argentina	
1982	Spain	Italy	
1986	Mexico	Argentina	
1990	Italy	West Germany	
1991		China	United States
1994	United States	Brazil	
1995	Sweden		Norway
1998	France	France	
1999	United States		United States
2002	Korea and Japan	Brazil	
2003	United States		Germany
2006	Germany	Italy	
2007	China		Germany
2010	South Africa	Spain	
2011	Germany		Japan

Documents

Thomas Edison on the Phonograph (1878)

In this article written for the North American Review, *Thomas Edison, one of the greatest inventors of the era and a vigorous promoter of his technological innovations, discusses the myriad possibilities for use of a recording machine. In his vision of the future of sound recording, written in 1878, he predicts every use the recording machine or some form of it had over the ensuing 100 years.*

Of all the writer's inventions, none has commanded such profound and earnest attention throughout the civilized world as has the phonograph. This fact he attributes largely to that peculiarity of the invention which brings its possibilities within range of the speculative imaginations of all thinking people, as well as to the almost universal applicability of the foundation principle, namely, the gathering up and retaining of sounds hitherto fugitive, and their reproduction at will. From the very abundance of conjectural and prophetic opinions which have been disseminated by the press, the public is liable to become confused, and less accurately informed as to the immediate result and effects of the phonograph than if the invention had been one confined to certain specific applications, and therefore of less interest to the masses. The writer has no fault to find with this condition of the discussion of the merits and possibilities of his invention; for, indeed, the possibilities are so illimitable and the probabilities so numerous that he thought subject to the influence of familiar contacts himself in a somewhat chaotic condition of mind as to where to draw the dividing line. In point of fact, such line cannot with safety be defined in ordinary inventions at so early a stage of their development. In the case of an invention of the nature and scope of the phonograph, it is practically impossible to indicate it to-day, for to-morrow a trifle may extend it almost indefinitely. There are, however, certain stages in the developing process which have thus far been actually reached; certain others which are clearly within reach; and others which, though they are in the light of to-day classed as possibilities, may to-morrow become probable, and a little later actual achievements. It is the intention of the writer in this article to confine himself to the actual and the probable, to the end that a clearer conception of the immediate realizations of the phonograph may be had. He concedes to the public press and the world of science the imaginative work of pointing and commenting upon the possible. It is in view of the liberal manner in which this has already been done, and the handsome treatment he has received at their hands, that he for the first time appears in persona to discuss and comment upon the merits of one of his own inventions.

In order to furnish a basis upon which the reader may take his stand, and accept or combat the logic of the writer in his presentment of the probabilities of the phonograph, a few categorical questions are put and answers given upon the essential features of the principle involved:

1. Is a vibrating plate or disk capable of receiving a complex motion which shall correctly represent the peculiar property of each and all the multifarious vocal and other sound-waves? The telephone answers affirmatively.
2. Can such complex movement be transmitted from such plate, by means of a single embossing-point attached thereto, to effect a record upon a plastic material by indentation, with such fidelity as to give to such

indentations the same varied and complex form; and, if so, will this embossing-point, upon being passed over the record thus made, follow it with such fidelity as to retransmit to the disk the same variety of movement, and thus effect a restoration or reproduction of the vocal or other sound waves, without loss of any property essential to producing upon the ear the same sensation as if coming direct from the original source?

The answer to this may be summed up in a statement of the fact that, by the application of power for uniformity of movement, and by attention to many seemingly unimportant and minor details, such as the form and material of the embossing point, the proper dampening of the plate, the character of the material embossed, the formation of the mouth-piece over the plate, etc., the writer has at various times during the past weeks reproduced these waves with such degree of accuracy in each and every detail as to enable his assistants to read, without the loss of a word, one or more columns of a newspaper article unfamiliar to them, and which were spoken into the apparatus when they were not present. The only perceptible loss was found to be in the quality of the utterance a non-essential in the practical application of the apparatus. Indeed, the articulation of some individuals has been very perceptibly improved by passage through the phonograph, the original utterance being mutilated by imperfection of lip and mouth formation, and these mutilations eliminated or corrected by the mechanism of the phonograph.

3. Can a record be removed from the apparatus upon which it was made, and replaced upon a second without mutilation or loss of effective power to vibrate the second plate? This is a mere mechanical detail, presenting no greater obstacle than having proper regard for the perfect interchangeableness of the various working parts of the apparatus not so nice a problem as the manufacture of the American watch.

4. What as to facility of placing and removing the record sheet, and as to its transportation by mail? But ten or fifteen seconds suffice for such placing or removal. A special envelope will probably be required for the present, the

weight and form of which, however, will but slightly increase the cost of postage.

5. What as to durability? Repeated experiments have proved that the indentations possess wonderful enduring power, even when the reproduction has been effected by the comparatively rigid plate used for their production. It is proposed, however, to use a more flexible plate for reproducing, which, with a perfectly smooth stone point diamond or sapphire will render the record capable of from 50 to 100 repetitions, enough for all practical purposes.

6. What as to duplication of a record and its permanence? Many experiments have been made with more or less success, in the effort to obtain electrotypes of a record. This work has been done by others, and, though the writer has not as yet seen it, he is reliably informed that, very recently, it has been successfully accomplished. He can certainly see no great practical obstacle in the way. This, of course, permits of an indefinite multiplication of a record, and its preservation for all time.

7. What are the requisite force of wave impinging upon the diaphragm and the proximity of the mouth to the diaphragm to effect a record?

These depend in a great measure upon the volume of sound desired in the reproduction. If the reproduction is to be made audible to an audience, considerable force is requisite in the original utterance; if for the individual ear, only the ordinary conversational tone (even a whisper has been reproduced). In both cases the original utterances are delivered directly in the mouth piece of the instrument. An audible reproduction may, however, be had by speaking at the instrument from a distance of from two to three feet in a loud tone. The application of a flaring tube or funnel to collect the sound-waves and the construction of an especially delicate diaphragm and embossing-point, etc., are the simple means which suggest themselves to effect this. The writer has not as yet given this stage of the development much attention, but sees no practical difficulty in gathering up and retaining a sectional part of the sound-waves diffused about the original source, within a radius of, say, three feet (sufficiently removed not to be annoying to a speaker or a singer).

The foregoing presentment of the stage of development reached by the several essential features of the phonograph demonstrates the following as faits accomplis:

1. The captivity of all manner of sound-waves heretofore designated as fugitive, and their permanent retention.
2. Their reproduction with all their original characteristics at will, without the presence or consent of the original source, and after the lapse of any period of time.
3. The transmission of such captive sounds through the ordinary channels of commercial intercourse and trade in material form, for purposes of communication or as merchantable goods.
4. Indefinite multiplication and preservation of such sounds, without regard to the existence or non-existence of the original source.
5. The captivation of sounds, with or without the knowledge or consent of the source of their origin.

The probable application of these properties of the phonograph and the various branches of commercial and scientific industry presently indicated will require the exercise of more or less mechanical ingenuity. Conceding that the apparatus is practically perfected in so far as the faithful reproduction of sound is concerned, many of the following applications will be made the moment the new form of apparatus, which the writer is now about completing, is finished. These, then, might be classed as actualities; but they so closely trench upon other applications which will immediately follow, that it is impossible to separate them: hence they are all enumerated under the head of probabilities, and each specially considered. Among the more important may be mentioned: Letter-writing, and other forms of dictation books, education, reader, music, family record; and such electrotype applications as books, musical-boxes, toys, clocks, advertising and signaling apparatus, speeches, etc., etc. The apparatus now being perfected in mechanical details will be the standard phonograph, and may be used for all purposes, except such as require special form of matrix, such as toys, clocks, etc., for an indefinite repetition of the same thing. The main utility of the phonograph, however, being for the purpose of letter-writing and other forms of dictation, the design is made with a view to its utility for that purpose. The general principles of construction are, a flat plate or disk, with spiral groove on the face, operated by clock-work underneath the plate; the grooves are cut very closely together, so as to give a great total length to each inch of surface a close calculation gives as the capacity of each sheet of foil, upon which the record is had, in the neighborhood of 40,000 words. The sheets being but ten inches square, the cost is so trifling that but 100 words might be put upon a single sheet economically. Still, it is problematical whether a less number of grooves per inch might not be the better plan it certainly would for letters but it is desirable to have but one class of machine throughout the world; and as very extended communications, if put upon one sheet, could be transported more economically than upon two, it is important that each sheet be given as great capacity as possible.

The writer has not yet decided this point, but will experiment with a view of ascertaining the best mean capacity. The practical application of this form of phonograph for communications is very simple. A sheet of foil is placed in the phonograph, the clock-work set in motion, and the matter dictated into the - mouth-piece without other effort than when dictating to a stenographer. It is then removed, placed in a suitable form of envelope, and sent through the ordinary channels to the correspondent for whom designed. He, placing it upon his phonograph, starts his clock-work and listens to what his correspondent has to say. Inasmuch as it gives the tone of voice of his correspondent, it is identified. As it may be lied away as other letters, and at any subsequent time reproduced, it is a perfect record. As two sheets of foil have been indented with the same facility as a single sheet, the writer may thus keep a duplicate of his communication. As the principal of a bossiness hose, or his partners now dictate the important bossiness communications to clerks, to be written out, they are required to do no more by the phonographic method, and do thereby dispense with the clerk, and maintain perfect privacy in their communications. The phonograph letters may be dictated at home, or in the office of a friend, the presence of a stenographer not being required. The dictation may be as rapid as the thoughts can be formed, or the lips utter them. The recipient may listen to his letters being read at a rate of from 150 to 200 words per minute, and at the same time busy himself about other matters. Interjections, explanations, emphasis, exclamations, etc., may be thrown into such letters, ad infinitum. In the early days of the phonograph, ere it has become universally adopted, a correspondent in Hong-Kong may possibly not be supplied with an apparatus, thus necessitating a written letter of the old-fashioned sort. In that case the writer would use his phonograph simply as a dictating-machine, his clerk writing it out from the phonograph at leisure, causing as many words to be uttered at one time as his memory was capable of retaining until he had written them down. This clerk need not be a stenographer, nor need he have been present when the letter was dictated, etc. The advantages of such an innovation upon the present slow, tedious, and costly methods are too numerous, and too readily suggest themselves, to warrant their enumeration, while there are no disadvantages which will not disappear coincident with the general introduction of the new method.

Dictation. All kinds and manner of dictation which will permit of the application of the mouth of the speaker to the mouthpiece of the phonograph may be as readily effected by the phonograph as in the case of letters. If the matter is for the printer, he would much prefer, in setting it up in type, to use his ears in lieu of his eyes. He has other use for them. It would be even worth while to compel witnesses in court to speak directly into the phonograph, in order to thus obtain au unimpeachable record of their testimony. The increased delicacy of the phonograph, which is in the near future, will enlarge this field rapidly. It may then include all the sayings of not only the witness, but the judge and the counsel. It will then also comprehend the utterances of public speakers. Books may be read by the charitably-inclined professional reader, or by such readers especially employed for that purpose, and the record of such book used in the asylums of the blind, hospitals, the sick-chamber, or even with great profit and amusement by the lady or gentleman whose eyes and hands maybe otherwise employed; or, again, because of the greater enjoyment to be had from a book when read by an elocutionist than when read by the average reader. The ordinary record-sheet, repeating this book from fifty to a hundred times as it will, would command a price that would pay the original reader well for the slightly-increased difficulty in reading it aloud in the phonograph.

Educational Purposes. As an elocutionary teacher, or as a primary teacher for children, it will certainly be invaluable. By it difficult passages may be correctly rendered for the pupil but once, after which he has only to apply to his phonograph for instructions. The child may thus learn to spell, commit to memory a lesson set for it, etc., etc. A song sung on the phonograph is reproduced with marvelous accuracy and power. Thus a friend may in a morning-call sing us a song which shall delight an evening company, etc. As a musical teacher it will be used to enable one to master a new air, the child to form its first songs, or to sing him to sleep.

Family record. For the purpose of preserving the sayings, the voices, and the last words of the dying member of the family as of great menthe phonograph will unquestionably outrank the photograph. In the field of multiplication of original matrices, and the repetition of one and the same thing, the successful electrotyping of the original record is an essential. As this is a problem easy of solution, it properly ranks among the probabilities. It comprehends a vast field.

The principal application of the phonograph in this direction is in the production of Phonographic Books. A book of 40,000 words upon a single metal plate ten inches square thus becomes a strong probability. The advantages of such books over those printed are too readily seen to need mention. Such books would be listened to where now none are read. They would preserve more than the mental emanations of the brain of the author; and, as a bequest to future generations, they would be unequaled. For the preservation of languages they would be invaluable. The only element not absolutely assured, in the result of experiments thus far made which stands in the way of a perfect reproduction at will of Adelina Pattis' voice in all its purity is the single one of quality, and even that is not totally lacking, and will doubtless be wholly attained. If, however, it should not, the musical-box, or cabinet, of the present, will be superseded by that which will give the voice and the words of the human songstress. A doll which may speak, sing, cry, or laugh, may be safely promised our children for the Christmas holidays ensuing. Every species of animal or mechanical toys such as locomotives, etc. may be supplied with their natural and characteristic sounds.

Clocks. The phonographic clock will tell you the hour of the day; call you to lunch; send your lover home at ten, etc.

Advertising, etc. This class of phonographic work is so akin to the foregoing, that it is only necessary to call attention to it.

Speech and other Utterances. It will henceforth be possible to preserve for future generations the voices as well as the words of our Washingtons, our Lincolns, our Gladstones, etc., and to have them give us their greatest orations every town and hamlet in the country, upon our holidays.

Lastly, and in quite another direction, the phonograph will perfect the telephone, and revolutionize present systems of telegraphy. That useful invention is now restricted in its field of operation by reason of the fact that it is a means of communication which leaves no record of its transactions, thus restricting its use to simple conversational chit-chat, and such an important details of business as are not considered of sufficient importance to record. Were this different, and our telephone-conversation automatically recorded, we should find the reverse of the present status of the telephone. It would be expressly resorted to as a means of perfect record. In writing our agreements we incorporate in the writing the summing up of our understanding using entirely new and different phraseology from that which we used to express our understanding of the transaction in its discussion, and not infrequently thus begetting perfectly innocent causes of misunderstanding. Now, if the telephone, with the phonograph to record its sayings, were used in the preliminary discussion, we would not only have the full and correct text, but every word of the whole matter capable of throwing light upon the subject. Thus it would seem clear that the men would find it more advantageous to actually separate a half-mile or so in order to discuss important business matters, than to discuss them verbally, and then make an awkward attempt to clothe their understanding in a new language. The logic which applies to transactions between two individuals in the same office, applies with the greater force to two at a distance who must discuss the matter between them by the telegraph or mail. And this latter case, in turn, is reinforced by the demands of an economy of time and money at every mile of increase of distance between them.

How can this application be made will probably be asked by those unfamiliar with either the telephone or phonograph. Both these inventions cause a plate or disk to vibrate, and thus produce sound-waves in harmony with those of the voice of the speaker. A very simple device may be made by which the one vibrating disk may be made to do duty for both the telephone and the phonograph, thus enabling the speaker to simultaneously transmit and record his message. What system of telegraphy can approach that? A similar combination at the distant end of the wire enables the correspondent, if he is present, to hear it while it is being recorded. Thus we have a mere pas-sage of words for the action, but a complete and durable record of those words as the result of that action. Can economy of time or money go further than to annihilate time and space, and bottle up for posterity the mere utterance of man, without other effort on his part than to speak the words?

In order to make this adaptation, it is only requisite that the phonograph shall be made slightly more sensitive to record, and the telephone very slightly increased in the vibrating force of the receiver, and it is accomplished. Indeed, the Carbon Telephone, invented and perfected by the writer, will already well nigh effect the record on the phonograph; and, as he is constantly improving upon it, to cause a more decided vibration of the plate of the receiver, this addition to the telephone may be looked for coincident with the other practical applications of the phonograph, and with almost equal certainty.

The telegraph company of the future and that no distant one will be simply an organization having a huge system of wires, central and sub-central stations, managed by skilled attendants, whose sole duty it will be to keep wires in proper repair, and give, by switch or shunt arrangement, prompt attention to subscriber No. 923 in New York, when he signals his desire to have private communication with subscriber No. 1001 in Boston, for three minutes. The minor and totally inconsequent details which seem to arise as obstacles in the eyes of the groove-traveling telegraph-man, wedded to existing methods, will wholly disappear before that remorseless Juggernaut the needs of man; for, will not the necessities of man surmount trifles in order to reap the full benefit of an invention which practically brings him face to face with whom he will; and, better still, doing the work of a conscientious and infallible scribe? Thomas A. Edison.

Source: Edison, Thomas A., "The Phonograph and Its Future," *North American Review* 126, no. 262, May 1878, pp. 527–36.

P. T. Barnum: "The Art of Money-Getting" (1880)

Phineas T. Barnum was an author, publisher, politician, showman, and one of the great marketing geniuses in American history. He is famously credited for the saying "There's a sucker born every minute." Though there is no evidence that Barnum actually said this, he never denied it. This excerpt suggests that his credo was closer to "there's a customer born every minute."

BE POLITE AND KIND TO YOUR CUSTOMERS
Politeness and civility are the best capital ever invested in business. Large stores, gilt signs, flaming advertisements, will all prove unavailing if you or your employees treat your patrons abruptly. The truth is, the more kind and liberal a man is, the more generous will be the patronage bestowed upon him. "Like begets like." The man who gives the greatest amount of goods of a corresponding quality for the least sum (still reserving for himself a profit) will generally succeed best in the long run. This brings us to the golden rule, "As ye would that men should do to you, do ye also to them" and they will do better by you than if you always treated them as if you wanted to get the most you could out of them for the least return. Men who drive sharp bargains with their customers, acting as if they never expected to see them again, will not be mistaken. They will never see them again as customers. People don't like to pay and get kicked also.

One of the ushers in my Museum once told me he intended to whip a man who was in the lecture-room as soon as he came out.

"What for?" I inquired.

"Because he said I was no gentleman," replied the usher.

"Never mind," I replied, "he pays for that, and you will not convince him you are a gentleman by whipping him. I cannot afford to lose a customer. If you whip him, he will never visit the Museum again, and he will induce friends to go with him to other places of amusement instead of this, and thus you see, I should be a serious loser."

"But he insulted me," muttered the usher.

"Exactly," I replied, "and if he owned the Museum, and you had paid him for the privilege of visiting it, and he had then insulted you, there might be some reason in your resenting it, but in this instance he is the man who pays, while we receive, and you must, therefore, put up with his bad manners."

My usher laughingly remarked, that this was undoubtedly the true policy; but he added that he should not object to an increase of salary if he was expected to be abused in order to promote my interest.

Source: Barnum, P. T., "The Art of Money-Getting, or, Golden Rules for Making Money." Originally published 1880. Available at http://www.gutenberg.org/files/8581/8581-h/8581-h.htm.

The Modern Olympics (1896)

The following selection by Pierre de Coubertin, a Frenchman who was instrumental in organizing the revival of the Olympic Games, describes the first modern games held in Athens in 1896.

The Olympic Games which recently took place at Athens were modern in character, not alone because of their programs, which substituted bicycles for chariot races, and fencing for the brutalities of pugilism, but because in their origin and regulations they were international and universal, and consequently adapted to the conditions in which athletics have developed at the present day. The ancient games had an exclusively Hellenic [Greek] character; they were always held in the same place, and Greek blood was a necessary condition of admission to them. It is true that strangers were in time tolerated; but their presence at Olympia was a tribute paid to the superiority of Greek civilization than a right exercise in the name of racial equality. With the modern games it is quite otherwise. Their creation is the work of "Barbarians." It is due to the delegates of the athletic associations of all countries assembled in Paris in 1894. It was there agreed that every county should celebrate the Olympic games in turn. The first place belonged by right to Greece; it was accorded by unanimous vote; and in order to emphasize the permanence of the institution, its wide bearings, and its essentially cosmopolitan character, an international committee was appointed, the members of which were to represent the various nations, European and American, with whom athletics are held in honor. The presidency of this committee falls to the country in which the next games are to be held. . . . Easter Monday, April 6, the streets of Athens wore a look of extraordinary animation. All the public buildings were draped in bunting; multicolored streamers floated in the wind; green wreaths decked the house-fronts. Everywhere were the two letters "O.A.," the Greek initials of the Olympic games, and the two dates, B.C. 776, A.D. 1896, indicating their ancient past and their present renascence. At two o'clock in the afternoon the crowd began to throng the Stadion and to take possession of the seats. It was a joyous and motley concourse. The skirts and braided jackets of the palikars contrasted with the somber and ugly European habiliments. The women used large paper fans to shield them from the sun, parasols, which would have obstructed the view, being prohibited. The king and queen drove up a little before three o'clock, followed by Princess Marie, their daughter, and her fiancé, Grand Duke George of Russia.

The crown prince, taking his stand in the arena, facing the king, then made a short speech, in which he touched upon the origin of the enterprise, and the obstacles surmounted in bringing it to fruition. Addressing the king, he asked him to proclaim the opening of the Olympic games, and king, rising, declared them opened. It was a thrilling moment. Fifteen hundred and two years before, the Emperor Theodosius had suppressed the Olympic games, thinking, no doubt, that in abolishing this hated survival of paganism he was furthering the cause of progress; and here was a Christian monarch, amid the applause of an assemblage composed almost exclusively of Christians, announcing the formal annulment of the imperial decree. [...]

The Greeks are novices in the matter of athletic sports, and had not looked for much success in their own country. One event only seemed likely to be theirs from its very nature—the long-distance run from Marathon. [...] A young peasant named Loues, from the village of Marousi, was the winner in two hours and fifty-five minutes. He reached his goal fresh and in fine form. He was followed by two other Greeks. . . . When Loues came in to the Stadion, the crowd, which numbered sixty thousand persons, rose to its feet like one man, swayed by extraordinary excitement. [...]

Every night while the games were in progress the streets of Athens were illuminated. There were torch-light processions, bands played the different national hymns, and the students of the university got up ovations under the windows of the foreign athletic crews, and harangued them in the noble tongue of Demosthenes. [...]

There were nocturnal festivities on the Acropolis, where the Parthenon was illuminated with colored lights, and at the Piraeus, where the vessels were hung with Japanese lanterns. Unluckily, the weather changed, and the sea was so high on the day appointed for the boat-races, that the project was abandoned. The distribution of prizes was likewise postponed for twenty-four hours. It came off with much solemnity, on the morning of April 15, in the Stadion. The sun shone again, and sparkled on the officers' uniforms. [...]

The prizes were an olive branch from the very spot, at Olympia, where stood the ancient Altis, a diploma drawn by a Greek artist, and a silver medal . . . On one side of the medal is the Acropolis, with the Parthenon and the Propylaea; on the other a colossal head of the Olympian Zeus . . .

After the distribution of prizes, the athletes formed for the traditional procession around the Stadion. Loues, the victor of the Marathon, came first, bearing the Greek flag. Then the Americas, the Hungarians, the French, the Germans. The ceremony, moreover, was made more memorable by a charming incident. One of the contestants, Mr. Robertson, an Oxford student, recited an ode which he had composed, in ancient Greek and in the Pindaric mode, in honor of the games. Music had opened them, and Poetry was present at their close; and thus was the bond once more renewed which in the past united the muses with feats of physical strength, the mind with the well-trained body. [. . .]

Should the institution prosper—as I am persuaded, all civilized nations aiding, that it will—it may be a potent, if indirect factor in securing universal peace. Wars break out because nations misunderstand each other. We shall not have peace until the prejudices which now separate the individual races shall have been outlived. To attain this end, what better means than to bring the youth of all countries periodically together for amicable trials of muscular strength and agility? The Olympic games, with the ancients, controlled athletics and promoted peace. It is not visionary to look to them for similar benefactions in the future.

Source: de Coubertin, Pierre, "The Olympic Games of 1896," *Century Magazine* 53, no. 1, November 1896, pp. 803–16

Spalding's Official Base Ball Guide (1910)

Albert Spalding was a player, owner, and baseball entrepreneur. He achieved great success on the field, eventually owning the Chicago White Stockings. But he made his fortune in the sporting goods industry. By 1910, when this particular guide was published, baseball had been well established as the nation's past time. This guide begins with a summary of the previous season's major events. Inherent in this narrative is an optimistic view of the future of organized baseball.

In many ways the Base Ball season of 1909 was a shower of sunbeams for all those who were connected with its transition. Prosperity shone from an unclouded sky. It enveloped alike the major leagues and the minor leagues. There were some clubs which were less fortunate than their neighbors, but it will be difficult to expect anything better, no matter how long continued our competitions for national and local championships. Even the less fortunate were not so unfortunate as some clubs had been in seasons prior, which is not only encouraging but a certain index of the steady progress which Base Ball is making toward that standard where its fixed values will be in excess of its probabilities. From an artistic standpoint it is rather difficult to discriminate accurately as to evolution. There are some who maintain that the Base Ball of the present is better than that of the past. It is doubtful if this can be thoroughly proved. It is a presumptuous task on the part of anybody to attempt to prove it. There are too many attendant features to be considered when-ever one becomes reminiscent, and more than that not all of us are in position where we can be reminiscent with accuracy, for there are comparatively few of the modern school who were spectators of the Base Ball which was played in the '70's. One quality may well be attributed to the Base Ball of 1909, as well as to that of 1876, and that is the pleasure afforded to those who witnessed the contests. We have no record that enthusiasm was less plentiful some thirty years ago. On the contrary, it seems that the Base Ball of those days was welcomed with as much spontaneous approval as that of a more recent period, and after all what test is there to be devised which shall be more comprehensive? The "fan" of the '70's, with all his enthusiasm, was not more demonstrative than the "fan" of the '90;s, and those of both periods attest their love for the game by the devotion with which they follow it, and one human being can ask no more of another. The realities of Base Ball have increased enormously in value. Permanency to the sport has been appreciated by those who are sponsors for it. They have been generous in outlay for the creature comfort of the spectators. They should be. It is a matter of mutual respect. The better the conveniences the greater the attendance. The greater the attendance the better the conveniences. It works both ways. Millions of dollars are invested in Base Ball where the sum was once denoted by thousands. These millions of dollars by no possibility can be considered unwise investment and expenditure. The glorious amusement which is afforded to more than 60,000,000 persons during the outdoor season is one of the finest pleasures of our modern civilization. This, too, is to be considered solely as the spectacular and exhibitive side of the sport, for not less than one-third of the total population of the republic derives fully as much pleasure in participating in the game in some capacity or another as amateurs. The outlook for the season of 1910 is better than that of 1909. If the signs are not misleading there will be more and as fine

Base Ball as there was last Summer. There is absolutely nothing in sight at the present time which would warrant the prediction of anything but multiplying successes, and the individual who makes any effort to upset such capital conditions is an enemy to the grandest sport in the world and a peevish foe to his own fellow beings.

Source: *Spalding's Official Baseball Guide: 1910*, New York: American Sports Publishing Co., 1910. (Official indoor base ball guide containing the constitution, 1910. Spalding Base Ball Guides, 1889–1939. Library of Congress, General Collection)

Vaudeville Program (1921)

This is a program from a typical vaudeville show. This particular show was at the Palace Theater, located in Times Square in Manhattan. The Palace was considered to be the premier theater on the vaudeville circuit. It opened in 1913 and played its last vaudeville act in 1935.

**B. F. Keith's
PALACE THEATRE**
Edward F. Albee, President
Commencing Monday Matinee, January 24th, 1921
Daily at 2:00 and 8:00 PM
Order of this Program Subject to Change

PALACE ORCHESTRA
Mr. Frederick F. Daab, Conductor

PALACE NEWS PICTORIAL
Incidental Music

PERCY ATHOS and CO.
With Gertrude Jackson and Edythe Le Roy
"The Poetry of Motion"

AL MAMAUX
The Famous Pitcher of the Brooklyn National Champions
—and—

JIMMIE RULE
The Popular Songwriter

HERMINE SHONE
Assisted by BILLY RHODES & CO.
In a Fantastic Comedy
"THE NEW MOON"
By Edgar Allan Woolf
Scene 1—The Flower Garden of the Gregan Home—Derrynans,
Ireland
Scene 2—A Quaker Meeting House
Scene 3—A Chinese Pagoda
Entire Production Staged by Edgar Allan Woolf

3—**MISSES DENNIS**—3
Ann-Cherry-Ruth
In Songs

The Musical Comedy Stars
Bert—**CLARK AND ARCARO**—Flavia
In "A Wayward Conceit"

PEARL REGAY
Assisted by ROY SHELDON and the Rialto Versatile Fige
"TERPSICHORE MEETS SYNCOPATION"

INTERMISSION

"TOPICS OF THE DAY"

ETHEL LEVEY
The Internationally Famous Singing Comedienne

Lou—**CLAYTON and EDWARDS**—Cliff
"Don't Do That"

MIRANO BROS.
The Flying Torpedoes

EXIT MARCH

Source: Program from the Palace Theatre, New York, January 24,
1921. Oscar Hammerstein II Collection, Library of Congress.

Television Patents (1923 and 1927)

The invention of television was essentially a two-man race between the ultimate winner, Philo T. Farnsworth, and Vladymir K. Zworykin. Farnsworth was a dying breed, the lone inventor working in his own lab, responsible for financing his own work. Zworykin, on the other hand, headed the RCA television research team. His work was financed by one of the wealthiest corporations in the world, and he had a team of assistants at his beck and call.

V. K. Zworykin, patent for "Television System," 1923

My invention relates, in general to television systems.

One of the objects of my invention is to provide a system for enabling a person to see distant moving objects or views by radio.

Another object of my invention is to eliminate synchronizing devices heretofore employed in television systems.

Still another object of my invention is to provide a system for broadcasting, from a central point, moving pictures, scenes from plays, or similar entertainments . . .

U.S. Patent US2141059. Filed December 29, 1923.

Philo T. Farnsworth, patent for "Television System," 1927

This invention relates to a television apparatus and process, that is, it is directed to an apparatus and process for the instantaneous transmission of a scene or moving image of an object located at a distance in which the transmission is by electricity.

. . .

. . . None of these prior attempts at television have proven successful. They have resulted at best in the production of a crude moving silhouette of the object to be transmitted. This has generally been due to the fact that the mechanically moving parts of the prior apparatus have not been able to travel at the necessary speed requirements with the synchronism required in a television apparatus.

An object of the present invention is to provide a method and apparatus for television, which is adapted to transmit electrically a true moving image in full light shades of the object to be transmitted.

Another object of the present invention is to provide a method and apparatus for television in which the conversion and dissecting of the light shades of the object to be transmitted, to electricity and the reconversion of such electricity to form an image is accomplished in the following manner . . .

U.S. Patent US1773980. Filed January 7, 1927.

Theater during the Harlem Renaissance (1939)

The Apollo Theater was a popular venue that featured black talent during the Harlem Renaissance. As such, it became a thriving hub of music, theater, and other sorts of entertainment that became associated with Harlem during this period. In the following July 1939 Federal Writers' Project interview, performer Lilly Lindo describes her experiences in the Apollo Theater.

Lilly Lindo, one of the Apollo Theatre dancing girls, isn't as happy as she looks when she trips out on the stage four times each day, seven days a week. In between shows and after the last show at night she rehearses for the next week's bill. . . .

"I been doin' this for goin' on two years now, hopin' an' whishin' that some day I'll get a break an' be sumbody. I want t'seemah name in 'lectric lights an' in alla newspapers. — I knows I'm black, an' I knows black folks has gotta go a long ways befo' they arrive. But I got one thing in th' back a this head a mine, an' that is 'Color Can't Conquer Courage'. I'm gonna be a Florence Mills. . . . Does you remember her, Miss?

"Y'knows when she started dancin' she was oney 5 years old? At an entertainment her Sunday School was puttin' on it was, an' she kep' on from there to the nickelodeons on 135th Street an' on, an' on, til she became the sensation of two continents. She danced an' sung for kings, princes an' all the rest a royalty. Lawd, am I wishin' an' hopin' that one a these nights some a them white folks who come to Harlem lookin' for talent will see sumthin' in me an' give me a chance where I whouldn't have t'do four shows a day for 7 days a week.

"Florence Mills knocked 'em dead ev'vy time she came on the stage. The Duke a Win'sor, (then he was the Prince a Wales) saw her 'strut her stuff' thirteen times. They even call her the Negro Ambassador to the World, but things like that never went to her head. Her spirit was typical of the Negro, and did she have pride in her own people! Whenever she was playin' in a show on Broadway she always seed to it that it came to Harlem even for a week so that her own people who didn't have money enough to go down on Broadway would not be denied the privilege of seein' her. Lawd, I can see an' hear her now, singin': 'I'm a little Blackbird lookin' for a Bluebird', in her small warblin' voice, her figgitin' feet dancin' as though she was walkin' on fine wires an' had 'lectric sparks goin' through her body. Jesus! she shore did her stuff with enjoyment. I'm gonna be that sumday, shore enough. I'm 23 now. Keep watchin' the newspapers . . . you gonna read about me. Florence Mills was one a God's chosen chillren. She make as much as three thousan' five hun'red dollars a week an' she didn't leave 133rd Street either, until God saw fit t'take her offa this wicked earth, an' she was moved outa there. Sometime I think God ain' fair as He should be. Florence Mills die when she reached the top. She didn' enjoy the money she made. She was in demand. They had big plans for her an' all of a sudden God came on the scene. She was one of His chill'ren; He step right in an' clip her wings. Her shufflin' feet danced her way t'Glory. She was a God-given Genius. People like Florence Mills make this world a better place t'live in. She did a helluva lot t'wipe out race prejudice. . . . If all they say about the Hereafter is true, then the Heavenly Gates must a swung ajar for Florence Mills t'enter an' Shine in Heaven, 'cause she sure did shine down here. That was some year an' month a dissapointments in Harlem, November 1927. The Republicans swep' Harlem, Marcus Garvey was bein' deported an' our Queen a Happiness died.

Source: Folklore Project, Federal Writers' Project, U.S. Works Progress Administration (WPA), 1936–1940. Library of Congress.

Statement by Representative Henry A. Waxman on the Use of Steroids in Baseball (2005)

After a devastating strike in 1994 that cancelled the World Series, baseball rebounded over the next decade with some of the greatest individual seasons in the history of the game. The single season home run record was broken numerous times, and the career home run record fell as well. As it turned out, however, those records would be called into question due to the alleged use of performance enhancing drugs (steroids) by players. The steroids issue eventually reached the halls of Congress.

Mr. Chairman, thank you for holding this hearing.

Today's hearing is about steroid use in professional baseball, its impact on steroid use by teenagers, and the implications for federal policy. These are important questions for baseball, its fans, and the nation.

Major League Baseball and the Players' Association say that this subject should be left to the bargaining table. They're wrong. This is an issue that needs debate in Congress—and discussion around the family dinner table.

Steroids are a drug problem that affects not only elite athletes, but also the neighborhood kids who idolize them.

And this issue is a challenge not just for baseball, but for our whole society.

More than 500,000 teenagers across the country have taken illegal steroids, risking serious and sometimes deadly consequences. Today, the Garibaldis and Hootens will testify about what steroids have done to their sons and their families. And I commend them for their courage.

There is an absolute correlation between the culture of steroids in high schools and the culture of steroids in major league clubhouses. Kids get the message when it appears that it's okay for professional athletes to use steroids. If the pros do it, college athletes will, too. And if it's an edge in college, high school students will want the edge, too.

There is a pyramid of steroid use in society. And today, our investigation starts where it should: with the owners and players at the top of the pyramid.

Congress first investigated drugs and professional sports, including steroids over 30 years ago. I think perhaps the only two people in the room who will remember this are me and Commissioner Selig, because I believe he became an owner in 1970.

In 1973, the year I first ran for Congress, the House Committee on Interstate and Foreign Commerce concluded a year-long investigation that found—and I quote—"drug use exists . . . in all sports and levels of competition . . . In some instances, the degree of improper drug use—primarily amphetamines and anabolic steroids—can only be described as alarming."

The Committee's chairman—Harley Staggers—was concerned that making those findings public in a hearing would garner excessive attention and might actually encourage teenagers to use steroids. Instead, he quietly met with the commissioners of the major sports, and they assured him the problem would be taken care of.

Chairman Staggers urged Baseball Commissioner Bowie Kuhn to consider instituting tough penalties and testing. And he trusted Commissioner Kuhn to do that. In fact, in a press release in May 1973, Chairman Staggers said—and again I quote—

"Based on the constructive responses and assurances I have received from these gentlemen, I think self-regulation will be intensified, and will be effective."

But as we now know from 30 years of history, baseball failed to regulate itself.

Let's fast forward to 1988. Jose Canseco was widely suspected of using steroids. Fans in opposing parks even chanted the phrase "steroids" when he came to bat. But according to Mr. Canseco, no one in major league baseball talked with him or asked him any questions about steroids. He was never asked to submit to a drug test. Instead, he was voted the American League's Most Valuable Player.

In 1991, Fay Vincent, then baseball's commissioner, finally took unilateral action and released a Commissioner's Policy that said "the possession, sale, or use of any illegal drug or controlled substance by Major League players and personnel is strictly prohibited | This prohibition applies to all illegal drugs and controlled substances, including steroids." This policy didn't give Major League Baseball the right to demand that players take mandatory drug tests, but it was a step in the right direction and demonstrated the league's authority to act on its own to respond to allegations of steroid use.

In 1992, Bud Selig was appointed commissioner and replaced Mr. Vincent. One year later, in 1993, the Centers for Disease Control reported that 1 in 45 teenagers had used illegal steroids.

In 1995, the first of a series of detailed investigative reports about steroid use in baseball was published. The Los Angeles Times quoted one major league general manager who said: "We all know there's steroid use, and it's definitely become more prevalent—I think 10% to 20%." Another general manager estimated that steroid use was closer to 30%.

In response to that story, Commissioner Selig said, "If baseball has a problem, I must say candidly that we were not aware of it. But should we concern ourselves as an industry? I don't know."

In 1996, Ken Caminiti, who was using steroids, won the Most Valuable Player Award. That same year, Pat Courtney, a major league spokesman, commented on steroids and said, "I don't think the concern is there that it's being used."

In 1997, the Denver Post investigated the issue, reporting that as many as 20% of big league ballplayers used illegal steroids.

In 1998, baseball hit the height of its post-baseball strike resurgence, as Sammy Sosa and Mark McGwire both shattered Roger Maris's home run record.

In 1999, the Centers for Disease Control reported that 1 in 27 teenagers had used illegal steroids.

In July 2000, a Boston Red Sox infielder had steroids seized from his car. Three months later, the New York Times published a front-page story on the rampant use of steroids by professional baseball players. And here's what a major league spokesman said the very same year: "steroids have never been much of an issue."

In June 2002, Sports Illustrated put steroids on its cover and reported that baseball "had become a pharmacological trade show." One major league player estimated that 40% to 50% of major league players used steroids.

After that Sports Illustrated article, Major League Baseball and the players' union finally agreed to a steroid testing regimen. Independent experts strongly criticized the program as weak and limited in scope. But in 2003, when the first results were disclosed, Rob Manfred, baseball's Vice President for labor relations, said, "A positive rate of 5% is hardly a sign that you have rampant use of anything."

The same year, the Centers for Disease Control reported that 1 in 16 high school students had used illegal steroids.

The allegations and revelations about steroid use in baseball have only intensified in recent months. We have learned that Jason Giambi, a former most valuable player, Gary Sheffield, and Barry Bonds, who has won the most valuable player award seven times, testified before a federal grand jury in San Francisco about their steroid use.

And just last month, Jose Canseco released a book alleging that steroid use in baseball was widespread in the 1990s, that it involved some of baseball's biggest stars, and that he had personally injected other players with steroids.

In response to these unproven but serious accusations, Sandy Alderson, a senior major league official, said, "I'd be surprised if there were any serious follow-up." And Bud Selig was quoted as saying: "As a sport, we have done everything that we could."

That brings us to today.

For thirty years, Major League Baseball has told us to trust them. But the league hasn't honored that trust. And it hasn't acted to protect the integrity of baseball or sent the right 4 messages to the millions of teenagers who idolize ballplayers.

Major League Baseball isn't the only reason 1 in 16 teenagers are using illegal steroids. But it is part of the reason. Baseball had a responsibility to do the right thing, and it didn't do it. I don't see any other way to read the thirty- year history.

Major league baseball is absolutely right that it couldn't impose mandatory testing on the players. It needed the union's agreement to that. But there were many other steps that Major League Baseball could have taken—but didn't—in the 1980s and the 1990s.

Baseball's constitution says that the commissioner can—and I quote—"investigate *any act* alleged or suspected to be not in the best interests of the national game of Baseball." The collective bargaining agreement expressly recognizes that the baseball commissioner retains inherent authority to take actions necessary for—and again I quote—"the preservation of the integrity of, or the maintenance of public confidence in, the game of baseball."

But Major League Baseball never exercised this authority to investigate steroid use. Its position boils down to this: We don't know what happened, we don't know who did it, and we don't know what they did or how they did it.

But we fixed it. Trust us again.

We wrote the Commissioner yesterday because we already see significant differences between what Major League Baseball says its new drug policy will accomplish and what is actually in the policy. And we will ask questions about that today.

Over the past century, baseball has been part of our social fabric. It helped restore normalcy after war, provided the playing field where black athletes like Jackie Robinson broke the color barrier, and inspired civic pride in communities across the country.

Now America is asking baseball for integrity. An unequivocal statement against cheating. An unimpeachable policy. And a reason for all of us to have faith in the sport again.

At the end of the day, the most important things Congress can do are to find as many of the facts as we can and to do our part to change the culture of steroids that has become part of baseball and too many other sports.

That's why I'm intrigued with the idea of one federal policy that applies to all sports and to all levels of competition—from high school to the pros—and that provides a strong disincentive to using steroids. If we are going to do something for our nation's kids, it seems we are long past the point where we can rely on Major League Baseball to fix its own problems.

Thank you, Mr. Chairman, and thank you to the witnesses, for helping us fulfill our responsibility in Congress.

Mr. Chairman, my staff has prepared a background memo that provides additional detail about some of the points I have discussed this morning. I ask unanimous consent to make this part of the hearing record.

Source: Opening Statement of Rep. Henry A. Waxman, Ranking Minority Member Committee on Government Reform, "Restoring Faith in America's Pastime: Evaluating Major League Baseball's Efforts to Eradicate Steroid Use," *The Mitchell Report: The Illegal Use of Steroids in Major League Baseball, Day 2. Hearing before the Committee on Oversight and Government Reform*, February 13, 2008. Serial No. 110–63. Washington, D.C.: Government Printing Office, 2008.

7

Directory of Organizations

This chapter includes a selective list of organizations, associations, and agencies, along with a brief description of the relevance of each to the book topic, including contact information (web or postal [if no web address available]).

Sports Leagues

National Football League
The National Football League (NFL) is the highest level of professional football (American football, as opposed to what the rest of the world knows as football, which Americans call soccer) in the world. The league was formed by 11 teams in 1920 and was known as the American Professional Football Association. The name was officially changed in 1922. The league itself is an unincorporated 501(c)(6) nonprofit association. The 32 franchises in the league are individually owned and are for profit entities, with the exception of the Green Bay Packers. The NFL has the highest average attendance per game of any professional sports league in the world.

National Football League
Commissioner Roger Goodell
280 Park Ave., 15thFloor
New York, NY 10017
Website: http://www.nfl.com/

NFL Players Association
The National Football League Players Association (NFLPA) is the union for professional football players in the National Football League. Established in 1956, the NFLPA has a long history of ensuring proper recognition and representation of players' interests. The NFLPA represents all players in matters concerning wages, hours, and working conditions, and it protects their rights as professional football players. It also ensures that the terms of the collective bargaining agreement are met, negotiates and monitors retirement and insurance benefits, provides assistance to charitable and community organizations, and enhances and defends the image of players and their profession on and off the field.

NFL Players Association
1133 20th St., NW
Washington, D.C. 20036
Telephone: 202-756-9100
Website: https://www.nflplayers.com/default.aspx

Major League Baseball
Major League Baseball (MLB) is the highest level of professional baseball in the world. The league consists of 30 individually owned franchises organized into two leagues. Professional baseball began in 1876 with the formation of the National League of Professional Baseball Clubs (NL). The American League (AL) was formed in 1901 as a competitor. After two seasons, the two leagues entered into a working agreement. In 2000, the two leagues formally merged into a single organization. MLB is the oldest continually operating professional sports league in the world.

The Office of the Commissioner of Baseball
Allan H. (Bud) Selig, Commissioner
245 Park Ave., 31st Floor
New York, NY 10167
Telephone: 212-931-7800
Website: http://mlb.mlb.com/index.jsp

Major League Baseball Players Association
The Major League Baseball Players Association (MLBPA) is the collective bargaining representative for all current Major League Baseball players. The MLBPA also assists players with grievances and salary arbitration. It works closely with MLB in ensuring that

the playing conditions for all games involving MLB players, whether the games are played in MLB stadiums or elsewhere, including internationally, meet proper safety guidelines. The MLBPA also serves as the group licensing agent on behalf of the players.

Major League Baseball Players Association
12 East 49th St., 24thFloor
New York, NY 10017
Telephone: 212-826-0808
Website: http://mlb.mlb.com/pa/index.jsp

National Hockey League
The National Hockey League (NHL) is an unincorporated non-profit association of professional hockey teams. The league consists of 30 individually owned franchises located in the United States and Canada. The NHL is the highest level of professional hockey in the world. The NHL was first organized in Montreal in 1917 with only four teams. It succeeded the National Hockey Association (NHA), which had been formed in 1909. The NHA was also a professional league. Difficulties arising from World War I and disagreements among owners led to the suspension of the league in 1917 and the subsequent formation of the NHL.

National Hockey League
Commissioner Gary B. Bettman
1185 Avenue of the Americas, 12th Floor
New York, NY 10036
Telephone: 212-789-2000
Website: http://www.nhl.com/

National Hockey League Players Association
The National Hockey League Players' Association (NHLPA) is the labor union for the professional hockey players in the NHL. Established in 1967, and with headquarters in Toronto, the NHLPA's principal role is to represent NHL players and to guarantee that their rights as players are upheld under the terms of the collective bargaining agreement. While the management of daily operations is the responsibility of the NHLPA executive director, the ultimate control over all NHLPA activities resides with the players, who each year elect representatives from the 30teams in the league to form an executive board.

National Hockey League Players Association
20 Bay St., Suite 1700
Tornoto, ON M5J 2N8
Website: http://www.nhlpa.com/

National Basketball Association
The National Basketball Association (NBA) is the highest level of
professional basketball in the world. It consists of 30 franchises
located in the United States and Canada. Players in the NBA boast
the highest average salary of any professional athletes in
the world. The league was founded in 1946 as the Basketball
Association of America. It was renamed the NBA in 1949
after merging with the rival National Basketball League. In 1976,
the NBA merged with the competing American Basketball
Association.

National Basketball Association
Commissioner David Stern
Olympic Tower
645 5th Ave.
New York, NY 10022
Website: http://www.nba.com/

National Basketball Association Players Association
The National Basketball Players Association (NBPA) is the union
for current professional basketball players in the NBA. Established in 1954, the NBPA mission is to ensure that the rights of
NBA players are protected and that every conceivable measure
is taken to assist players in maximizing their opportunities and
achieving their goals, both on and off the court. Whether it is
negotiating a collective bargaining agreement, prosecuting a
grievance on a player's behalf, or counseling a player on benefits
and educational opportunities, the NBPA advocates on behalf of
the best interest of all NBA players. Union members enjoy expansive benefits and are among the most recognizable entertainers
and athletes in the world.

National Basketball Association Players Association
310 Lenox Ave.
New York, NY 10027
Telephone: 212-655-0880
Website: http://www.nbpa.org/

National Association for Stock Car Auto Racing
The National Association for Stock Car Auto Racing (NASCAR) is a privately owned and operated business that sanctions and governs auto racing events. It was founded by Bill France, Sr. in 1947. The family continues to own NASCAR, which is the largest overseer of stock car racing in the United States, sanctioning over 1,500 races on more than 100 tracks throughout the United States and Canada. The NFL is the only professional sport that attracts more television viewers in the United States each year than NASCAR.

NASCAR Corporate Office
One Daytona Blvd.
Daytona Beach, FL 32114
Telephone: 386-253-0611
http://www.nascar.com/

National Collegiate Athletic Association
The National Collegiate Athletic Association (NCAA) was founded in 1906 to protect college athletes from the dangerous and exploitive athletic practices of the time. It continues to implement that principle with increased emphasis on both athletics and academic excellence.

Office of the President
NCAA
Dr. Mark A. Emmert
P.O. Box 6222
Indianapolis, IN 46206
Website: http://www.ncaa.org/

Professional Golf Association
The Professional Golf Association (PGA) of America is the world's largest working sports organization, comprised of 27,000 male and female golf professionals who are the recognized experts in teaching and managing the game of golf. Since its founding in 1916, The PGA of America has enhanced its leadership position by growing the game of golf through its premier spectator events, world-class education and training programs, significant philanthropic outreach initiatives, and golf promotions.

Professional Golf Association
Commissioner Tim Finchem

100 Avenue of the Champions
Palm Beach Gardens, FL 33418
Telephone: 561-624-8400
Website: http://www.pga.com/home/

Ladies Professional Golf Association
The Ladies Professional Golf Association (LPGA) is one of the longest-running women's professional sports associations in the world. Founded in 1950, the organization has grown from its roots as a playing tour into a nonprofit organization involved in every facet of golf. The LPGA Tour and the LPGA Teaching & Club Professionals comprise the backbone of what has become the premier women's professional sports organization in the world today. The LPGA maintains a strong focus on charity through its tournaments, programs, and the formation of The LPGA Foundation.

Ladies Professional Golf Association
Commissioner Michael Whan
100 International Golf Dr.
Daytona Beach, FL 32124-1092
Telephone: 386-274-6200
Website: http://www.lpga.com/

Association of Tennis Professionals
The Association of Tennis Professionals (ATP) was formed in 1972 to protect the interests of male professional tennis players. Since 1990, the association has organized the worldwide tennis tour for men. In 1990, the organization was called the ATP Tour. In 2001, was renamed the ATP and the tour was known as the ATP Tour. In 2009, it was once again renamed and is now the ATP World Tour. In 1973, the ATP established a computer ranking system that provides a fair analysis of a player's performance. It continues to be the official ranking system in men's professional tennis.

Association of Tennis Professionals
Chairman Brad Drewett
ATP International Group
P.O. Box N662
Sydney
NSW 1220
Australia
Telephone: 61-2-92502300
Website: http://www.atpworldtour.com/

Women's Tennis Association
The Women's Tennis Association (WTA) was founded in 1973. It is the principal organizing body of professional tennis for women, overseeing the WTA Tour, which is the worldwide professional tennis tour for women. The WTA is the world's leading professional sports association for women, with over 2,400 players.

Women's Tennis Association
Chairman Stacey Allaster
1 Progress Plaza #1500
St. Petersburg, FL 33701-4335
Telephone: 727-895-5000
Website: http://www.wtatennis.com/

Recording Studios and Licensing

Music Publishers Association of the United States
The Music Publishers Association was founded in 1895, making it the oldest music trade organization in the United States. The association represents music publishers in dealings with music retailers, educators, and all users of music. While the association addresses issues pertaining to every area of music publishing, its primary focus is on the relationship between publishers and educational and concert users.

Music Publishers Association
243 5thAve., Suite 236
New York, NY 10016
Website: http://www.mpa.org/

American Society of Composers, Authors and Publishers
American Society of Composers, Authors and Publishers (ASCAP) is a membership association of composers, songwriters, lyricists, and music publishers in the United States. ASCAP also represents musicians throughout the world through various agreements with affiliated international societies. ASCAP was created by musicians and music publishers, and continues to be run by them. The board of directors is composed from its membership. ASCAP looks out for its members, protecting the intellectual property rights to their creations by licensing and distributing royalties for the non dramatic public performances of their copyrighted works.

ASCAP New York
One Lincoln Plaza
New York, NY 10023
Telephone: 212-621-6000
Website: http://www.ascap.com/

Broadcast Music Inc. (BMI)
Formed in 1939 as a nonprofit performing rights organization, BMI
was the first to offer representation to songwriters of a variety of
types of music, including blues, country, jazz, gospel, rhythm and
blues, folk, Latin, and rock. BMI was founded by radio executives
to provide competition in the field of performing rights, to ensure
royalty payments to writers and publishers of music not represented by the existing performing rights organization and to provide an alternative source of licensing for all music users.

BMI
7 World Trade Center
250 Greenwich St.
New York, NY 10007-0030
Telephone: 212-220-3000
Website: http://www.bmi.com/

SESAC
SESAC was founded in 1930 to serve European composers not
adequately represented in the United States. Though the company name was once an acronym for Society of European Stage
Authors & Composers, today it is simply SESAC and not an
abbreviation of anything. With an international reach and a vast
repertory that spans virtually every genre of music, SESAC is
the fastest growing and most technologically adept of the nation's
performing rights companies. SESAC represents songwriters and
publishers and ensures they are paid royalties based upon how
frequently their songs are played.

SESAC
55 Music Square East
Nashville, TN 37203
Telephone: 615-320-0055
Website: http://www.sesac.com/

Bertelsmann Music Group
Bertelsmann Music Group (BMG) is a joint venture between the international media company Bertelsmann and Kohlberg Kravis Roberts & Co., a global asset manager. BMG is an international group of music companies focused on the management of music rights. BMG covers the entire range of rights administration, development, and funding of new master recordings. Since its founding in 2008, BMG has established a presence in eight core music markets and represents the rights of songs and recordings.

BMG Rights Management GmbH
SpreePalais
Anna-Louisa-Karsch-Str. 2
10178 Berlin
Telephone: +49 (0) 30-300 133 300
Fax: +49 (0) 30-300 133 328
Email: info@bmg.com
Website: http://www.bmg.com/

Sony Music Entertainment
Sony Music Entertainment is a global recorded music company with a roster that includes a broad array of artists from around the globe. It is home to more than a dozen U.S. record labels representing music from every genre. Included among its labels are Columbia, RCA, and Epic. Sony Music Entertainment is a wholly owned subsidiary of Sony Corporation of America.

Sony Network Entertainment International LLC
6080 Center Dr., 10th Floor
Los Angeles, CA 90045
Website: http://www.sonymusic.com/

RCA Records
RCA Music Group operates RCA Records. RCA produces CDs for its artists and distributes other media formats, such as digital downloads and streaming video. A unit of Sony Music Entertainment, RCA Music traces its roots back to the 1920s

RCA Recording Studios
1540 Broadway #34

New York, NY 10036
Telephone: 212-833-8000
Website: http://www.rcarecords.com/

Epic Records
Epic Records is a U.S. label owned by Sony Music Entertainment.
It was created in 1953 by CBS to market jazz, pop, and classical
music that did not fit the theme of the mainstream Columbia
Records label. It has since expanded to represent a much greater
variety of musical genres.

Website: http://www.epicrecords.com/

EMI Music North America
EMI Music Group North America is the home of two of the top
pop labels in the United States: Capitol Records and Virgin
Records. EMI Music North America was formed in 2007 when
EMI Music reorganized the business into three geographic divi-
sions: International, UK & Ireland, and North America.

EMI Music North America
150 5th Ave.
New York, NY 10010
Telephone: 212-786-8000

Atlantic Records Group
Atlantic was formed in 1947. Atlantic Records and Elektra
Records merged in 2004 to form Atlantic Records Group. The
company is currently owned by Warner Music Group. In addition
to its Atlantic Records label, it distributes Elektra Records
imprints, among others.

Atlantic Records
1290 Avenue of the Americas
New York, NY 10104
Telephone: 212-707-2000

Warner Music Group
Warner Music Group (WMG) is comprised of numerous record labels,
including Atlantic and Warner Brothers. It also owns the music publisher Warner/Chappell Music. Besides recording and publishing
music, WMG offers services to musicians, including management,

merchandising, touring, and fan club management. WMG was formed in 2004 when it was spun off from its parent company, Time Warner. Prior to that, it was known as WEA (Warner Brothers, Elektra, Atlantic), three of the leading recording labels of the time. During the summer of 2011, WMG was purchased by Access Industries, Inc.

Warner Music Group
75 Rockefeller Plaza
New York, NY 10019
Telephone: 212-275-2000
Website: http://www.wmg.com/

Motown Record Corporation
Motown is a recording company founded by Berry Gordy, Jr. in Detroit in 1960. It played an important role in the racial integration of American popular music. Motown relocated to Los Angeles in 1972. In 1988, Gordy sold Motown to MCA and Boston Ventures. It is now a subsidiary of Def Jam Music Group, which is in turn owned by Vivendi, a subsidiary of Universal Music Group.

Motown Record Corporation
1755 Broadway
New York, NY 10019
Telephone: 212-373-0750
Website: http://www.motown.com/

Capitol Records
Capitol Records is a major U.S. recording label. It also distributes through a sister label, Priority Records. Capitol, founded in 1942, is now part of United Kingdom–based EMI Group and operates as part of EMI Music North America.

Capitol Records
1750 N. Vine St.
Los Angeles, CA 90028-5209
Telephone: 323-462-6252
Website: http://www.capitolrecords.com/

Columbia Records
Columbia Records can trace its roots to the late nineteenth century. In addition to recorded CDs, the label markets DVDs and distributes digital music and videos. Columbia, the oldest

surviving brand name in pre-recorded sound, is a division of Sony Music Entertainment.

Columbia Records
550 Madison Ave.
New York, NY 10022-3211
Website: http://www.columbiarecords.com/

Movie Theater and Cinema Chains

National Association of Theatre Owners
The National Association of Theatre Owners (NATO) is the largest exhibition trade organization in the world, representing movie theaters in 50 countries worldwide. Its membership includes the largest cinema chains in the world as well as independent theater owners. NATO helps influence federal policymaking and works with movie distributors on all areas of mutual concern, from new technologies to legislation, marketing, and First Amendment issues. NATO tracks industry data for its members, providing them with information on film grosses, patron demographics, membership contact information, and film exhibition data.

National Association of Theatre Owners
750 First St., NE, Suite 1130
Washington, D.C. 20002
Telephone: 202-962-0054
Email: nato@natodc.com
Website: http://www.natoonline.org/

Regal Entertainment Group
Regal Entertainment Group operates more than 500 theaters with over 6,500 screens, making it the largest movie theater circuit in the United States. The organization focuses on the acquisition, development, and operation of multi screen theatres located in mid-sized metropolitan markets and suburban areas of larger metropolitan markets.

Regal Entertainment Group
7132 Regal Ln.
Knoxville, TN37918
Telephone: 865-922-1123
Website: http://www.regmovies.com/

AMC Entertainment, Inc.
AMC Theatres, known as AMC Entertainment, was founded in Kansas City, Missouri, in 1920. It is the second largest movie theater chain in North America. It is one of four national cinema chains in the United States that survived the 2001 and 2002 recession. AMC also owns theaters in Canada, the United Kingdom, France, Hong Kong, and Spain.

AMC Entertainment, Inc.
P.O. Box 725489
Atlanta, GA 31139-9923
Website: http://www.amctheatres.com/

Cinemark Theatres
Cinemark Theatres is a chain of movie theaters owned by Cinemark Holdings, Inc., the third largest theater circuit in the United States, with more than 3,800 screens and the most geographically diverse circuit in Latin America, with screens in 13 countries. In addition to Cinemark Theatres, the company owns Tinseltown USA, Century, and CineArts theaters. The latter features independent films.

Cinemark USA, Inc.
3900 Dallas Parkway, Suite 500
Plano, TX 75093-7865
Telephone: 800-246-3627
Website: http://www.cinemark.com/

Carmike Cinemas, Inc.
Carmike Cinemas was founded in 1982. It owns and operates a chain of movie theaters across the United States. It is the fourth largest theater company in the United State, operating approximately 2,200 screens. Carmike theaters are located primarily in rural and suburban areas with populations less than 200,000.

Carmike Cinemas, Inc.
1301 First Ave.
P.O. Box 391
Columbus, GA 31901-0391
Telephone: 706-576-3400
Website: http://www.carmike.com/

Cineplex Entertainment
Cineplex is the largest motion picture exhibitor in Canada, with more than 1,300 screens under its control. It is the largest exhibitor of digital, 3D, and IMAX projection technologies in the country.

Cineplex Entertainment
1303 Yonge St.
Toronto, ON, M4T 2Y9
Telephone: 800-313-4461
Fax: 416-323-7228
Website: http://www.cineplex.com/default.aspx

Rave Cinemas
Rave Cinemas was founded in 1999 as Rave Motion Pictures. Rave Cinemas made its mark by equipping its theaters with state-of-the-art technology and amenities for patrons, including oversized, reclining stadium seats with cup holders and trays; multiple concession stands; all digital projection; 3D technology; and large screen formats. Rave Cinemas was also a pioneer in the adoption of current satellite technology and is a leader in alternative content programming from live sports to concerts and opera.

Rave Cinemas
2101 Cedar Springs Rd., Suite 800
Dallas, TX 75201
Telephone: 214-880-6300
Fax: 214-880-6480
Email: information@ravecinemas.com
Website: http://www.ravecinemas.com/

Marcus Theatres
The Marcus Corporation was founded in 1935 with the purchase of a single movie theatre in Ripon, Wisconsin. The corporation today has two divisions: Marcus Theatres and Marcus Hotels and Resorts. Marcus Theatres owns approximately 700 screens at locations in the upper Midwest.

The Marcus Corporation
100 East Wisconsin Ave., Suite 1900
Milwaukee, WI 53202-4125
Telephone: 414-905-1100
Fax: 414-905-2879

Email: joanvoelzke@marcuscorp.com
Website: http://www.marcuscorp.com/

National Amusements
Michael Redstone founded National Amusements in 1936 as the
Northeast Theatre Corporation. The company is still owned by his
family. National Amusements is the parent company of both Viacom
and CBS Corporation, and is a partner in the advance sale movie ticket
website MovieTickets.com. In addition, they operate 1,500 screens in
the United States, United Kingdom, Latin America, and Russia.

National Amusements
846 University Ave.
P.O. Box 9108
Norwood, MA 02062-9108
Telephone: 781-461-1600
Website: http://www.national-amusements.com/

Theaters

The Broadway League
This web site provides information on special Broadway events
and programs, as well as industry information such as theatre
grosses and scheduled shows.

Website: http://www.broadwayleague.com/

Broadway Theaters

Broadway refers to theatrical performances in one of the 40 professional theatres with 500 or more seats located in the Theatre
District of Manhattan. The theaters are located along Broadway
and at Lincoln Center. Broadway, along with the West End theatres in London, is considered to be the highest level of professional theatre in the English-speaking world.

Ambassador Theatre
The Ambassador is one of 17 Broadway theatres owned by the
Shuberts. It is unusual in that it is situated diagonally on its site
to fit the maximum number of seats. Its external appearance,
indistinguishable from many other Broadway houses, does not

hint at the strange layout within. The theatre opened on February 11, 1921. The Shuberts sold the property in 1935, and for the next two decades it was used as a movie theater and television studio. In 1956, the Shuberts assumed ownership again and returned it to its original use.

Ambassador Theatre
219 West 49th St.
New York, NY 10019
Website: http://ambassadortheater.com/

American Airlines Theatre
The American Airlines Theatre is a reclamation project of the New 42nd Street, an organization dedicated to preserving historic theatres. Originally named the Selwyn Theatre, it was constructed in 1918 with a seating capacity of 1,180. At the time of its opening, the design had several innovations, including separate smoking rooms for men and women, and telephones in every dressing room. It fell into disrepair and in 1997 underwent renovation, reopening on June 30, 2000, under the name of its principal sponsor but with almost 400 fewer seats.

American Airlines Theatre
227 West 42nd St.
New York, NY 10036
Website: http://www.roundabouttheatre.org/Your-Visit/Venues—Theatres/American-Airlines-Theatre.aspx

Brooks Atkinson Theatre
The Brooks Atkinson was called the Mansfield Theatre when it opened in 1926. In 1945, it was leased to CBS for television productions. In 1960, it was renamed after the theater critic of the *New York Times* and returned to legitimate use.

Brooks Atkinson Theatre
256 West 47th St.
New York, NY 10036
Website: http://brooksatkinsontheater.com/

Ethel Barrymore Theatre
243 West 47th St.

New York, NY 10036
Website: http://www.shubertorganization.com/

The Ethel Barrymore Theatre opened on December 20, 1928, with *The Kingdom of God*, a play selected by leading lady Ethel Barrymore, for whom the theatre is named. Over the next dozen years, she returned to star in several more shows. Many venues were built by the Shuberts for their star performers. The Ethel Barrymore is the only one still surviving. It has been used continuously as a legitimate house, unlike many of the older theatres that have been used for a variety of purposes throughout the years.

Vivian Beaumont Theatre at Lincoln Center
The Vivian Beaumont Theater, which opened in 1965, is located in the Lincoln Center. It differs from traditional Broadway theaters because of its use of stadium seating and its thrust stage configuration. It is New York City's only Broadway-class theater that is not located in the theater district. The theater is named after major donor Vivian Beaumont Allen.

Vivian Beaumont Theatre at Lincoln Center
150 West 65th St.
New York, NY 10023
Website: http://www.lct.org/

Belasco Theatre
The Belasco opened in 1907 as the Stuyvesant Theatre. It was renamed after David Belasco in 1910. It featured an elaborate interior with Tiffany lighting, rich woodwork, murals, and a 10-room apartment that Belasco lived in. It was outfitted with the most advanced stagecraft of the day. The Shuberts purchased the building in 1949 and leased it to NBC before returning it to theatrical use for good in 1952.

Belasco Theatre
111 West 44th St.
New York, NY 10036
Website: http://www.shubertorganization.com/

Booth Theatre
The Booth Theatre is the smallest of the Shubert Broadway theaters, with a seating capacity of only 766. It is named after the actor

Edwin Booth, older brother of the infamous John Wilkes Booth. It opened in 1913, along with the Shubert Theatre. They were designed as a matching pair and abut one another, the Booth on 45th Street and the Shubert on 44th Street.

Booth Theatre
222 West 45th St.
New York, NY 10036
Website: http://www.shubertorganization.com/

Broadhurst Theatre
Playwright George H. Broadhurst built his theatre in association with the Shuberts in 1917. The playhouse is still in the Shubert family and has remained one of the organization's most consistently booked theatres.

Broadhurst Theatre
235 West 44th St.
New York, NY 10036
Website: http://www.shubertorganization.com/

The Broadway Theatre
The Broadway Theatre is one of only five Broadway theaters that actually open onto the street named Broadway. It opened in 1924 as B. S. Moss's Colony, a premiere movie house. The theatre was renamed the Broadway when it converted to stage performances in 1930. In 1934, it returned to a movie theater for another six years. Then in 1940, it returned to stage production and, except for a brief stint as a movie theatre in the 1950s, has remained a venue for live theatre ever since. It is the largest of the Shubert Broadway houses, with a seating capacity of 1,761.

The Broadway Theatre
1681 Broadway
New York, NY 10019
Website: http://www.shubertorganization.com/

Circle in the Square Theatre
The original Circle in the Square was founded in 1951 and was located in Greenwich Village. The current theatre was opened in 1972 and is one of two theatres in the Paramount Plaza tower. The Circle in the Square is one of the smallest Broadway theatres,

seating only 776. It is located below street level, and along with the Vivian Beaumont, is one of only two Broadway theaters with a thrust stage. The building is also home to the Circle in the Square Theatre School.

Circle in the Square Theatre
235 West 50th St.
New York, NY 10019
Website: www.circle-in-the-square.com/

Cort Theatre
The Cort Theatre was built in 1912 by John Cort, a former vaudeville comedian who eventually moved into theater management. The Shuberts purchased the theatre in 1927, and it has remained under their control ever since.

Cort Theatre
138 West 48th St.
New York, NY 10036
Website: http://www.shubertorganization.com/

Foxwoods Theatre
The Foxwoods is the newest Broadway theatre, opening in 1998 on the site of the former Apollo and Lyric Theatres. Both theatres were condemned in the early 1990s and were among the 42nd Street theatres under the protection of the New 42nd Street historic preservation project. They were not salvageable, however, and were razed in 1996. Fortunately, some of the major architectural elements were saved and have been incorporated into the Foxwoods Theatre, including the dome from the Lyric and the proscenium arch from the Apollo

Foxwoods Theatre
214 West 43rd St.
New York, NY 10036
http://www.new42.org/new42.html

Samuel J. Friedman Theatre
The Friedman opened as the Biltmore on December 7, 1925, with a seating capacity of 903, making it one of the smallest houses on Broadway at the time. Today, it has an even more intimate 650 seats and is still one of the smallest venues. Like many of Broadway's

grand old theatres, it fell into disuse as a live performance theatre. CBS leased it for radio and television studio space during the 1950s. In 1987, an arsonist torched the Biltmore, and it lay neglected and decaying until 2001, when the Manhattan Theatre Club purchased the building and restored it. The theatre was renamed after the Broadway publicist Samuel J. Friedman on September 4, 2008.

Samuel J. Friedman Theatre
261 West 47th St.
New York, NY 10036
Website: http://mtc-nyc.org/index.html

Gershwin Theatre
The Gershwin Theatre is the largest venue on Broadway, with a seating capacity of 1,935. It was built in 1972 on the site of the historic Capitol Theatre. When it opened, it was called the Uris Theatre. In 1983, it was renamed for the Gershwin brothers. The American Theatre Hall of Fame is located in the lobby of the Gershwin Theatre.

Gershwin Theatre
222 West 51st St.
New York, NY 10019
Website: http://gershwintheatre.com/

John Golden Theatre
The John Golden Theatre was originally built in 1927 as the Theatre Masque. It was designed as part of a three-theatre complex that also included the Royale and the Majestic. The Shuberts purchased all three properties in 1930. In 1937, when John Golden assumed its management, he renamed the theatre after himself— the third theatre to bear such an honor. The Shuberts resumed control in 1946, and it is one of 17 Broadway theatres in their stable.

John Golden Theatre
252 West 45th St.
New York, NY
Website: http://www.shubertorganization.com/

Helen Hayes Theatre
The Helen Hayes Theatre is the smallest on Broadway. It opened in 1912 and bore the names Little Theatre, New York Times Hall,

and Winthrop Ames before obtaining its present moniker in 1983. It has only 597 seats, but this is nearly twice as many as when it was originally built. The theatre is famous for originating the "little theatre movement," which was one of the reasons for its original name.

Helen Hayes Theatre
240 West 44th St.
New York, NY 10036
Website: http://www.2st.com/

Al Hirschfeld Theatre
The Al Hirschfeld Theatre opened as a vaudeville house in 1924. It was built for Martin Beck, for whom it was originally named. It was constructed on a grade scale, with dressing rooms for 200 actors. It was renamed the Al Hirschfeld Theatre on June 21, 2003, in honor of the caricaturist famous for his drawings of Broadway celebrities. It is one of five theatres owned and operated by the Jujamcyn Theater group.

Al Hirschfeld Theatre
302 West 45th St.
New York, NY
Website: http://www.jujamcyn.com/

Imperial Theatre
249 West 45th St.
New York, NY 10036
Website: http://www.shubertorganization.com/

The Imperial became the Shuberts fiftieth New York venue when it opened in 1923.It was built to replace the outdated Lyric, which had opened in 1903. The auditorium is wider than it is deep, giving most audience members the feeling of being close to the stage.

Bernard B. Jacobs Theatre
The Bernard B. Jacobs Theatre opened in 1927 as The Royale. It was designed as part of a three-theatre complex that also included the Majestic and the Masque. The three theatres, each of a different size, enabled producers to move shows based on their ticket sales to the most appropriately sized venue. In 1930, the Shuberts took over all three theatres. During the Depression, control of the

Jacobs passed to John Golden, who renamed the theatre after himself. The Shuberts regained control in 1936 and reverted the name to The Royale. It was rechristened the Bernard B. Jacobs in 2005 in honor of the longtime president of the Shubert Organization.

Bernard B. Jacobs Theatre
242 West 45th St.
New York, NY 10036
Website: http://www.shubertorganization.com/

Walter Kerr Theatre
The Walter Kerr Theatre is one of five Broadway theatres owned and operated by Jujamcyn Theatres. It was known as the Ritz when the Shubert family opened it in 1921. Like many theatres, it housed radio and television studios during the 1940s and 1950s. It sat vacant for much of the two decades from 1965 until 1983 when Jujamcyn bought it. It was renovated and renamed after theatre critic Walter Kerr in 1990.

Walter Kerr Theatre
219 West 48th St.
New York, NY 10036
Website: http://www.jujamcyn.com/

Longacre Theatre
The Longacre, named for Longacre Square (now Times Square), was built in 1913 by producer Harry H. Frazee, who gained notoriety as the man who sold Babe Ruth to the New York Yankees, allegedly to finance one of his Broadway shows. Frazee fell into financial difficulties and in 1919, control of the theatre passed to the Shuberts, where it remains today.

Longacre Theatre
220 West 48th St.
New York, NY 10036
Website: http://www.shubertorganization.com/

Lunt-Fontanne Theatre
The Lunt-Fontanne opened as the Globe Theatre, in honor of London's Shakespearean theatre, on January 10, 1910. The original design and construction called for the roof to open up to reveal starlight and keep the theatre cooler in summer. Other innovations

included seats that could be individually cooled by ice or heated by hot air from vents underneath. After serving as a movie house for nearly three decades, it was purchased in 1957, renovated, and renamed the Lunt-Fontanne in 1958. It is one of the nine Broadway houses owned by the Nederlander Organization.

Lunt-Fontanne Theatre
205 West 46th St. 10036
New York, NY
Website: http://luntfontannetheatre.com/

Lyceum Theatre
The Lyceum is Broadway's oldest continually operating theatre. Built in 1903, it was purchased by the Shuberts in 1950. When it was built, the theatre featured a state-of-the-art ventilation system: the auditorium was kept cool in the summer and warm in the winter as air was passed over either ice chambers or steam coils on its way into the theatre. An apartment was built above the theatre with a door that overlooked the stage below. Today, the apartment houses the Shubert Archives.

Lyceum Theatre
149 West 45th St. 10036
New York, NY
Website: http://www.shubertorganization.com/

Majestic Theatre
The Majestic Theatre was built in 1927 as part of a three-theatre complex that also included the Royale and the Masque. The Majestic was sold, along with the Royale and the Masque, to the Shuberts in 1930. With 1,645 seats, the Majestic is one of the largest venues on Broadway.

Majestic Theatre
247 West 44th St.
New York, NY 10036
Website: http://www.shubertorganization.com/

Marquis Theatre
The Marquis Theatre, located on the third floor of the Marriott Marquis Hotel on Broadway, was opened in 1986. The theatre is one of nine operated by the Nederlander Organization. A theatre

is located inside the hotel because construction of the Marriott required the razing of five theatres. As a condition of construction, the developers were required to include a theatre within the hotel structure.

Marquis Theatre
1535 Broadway
New York, NY 10036
Website: http://marquistheatre.com/

Minskoff Theatre
The Minskoff Theatre is located in an office tower at One Astor Plaza, which is on the site of the famous Astor Hotel. The theatre is named after the builder and owner of the Astor Plaza, Sam Minskoff. It opened on March 13, 1973. With a seating capacity of 1,710, it is the sixth largest Broadway house.

Minskoff Theatre
200 West 45th St. 10036
New York, NY
Website: http://minskofftheatre.com/

Music Box Theatre
The Music Box Theatre was built in 1921 to house Irving Berlin's *Music Box Revue*. Over time, the Shuberts gained control of the theater, owning it equally with Berlin himself for a while. Since 2007, the Shuberts have been the sole owners, and the theatre is one of 17 they own on Broadway.

Music Box Theatre
239 West 45th St. 10036
New York, NY
Website: http://www.shubertorganization.com/

Nederlander Theatre
The Nederlander opened in 1921 as the National Theatre. In 1959, it was renamed the Billy Rose, and in 1979, the Trafalgar Theatre. When the Nederlander Organization took control in 1980, they renamed it the David T. Nederlander Theatre. It is one of nine Broadway houses owned by the organization. Only the Shuberts own more.

Nederlander Theatre
208 West 41st St.

New York, NY 10036
http://nederlandertheatre.com/

New Amsterdam Theatre
The New Amsterdam Theatre is, along with the Lyceum, the oldest surviving Broadway house. The theater opened in 1903 and the following year the Roof Garden, where burlesque was staged, was added. The Roof Garden no longer exists, but the theatre was restored to its former grandeur when the Walt Disney Corporation had it renovated in 1997 to be its flagship stage for Disney Theatrical Productions. The building was added to the National Register of Historic Places in 1980 and was closed five years later, having served the previous half century as a movie theater.

New Amsterdam Theatre
214 West 42nd St.
New York, NY 10036
Website: http://disney.go.com/live-events/index

Eugene O'Neill Theatre
The Eugene O'Neill Theatre began life in 1925 as a Shubert theatre. It was originally a hotel-theatre complex named after the nineteenth-century actor Edwin Forrest. It was renamed the Coronet in 1945 and took on its present name in 1959. The theatre was once owned by playwright Neil Simon, who sold it to its present owner, Jujamcyn Theaters, in 1982.

Eugene O'Neill Theatre
230 West 49th St.
New York, NY 10019
Website: http://www.jujamcyn.com/

Palace Theatre
The Palace Theatre opened in 1913 as a vaudeville house. It quickly became the crown jewel of the Keith-Albee circuit and the most desired booking of every performer. To play at The Palace became the pinnacle of every vaudevillian's career. With a seating capacity of 1,743, it is the fourth largest venue on Broadway.

Palace Theatre
1564 Broadway
New York, NY 10036
Website: http://palacetheatreonbroadway.com/

Richard Rodgers Theatre
The Richard Rodgers Theatre is one of the nine Broadway venues owned by the Nederlander Organization. It opened in 1925 as Chanin's 46th Street Theatre, and when it was sold to the Shuberts they dropped Chanin'sfrom the name. Nederlander purchased it in 1982. The Richard Rodgers has been home to 10Tony Award–winning shows for either best play or best musical, more than any other Broadway theater.

Richard Rodgers Theatre
226 West 46th St.
New York, NY 10036
Website: http://richardrodgerstheatre.com/

Gerald Schoenfeld Theatre
The Shuberts built the Gerald Schoenfeld Theatre (formerly the Plymouth) along with the contiguous Broadhurst in 1917. It is still owned by the Shubert organization today, one of the 17 houses they own on Broadway. It was renamed the Gerald Schoenfeld in 2005 to honor the late chairman of their organization.

Gerald Schoenfeld Theatre
236 West 45th St.
New York, NY 10036
Website: http://www.shubertorganization.com/

Shubert Theatre
The Shubert, constructed in 1913, is the namesake of the 17 Broadway theaters owned by the company. The theater was built jointly with the Booth Theatre. There is a pedestrian walkway, originally a private road, known as Shubert Alley, that runs alongside the two, connecting 44th and 45th streets between Broadway and 8th Avenue.

Shubert Theatre
225 West 44th St.
New York, NY10036
Website: http://www.shubertorganization.com/

Neil Simon Theatre
When the Neil Simon Theatre opened in 1927, it was known as the Alvin Theatre. In 1983, after the successful run of Simon's *Brighton Beach Memoirs*, the theater was renamed in his honor. The Neil Simon seats 1,445 and is one of the Nederlander Organization's nine Broadway theaters.

Neil Simon Theatre
250 West 52nd St.
New York, NY 10019
Website: http://www.neilsimontheatre.com/

Stephen Sondheim Theatre
The Stephen Sondheim Theatre, originally named Henry Miller's Theatre, was built in 1918 by the actor-producer Henry Miller, not to be confused with the author of the same name. When it opened, it was the first air-conditioned theater on Broadway. It served as a theater until 1968, when it began an inglorious slide down the ladder of acceptability. It became a movie theater, then a porn theater, before beginning to return to respectability as a disco and eventually a legitimate theater in the late 1990s. The theater was closed in 2004 for major renovation work, during which the interior was gutted and a new theater was constructed underneath the new 57-story Bank of America Tower, making it one of only two subterranean Broadway theaters, the other being the Circle in the Square. It was named in honor of American composer Stephen Sondheim in 2010.

Stephen Sondheim Theatre
124 West 43rd St.
New York, NY 10036
Website: http://www.roundabouttheatre.org/Your-Visit/Venues
—Theatres/Stephen-Sondheim-Theatre.aspx

St. James Theatre
The St. James Theatre, originally named the Erlanger, has a luminous provenance. It was built by Abe Erlanger, founder of the notorious Theatrical Syndicate, in 1927. Upon his death three years later, the building was taken over by the Astors, who renamed it the St. James. The Shuberts purchased it a few years later and sold it to William McKnight, chairman of the board of 3M, in 1957. McKnight turned the property over to his daughter and son-in-law who formed Jujamcyn Theaters, which owns five Broadway theaters.

St. James Theatre
246 West 44th St.
New York, NY 10036
Website: http://www.jujamcyn.com/

Studio 54
Studio 54was originally constructed as an opera house but gained fame as a trendy discotheque in the late 1970s and 1980s. In between, it changed hands and names several times, including a stint as a CBS television studio. Since 1998, it has been the home of the Roundabout Theatre Company.

Studio 54
254 West 54th St.
New York, NY 10019
Website: http://www.roundabouttheatre.org/studio54.htm

August Wilson Theatre
The August Wilson Theatre opened as the Guild Theatre in 1925. As was the case with many theaters, it became a radio studio during the 1940s. It returned to use as a legitimate stage in 1950 under the name ANTA Theatre. In 1981, it was purchased by Jujamcyn Theaters and is one of their five Broadway houses. In 2005, just two weeks after his death, the theater was named in honor of American playwright August Wilson.

August Wilson Theatre
245 West 52nd St.
New York, NY 10019
Website: http://www.jujamcyn.com/

Winter Garden Theatre
The Winter Garden is not the oldest theater owned by the Shuberts, but they have owned it longer than any of their other properties on Broadway. They leased the building beginning in 1911, when it was converted into a theater. They controlled it through periods of use as a movie house in the early years of the Great Depression and again during World War II. It was returned to exclusive theatrical use after the war. In 2001, it was restored to it to its 1920s glory.

Winter Garden Theatre
1634 Broadway
New York, NY 10019
Website: http://www.shubertorganization.com/

Movie Studios

Warner Brothers Entertainment, Inc.
Warner Brothers Entertainment, known commonly as Warner Bros., is a fully integrated, broad-based entertainment company. Warner Brothers is one of the major movie studios and has been since its founding in 1918. It is a subsidiary of Time Warner, and itself has numerous subsidiary companies in the film, television, and music industries.

Warner Brothers Entertainment
4000 Warner Blvd.
Burbank, CA 91522-0001
Telephone:
Get Directions
818-954-6000
Website: http://www.warnerbros.com

DreamWorks Pictures
DreamWorks Pictures was formed in 1994 by industry titans Steven Spielberg and Jeffrey Katzenberg, along with music executive David Geffen. In 2005, the studio was sold to Viacom, the owner of Paramount Pictures. In 2008, Reliance ADA Group worked with Steven Spielberg to purchase DreamWorks from Viacom. Reliance now owns 50 percent of DreamWorks. In 2004, DreamWorks Animation SKG, the animation division of Dream-Works, was spun off as a separate company whose films were distributed by Paramount.

DreamWorks
1000 Flower St., Bungalow 477
Glendale, CA 91201
Telephone: 818-733-7000
Website: http://www.dreamworksstudios.com/

The Walt Disney Company
Disney, as it is commonly known, was founded by Walt and Roy Disney in 1923 as the Disney Brothers Cartoon Studio. It has since diversified significantly and is now a multinational media conglomerate controlling television programming, films, and theme parks around the world. It is the largest grossing media

conglomerate in the world. It owns numerous subsidiaries, including Pixar Animation Studios, ABC, ESPN, Marvel Entertainment, and a 27 percent share of Hulu.

Walt Disney Studios
500 S Buena Vista St
Burbank, CA 91521-0007
Telephone:
818-560-1000
Website: http://disney.go.com/index

20th Century Fox
20th Century Fox, a subsidiary of Fox Entertainment Group, is one of the world's largest and oldest producers and distributors of motion pictures. The Fox Film Corporation, founded in 1915, merged with 20th Century Pictures, founded in 1933, to form 20th Century Fox. In 1986, two years after media mogul Rupert Murdoch purchased Fox and the television studios from Metromedia in separate deals, the new network, Fox Broadcasting Company, was launched.

20th Century Fox
10201 West Pico Blvd.
Los Angeles, CA 90035
Mail: P.O. Box 900
Beverly Hills, CA 90213
Telephone: 310-277-2211
Website: www.foxmovies.com

MGM
Metro-Goldwyn-Mayer is a motion picture, television, home video, and theatrical production and distribution company that dates back to 1924. It owns the world's largest library of modern films. MGM is owned by an investor consortium comprised of Providence Equity Partners, TPG, Sony Corporation of America, Comcast Corporation, DLJ Merchant Banking Partners, and Quadrangle Group.

MGM Studios
10250 Constellation Blvd.
Los Angeles, CA 90067
Telephone: 310-449-3000
Website: http://www.mgm.com/

Millennium Films
Millennium Films was founded in 1992 as Nu Image Inc. It develops, finances, produces, and distributes films. It is one of the oldest independent film companies in Hollywood. Besides the traditional Hollywood studios, Millennium also operates studios in Shreveport, Louisiana, and Sofia, Bulgaria. Nu Image created Millennium Films in 1996 to address the market's growing need for higher budget action movies.

Millennium Films
6423 Wilshire Blvd.
Los Angeles, CA 90048
Telephone: 310-388-6900
Website: http://www.millenniumfilms.com/

Nu Image
Nu Image is a production company and distributor of films. The company was founded in 1992. In 1996, Nu Image formed Millennium Films to address the market's growing need for higher budget action movies, while Nu Image continued to cater to the world home video market.

Nu Image
6423 Wilshire Blvd.
Los Angeles, CA 90048
Telephone: 310-388-6900
Website: www.nuimage.net

Lionsgate Entertainment
Lionsgate Entertainment was formed in Vancouver, British Columbia, in 1997. Lionsgate produces and distributes motion pictures, television programming, and digitally delivered content. The company also owns TV Guide Network and several cable channels.

Lionsgate Entertainment
2700 Colorado Ave.
Santa Monica, CA 90404
Telephone: 310-449-9200
Website: http://www.lionsgate.com/

Miramax Films
Miramax Films is a motion picture production, financing, and distribution company that was founded in 1979. Until it was

acquired by Disney in 1993, it was a privately owned company specializing in the distribution of independent and foreign films. Disney sold Miramax to Colony Capital in 2010.

Website: http://www.miramax.com

Summit Entertainment
Summit Entertainment is a theatrical motion picture development, financing, production, and distribution studio. The studio handles all aspects of marketing and distribution for both its own films and those it acquires from outside the studio. The company was founded in 1991 and is a subsidiary of Lionsgate Entertainment.

Summit Entertainment
2308 Broadway
Santa Monica, CA 90404-2916
Telephone: 310-315-6047
Website: http://www.summit-ent.com/

Overture Films
Overture Films is a fully integrated studio. They produce, acquire, market, and distribute motion pictures. Overture, a subsidiary of Liberty Media Corporation, was formed in 2006.

Overture Films
9242 Beverly Blvd., Suite 200
Beverly Hills, CA 90210
Telephone: 424-204 4000
Website: http://www.overturefilms.net/

Television Networks

BBC
The BBC is the largest broadcaster in the world, established in 1927 by a Royal Charter and funded by the license fee that is paid by U.K. households. The BBC uses the income from the license fee to provide television and radio programming as well as a website. The BBC broadcasts outside the U.K. via BBC World Service, which is funded by a government grant, not the same license fee that funds the BBC. BBC World Service broadcasts its news

service in 32 languages. The BBC also owns BBC Worldwide, a commercial enterprise whose profits are returned to the BBC for investment in new programming and services.

Telephone: 44 20 8743 8000
Website: http://www.bbc.co.uk

NBC
The National Broadcasting Company (NBC) was the first major broadcast network in the United States. It began life as radio network in 1926, when it was created by the Radio Corporation of America (RCA). Today, it is owned by NBC Universal, a joint venture of Comcast and General Electric (GE), which purchased NBC in 1986. NBC owns 10television stations and has approximately 200 affiliates across the nation. It develops, produces, and markets entertainment, news, and information to a global audience. NBC also owns a motion picture company, television production operations, and theme parks.

NBC
30 Rockefeller Plaza
New York, NY10112
Telephone: 212-664-4444
Website: http://www.nbc.com/

CBS
CBS (Columbia Broadcasting System) is one of the major U.S. broadcasting networks. It began as a radio network in 1926 as United Independent Broadcasters. Its parent company, CBS Corporation, has operations in virtually every field of media and entertainment, including broadcast and cable television, television production and syndication, radio, publishing, music, and motion pictures.

CBS Headquarters
51 West 52nd Street
New York, NY 10019-6188
Telephone: 212-975-4321
Website: http://www.cbs.com/

ESPN
ESPN is a multinational, multimedia sports entertainment company. ESPN is 80 percent owned by ABC, an indirect subsidiary of the Walt Disney Company. The Hearst Corporation owns the

remaining 20 percent. ESPN was founded in 1979 as a single, sports-oriented cable channel. Today, it owns a variety of sports broadcasting operations, ranging from cable television channels to sports radio and a website.

ESPN Communications
ESPN Plaza
Bristol, CT 06010
Telephone: 860-766-2000
Website: www.espn.com

Fox Broadcasting
Fox Broadcasting is owned by the Fox Entertainment Group, which is wholly owned and controlled by the media conglomerate News Corporation, which is part owned by Rupert Murdoch. Fox Broadcasting Company was formed in 1986 and grew from a fledgling fourth network into the highest rated broadcast network for the coveted 18- to 49-year-old demographic in the first decad of the twenty-first century.

FOX Broadcasting Co.
P.O. Box 900
Beverly Hills, CA 90213
Website: http://www.fox.com/

ABC
The American Broadcasting Company (ABC) is a television network that was created in 1943 from the former NBC blue radio network. It is currently owned by the Walt Disney Company. ABC is the largest broadcaster in the world by revenues.

ABC Studios
77 West 66th St., Suite 100
New York, NY 10023
Telephone: 212-456-7777
Website: http://abc.go.com/

Labor Unions

Screen Actors Guild
The Screen Actors Guild (SAG) is the nation's largest labor union representing television and film actors. SAG was established in

1933 with the mission of establishing equitable compensation levels, benefits, and working conditions for its members. SAG represents over 200,000 actors who work in film, television programs, commercials, and video games. SAG is associated with Associated Actors and Artistes of America, the primary association of performer's unions in the United States, and is an affiliate of the American Federation of Labor—Congress of Industrial Organizations (AFL-CIO).

Screen Actors Guild
5757 Wilshire Blvd., 7th Floor
Los Angeles, CA 90036-3600
Telephone: 323-954-1600
Website: http://www.sag.org

American Federation of Television and Radio Artists
The American Federation of Television and Radio Artists (AFTRA) is a national labor union representing performers and other artists working in the entertainment and news media. AFTRA represents artists in the television, radio, sound recording, internet, and digital programming industries. AFTRA negotiates wages, working conditions, residual payments, and benefits for its members. AFTRA is affiliated with the AFL-CIO and shares jurisdiction with the Screen Actors Guild.

AFTRA
260 Madison Ave.
New York NY 10016-2401
Telephone: 212-532-0800
Website: http://www.aftra.org

Actors' Equity Association
Actors' Equity Association (AEA), founded in 1913, is the labor union that represents theatrical performers in the United States. Also known as Equity, the union seeks to promote the art of live theater, foster its growth, and advance the status of theatrical performers within the industry. AEA negotiates wages and working conditions, and provides a wide range of benefits, including health and pension plans, for its members. AEA is a member of the AFL-CIO and is affiliated with Associated Actors and Artistes of America as well as the International Federation of Actors.

AEA National Headquarters
165 West 46th Street
New York, NY 10036
Telephone: 212-869-8530
Website: www.actorsequity.org

International Federation of Actors
The International Federation of Actors (FIA) is an international organization of performing arts unions, representing over 100 performers' unions around the world. FIA serves as a lobbyist for performing arts unions on the international stage. FIA was conceived in 1951 at the First European Congress of Actors. It began with primarily European members but eventually grew to encompass unions from across the globe.

International Federation of Actors
31, rue de l'Hopital
1000 Brussels
Belgium
Telephone: 32-02-234-5653
Website: http://www.fia-actors.com/en/index.html

Dramatists Guild of America
The Dramatists Guild of America was established over 80years ago and is the only professional association that advances the interests of playwrights, composers, lyricists, and librettists writing for the living stage.

The Dramatists Guild of America was established for the purpose of aiding dramatists in protecting both the artistic and economic integrity of their work. The Guild maintains model contracts for all levels of productions (including Broadway, regional, and smaller theaters) and encourages its members to use these contracts when negotiating with producers. These contracts embody the Guild's overarching objectives of protecting the dramatist's control over the content of his or her work and ensuring that the dramatist is compensated for each use of his or her work in a way that will encourage him or her to continue writing for the living stage.

In addition to its contract services, the Guild acts as an aggressive public advocate for dramatists' interests and assists dramatists in developing both their artistic and business skills through its publications, which are distributed nationally, and the educational programs that it sponsors around the country.

Dramatists Guild of America
1501 Broadway, Suite 701
New York, NY 10036
Telephone: 212-398-9366
Website: http://www.dramatistsguild.com

American Federation of Musicians
The American Federation of Musicians (AFM) is the largest organization in the world representing the interests of professional
musicians. Whether negotiating fair agreements, protecting
ownership of recorded music, securing benefits such as health
care and pension, or lobbying legislators, the AFM is committed
to raising industry standards and placing the professional musician in the foreground of the cultural landscape.

American Federation of Musicians
1501 Broadway, Suite 600
New York, NY10036
Telephone: 212-869-1330
Website: http://www.afm.org/

Stage Directors and Choreographers Society
Stage Directors and Choreographers Society (SDC) is the theatrical union that unites and protects professional stage directors
and choreographers throughout the United States. The SDC seeks
to foster a national community of professional stage directors and
choreographers by protecting members rights.

Stage Directors and Choreographers Society
1501 Broadway, Suite 1701
New York, NY 10036
Telephone: 800-541-5204
Website: http://www.sdcweb.org/

International Alliance of Theatrical Stage Employees, Moving Pic-
ture Technicians, Artists and Allied Crafts of the United States, Its
Territories and Canada (IATSE)
International Alliance of Theatrical Stage Employees, Moving Pic-
ture Technicians, Artists and Allied Crafts of the United States, Its
Territories and Canada (IATSE) was originally chartered by the
American Federation of Labor as the National Alliance of Theatri-
cal Stage Employees in 1893. The name has evolved over the

course of 117 years of geographic and craft expansion as well as technological advancement. Since the birth of the organization, the stagehands and projectionists have been joined by a great variety of other craftspersons in the numerous branches of the entertainment industry, including motion picture and television production, product demonstration and industrial shows, conventions, facility maintenance, casinos, audio visual, and computer graphics.

IATSE General Office
1430 Broadway, 20th Floor
New York, NY 10018
Telephone: 212-730-1770
Website: http://www.iatse-intl.org

MPAA
The Motion Picture Association of America (MPAA) was formed in 1922 by the presidents of the major movie studios. The MPAA serves as the voice and advocate of the American motion picture, home video, and television industries around the world. MPAA's members are the six major U.S. motion picture studios: Walt Disney, Paramount, Sony, Twentieth Century Fox, Universal, and Warner Brothers. The MPAA is responsible for the ratings system used in the U.S. movie industry.

MPAA
1600 Eye St., NW
Washington, D.C. 20006
Telephone: 202-293-1966
Website: http://www.mpaa.org

Cable Companies

Comcast
Comcast was originally founded as American Cable Systems in 1963. It was incorporated as Comcast Corporation in 1969 and is now the largest cable operator in the United States. It develops, manages, and operates cable networks and also delivers programming content. Comcast owns NBC Universal, which in turn owns entertainment and news cable networks, local television stations, and production studios.

Comcast Corp.
One Comcast Center
Philadelphia, PA 19103-2838
Telephone: 215-665-1700
Website: http://www.comcast.com/default.cspx

Time Warner Cable
Time Warner Cable provides cable and communication services across the country. Its mission is to connect people and businesses with information, entertainment, and each other through television, internet, and telephone services. Until 2009, it was owned by Time Warner. It is now an independent company.

Time Warner Cable
60 Columbus Cr.
New York, NY 10023-5800
Website: http://www.timewarnercable.com

Charter Communications
Charter Communications is the fourth largest cable operator in the United States. Charter provides video, internet, and telephone services to more than five million homes and businesses.

Charter Communications
12405 Powerscourt Dr.
St. Louis, MO 63131
Telephone: 314-965-0555
Website: www.charter.com

Cox Communication
Cox Enterprises, the parent company of Cox Communication, began with the purchase of a single newspaper in Dayton, Ohio, in 1920. Today it is the third largest cable entertainment and broadband services provider in the country. Cox developed the concept of bundling television, internet, and telephone services together, offering consumers the ability to consolidate their services with one provider.

Cox Communications
1400 Lake Hearn Dr.
Atlanta, GA 30319
Website: http://ww2.cox.com

Cablevision
Cablevision Systems Corporation was founded in 1973 as a cable television company with 1,500 households on Long Island. It is now one of the leading telecommunications, media, and entertainment companies in the United States. Its services include digital television, voice, high speed Internet, national television networks, and local media and programming properties.

Cablevision Systems Corp.
1111 Stewart Ave.
Bethpage, NY 11714
Website: http://www.cablevision.com

Satellite Companies

DirectTV
DirecTV is a direct broadcast satellite service that transmits digital satellite television and audio to households in the United States, Latin America, and the Caribbean. DirecTV was launched in 1994 and is now owned by the DirecTV Group, which is controlled by Liberty Media.

Website: http://www.directv.com/DTVAPP/index.jsp

DISH Network
DISH Network Corporation was founded in 1996. It is the fourth largest payTV provider in the United States, providing direct broadcast satellite service to commercial and residential customers. DISH also owns Blockbuster and is itself the media and entertainment portion of its former parent company, EcohStar Communications Corporation, founded in 1980. In 2008, DISH and EchoStar split, and EchoStar became the provider of the technology used by DISH Network.

Telephone: 800-823-4929
Website: http://www.dishnetwork.com/

Sirius Satellite Radio
Sirius Satellite Radio is a satellite radio service operating in the United States and Canada. It is owned by Sirius XM Radio. Sirius

began operating in 2002. Sirius carries a wide variety of genres, broadcasting commercial free and uncensored.

Website: http://www.sirius.com/

XM Satellite Radio
XM Satellite Radio (XM) is one of two satellite radio services in the United States and Canada. It is operated by Sirius XM Radio. It provides pay-for-service radio, which is analogous to cable television. Satellite radio is funded by subscription, not advertising, so it provides commercial free radio. It is not governed by U.S. Federal Communications Commission (FCC) regulations regarding over-the-air content, so like pay cable stations such as HBO, it offers fare unavailable on commercial radio.

Website: http://www.xmradio.com/

Major Symphony Orchestras

National Symphony Orchestra
The National Symphony Orchestra was founded in 1931. It became the artistic affiliate of the John F. Kennedy Center for the Performing Arts in 1986. The National Symphony regularly participates in events of national and international importance, including performances for state occasions, presidential inaugurations, and official holiday celebrations. It also tours internationally and performs for visiting heads of state.

The John F. Kennedy Center for the Performing Arts
2700 F St., NW
Washington, D.C. 20566
Telephone: 202-467-4600
Website http://www.kennedy-center.org/nso/

Boston Symphony Orchestra
The Boston Symphony Orchestra (BSO) is one of five American orchestras commonly referred to as the Big Five. The BSO plays most of its concerts at Boston's Symphony Hall and in the summer performs at the Tanglewood Music Center.

Telephone: 617-266-1492
Website: www.bso.org

Chicago Symphony Orchestra
The Chicago Symphony Orchestra is one of the five American orchestras commonly referred to as the Big Five. Founded in 1891, the symphony makes its home in Chicago's Orchestra Hall and plays a summer season at the Ravinia Festival.

The Chicago Symphony Orchestra
220 S. Michigan Ave.
Chicago, IL 60604
Telephone: 312-294-3000
Website: http://www.cso.org

New York Philharmonic
The New York Philharmonic, organized in 1842, is the oldest continuously operating symphony orchestra in the United States. It is one of the U.S. orchestras commonly referred to as the Big Five. The Philharmonic plays in Avery Fisher Hall at the Lincoln Center.

New York Philharmonic
Avery Fisher Hall
10 Lincoln Center Plaza
New York, NY 10023-6970
Website: http://nyphil.org/

Philadelphia Orchestra
The Philadelphia Orchestra is one of the Big Five American orchestras. It was founded in 1900. The orchestra's home is the Kimmel Center for the Performing Arts. From 1900 to 2001, the Philadelphia Orchestra performed at the Academy of Music. The orchestra still owns the Academy and returns there one week per year. The Philadelphia Orchestra's summer home is the Mann Center for the Performing Arts. It also has summer residencies at the Saratoga Performing Arts Center and the Bravo! Vail Valley Festival.

Philadelphia Orchestra
260 South Broad St., Suite 1600
Philadelphia, PA 19102
Telephone: 215-893-1900
Website: http://www.philorch.org

Cleveland Orchestra
The Cleveland Orchestra is one of the Big Five American orchestras. The orchestra was founded in 1918 and calls Severance Hall its home.

Cleveland Orchestra
Severance Hall
11001 Euclid Ave.
Cleveland, Ohio 44106
Telephone: 216-231-1111
Website: http://www.clevelandorchestra.com/

Los Angeles Philharmonic
The Los Angeles Philharmonic is one of the world's outstanding orchestras. It performs at home in the Walt Disney Concert Hall. Since 1922, it has performed summer concerts at the Hollywood Bowl. The orchestra's involvement with Los Angeles also extends far beyond regular symphony concerts in a concert hall, embracing the schools, churches, and neighborhood centers. Among its wide-ranging education initiatives is Youth Orchestra LA (YOLA). Central to YOLA is the Philharmonic's plan to build, with community partners, youth orchestras in communities throughout Los Angeles.

Los Angeles Philharmonic
Walt Disney Concert Hall
111 S. Grand Ave.
Los Angeles, CA90012
Telephone: 323-850-2000
Website: http://www.laphil.com/

SNL Kagan
SNL Kagan is a source for in-depth analysis and proprietary data on the media and communications business. Kagan tracks both quantitative impact and qualitative implications.

Kagan Media Appraisals
Telephone: 831-624-1536
Website: http://www.snl.com/Sectors/Media/Default.aspx

Nielsen
Nielsen is best known for its television ratings service. Nielsen ratings were developed by the company founded by Arthur Nielsen in 1923. Today, Nielsen helps media companies understand and measure their market. It provides audience measurement, advertising effectiveness, and overall marketing performance.

Nielsen
770 Broadway
New York, NY 10003-9595
Website: http://www.nielsen.com/us/en.html

Licensing Plays

Dramatists Play Service, Inc.
For 75 years, Dramatists Play Service, Inc. has provided plays by both established writers and new playwrights. Formed in 1936 by prominent playwrights and theatre agents, Dramatists Play Service was created to foster opportunity and provide support for playwrights by publishing acting editions of their plays and handling the nonprofessional and professional leasing rights to these works.

DPS
440 Park Avenue South
New York, NY 10016
Telephone: 212-683-8960
Website: http://www.dramatists.com/

Samuel French, Inc.
Samuel French was founded by Samuel French and Thomas Lacy to combine their existing interests in London and New York. It publishes plays and represents authors.

Samuel French, Inc.
45 West 25th St.
New York, NY 10010-2751
Telephone: 212-206-8990
Website: http://www.samuelfrench.com/

Dramatic Publishing
Publishing fine plays since 1885, Dramatic Publishing serves the authors, artists, and educators who comprise the world of theatre. They offer musicals, full-length and one-act plays, and theatrical books suitable for highschool, children's, professional and community theatre.

Dramatic Publishing
311 Washington St.
Woodstock, IL 60098-3308
Telephone: 800-448-7469
Website: http://www.dramaticpublishing.com/index.html

8

Resources

Sports

Abrams, Roger, "The Public Regulation of Baseball Labor Relations and the Public Interest," *Journal of Sports Economics* 4:4 (November 2003), pp. 292–301.

Abrams looks at the 1994 Major League Baseball (MLB) strike and the involvement of a federal district court judge in ending it. He then assesses whether the public interest is served by the existing system regulating the professional sports industry.

Abrams, Roger, *Legal Bases: Baseball and the Law*, Philadelphia: Temple University Press, 1998.

Abrams looks at the historical evolution of baseball and the law, covering topics ranging from collective bargaining and arbitration to baseball's antitrust exemption.

Abrams, Roger, *Sports Justice: The Law and the Business of Sports*, Lebanon, NH: University Press of New England, 2010.

Abrams looks at the application of law to a wide variety of sports and sports issues, including professional and amateur interests as well as discrimination.

Ahn, C. C. and Y. H. Lee, "Life–Cycle Demand for Major League Baseball," presented at the Western Economics Association International Conference, Denver, CO, 2003.

Ahn and Lee develop a life–cycle demand model for Major League Baseball.

Berri, David J. and Martin B. Schmidt, "On the Road with the National Basketball Association's Superstar Externality," *Journal of Sports Economics* 7:4 (November 2006), pp. 347–58.

Berri and Schmidt measure the impact of superstars on road attendance and television ratings.

Berri, David J., Martin B. Schmidt, and Stacey L. Brook, "Stars at the Gate: The Impact of Star power on NBA Gate Revenues," *Journal of Sports Economics* 5:1 (February 2004), pp. 33–50.

Berri and Schmidt examine the "superstar effect," arguing that some individual players are so popular that on their own they lead to an increase in ticket sales when they come to town.

Baker, Matthew, Thomas J. Miceli, and William J. Ryczek, "The Old Ball Game: Organization of 19th-Century Professional Base Ball Clubs," *Journal of Sports Economics* 5:3 (August 2004), pp. 277–91.

Baker, Miceli, and Ryczek argue that stock ownership of clubs won out over player cooperative forms of ownership of baseball teams in the late nineteenth century because the team production problem resulted in players of unknown ability migrating to teams in coop leagues.

Brandes, Leif, Franck Egon, and Stephan Nuesch, "Local Heroes and Superstars: An Empirical Analysis of Star Attraction in German Soccer," *Journal of Sports Economics* 9:3 (June 2008), pp. 266–86.

Brandes, Egon and Nuesch look at the German soccer market in an effort to determine whether the "superstar phenomenon" is driven by superior talent or popularity.

Cain, Louis P. and David D. Haddock, "Similar Economic Histories, Different Industrial Structures: Transatlantic Contrasts in the Evolution of Professional Sports Leagues," *Journal of Economic History* 65:4 (December 2005), pp. 1116–47.

Cain and Haddock compare and contrast the evolution of American baseball and British football leagues.

Coates, Dennis, and Brad Humphreys, "The Economic Consequences of Professional Sports Strikes and Lockouts," *Southern Economic Journal* **67:3 (January 2001), pp. 737–47.**

Coates and Humphreys look at the economic impact of work stoppages in professional football and basketball in effort to shed some light on the potential economic impact of the 1998–99 NBA lockout.

Coates, Dennis, and Brad Humphreys, "The Growth Effects of Sport Franchises, Stadia, and Arenas," *Journal of Policy Analysis and Management* **18:4 (1999), pp. 601–24.**

Coates and Humphreys investigate the relationship between professional sports franchises and venues, and their impact on personal income over the period of 1969 to 1994. They consider franchise relocations, stadium construction, and other sports-related factors.

Cooke, Andrew, *The Economics of Leisure and Sport,* **London: Routledge, 1994.**

Cooke discusses the use of core economic principles such as supply and demand, elasticity and pricing, government policy, and costs of production to offer insights into the entertainment industry.

Daly, George and William J. Moore, "Externalities, Property Rights and the Allocation of Resources in Major League Baseball," *Economic Inquiry* **19:1 (1982), pp. 77–95.**

Daly and Moore conduct an empirical analysis of two decades of Major League Baseball (MLB) player movement and do not find evidence to support claims that the reserve clause and amateur draft influence the wealth distribution between players and owners but not the allocation of talent among teams.

Drever, P. and J. MacDonald, "Attendances of South Australian Football Games," *International Review of Sports Sociology* **16:2 (1981), pp. 103–13.**

Drever and MacDonald develop a model to explain attendance at Australian football games.

Falter, Jean-Marc, Christophe Perignon, and Olivier Vercruysse, "Impact of Overwhelming Joy on Consumer Demand: The Case

of a Soccer World Cup Victory," *Journal of Sports Economics* 9:1 (February 2008), pp. 20–42.

Falter, Perignon, and Vercruysse test the impact of a country winning the World Cup on the demand for soccer in that country.

Feddersen, Arne and Armin Rott, "Determinants of Demand for Televised Live Football: Features of the German National Football Team," *Journal of Sports Economics* 12:3 (June 2011), pp. 352–69.

Feddersen and Rott analyze German soccer to identify the factors that determine the demand for televised broadcasts of the games.

Forrest, David, and Rob Simmons, "New Issues in Attendance Demand: The Case of the English Football League," *Journal of Sports Economics* 7:3 (August 2006), pp. 247–66.

Forrest and Simmons use an attendance model to look at the impact of the English Premier League on attendance at lower football leagues.

Fort, Rodney and Joel Maxcy, "The Demise of African American Baseball Leagues: A Rival League Explanation," *Journal of Sports Economics* 2:1 (February 2001), pp. 35–49.

Fort and Maxcy argue that the Negro Leagues posed an economic threat to MLB at the time of integration. They analyze the impact of integration and MLB behavior toward Negro League teams to determine the impact on players and franchises.

Fort, Rodney, "Subsidies as Incentive Mechanisms in Sports," *Managerial and Decision Economics* 25:2 (March 2004), pp. 95–102.

Fort demonstrates the inverse relationship between sports ticket prices and public subsidies to sports teams in his analysis of the NFL.

Fort, Rodney, "Inelastic Sports Pricing," *Managerial and Decision Economics* 25:2 (March 2004), pp. 87–94.

Fort looks at local television market revenues in MLB to show that firms pricing on the inelastic portion of the demand curve do exhibit profit maximizing behavior.

Fort, Rodney and John Fizel (Eds.), *International Sports Economics Comparisons,* **Westport, CT: Praeger Publishers, 2004.**

Fort and Fizel edit a volume that includes articles providing overviews and comparisons of sports from countries around the world.

Fort, Rodney, "The Golden Anniversary of 'The Baseball Players' Labor Market'," *Journal of Sports Economics* 6:4 (November 2005), pp. 347–58.

Fort documents the many contributions Simon Rottenberg made to the sports economics literature in his seminal article.

Garcia, Jaume and Placido Rodriguez, "The Determinants of Football Match Attendance Revisited: Empirical Evidence from the Spanish Football League," *Journal of Sports Economics* 3:1 (February 2002), pp. 18–38.

Garcia and Rodriguez estimate individual game attendance for Spanish football by analyzing the Spanish First Division Football League.

Gendzel, Glen, "Competitive Boosterism: How Milwaukee Lost the Braves," *Business History Review* 69:4 (Winter 1995), pp. 530–66.

Gendzel provides a specific example of the organization of sports leagues in his study of the relocation of the MLB Braves from Milwaukee to Atlanta.

Haupert, Michael J., "Pay, Performance, and Race During the Integration Era," *Black Ball* 2:1 (Spring 2009), pp. 37–51.

Haupert looks at historical contract data from both black and white professional baseball leagues in order to examine the differences in pay between players.

Haupert, Michael J., "Player Pay and Productivity in the Reserve Clause and Collusion Eras," *Nine: A Journal of Baseball History and Social Policy Perspectives* (Fall 2009), pp. 63–85.

Haupert looks at the differences in the way players were paid in segregated professional baseball leagues.

Haupert, Michael and James Murray, "Regime Switching and Wages in Major League Baseball Under the Reserve Clause," *Cliometrica* 6:2 (June 2012), 143–62.

Haupert and Murray look at the long run evolution of the factors determining the pay of major league baseball players.

Hausman, Jerry A. and Gregory K. Leonard, "Superstars in the National Basketball Association: Economic Value and Policy," *Journal of Labor Economics* **15:4 (October 1997), pp. 586–624.**

Hausman and Leonard show that when an NBA "superstar" is involved in a televised game, the ratings are substantially higher, generating revenue for both the home and visiting team. They estimate the value of Michael Jordan to each NBA team, based on this finding.

Hylan, Timothy R., Maureen J. Lage, and Michael Treglia, "The Coase Theorem, Free Agency, and Major League Baseball: A Panel Study of Pitcher Mobility from 1961 to 1992," *Southern Economic Journal* **62:4 (1996), pp. 1029–42.**

Hylan and colleagues test the Coase theorem using data for MLB pitchers and reject the invariance thesis of the theorem. They show that after free agency, pitchers with greater longevity in MLB were less likely to switch teams relative to their ability to do so before free agency. They also show that higher quality pitchers and pitchers on better teams or in large markets were also less likely to switch teams.

Johnson, Arthur T., "Congress and Professional Sports: 1951–1978," *Annals of the American Academy of Political and Social Science* **445 (September 1979), pp. 102–15.**

Johnson analyzes the relationship between government and professional sports by reviewing congressional activity relative to sports from the 1950s through the 1970s.

Johnson, Arthur T., "Municipal Administration and the Sports Franchise Relocation Issue," *Public Administration Review* **43:6 (November–December 1983), pp. 519–28.**

Johnson reviews the relationship between cities and professional sports franchises, and analyzes the legislative options available to protect local government interests.

Johnson, Arthur T., "Professional Baseball at the Minor League Level: Considerations for Cities Large and Small," *State & Local Government Review* **22:2 (Spring 1990), pp. 90–96.**

Johnson surveys local governments hosting minor league baseball teams and describes the relationship between cities and franchises. He suggests that the same negotiating dynamics that occur between MLB teams and cities also take place at the minor league level.

Johnson, B. K., P. A. Groothuis, and J.C. Whitehead, "The Value of Public Goods Generated by a Major League Sports Team: CVM," *Journal of Sports Economics* **2:1 (February 2001), pp. 6–21.**

Johnson and colleagues use the contingent valuation method to measure the value of public goods generated by the Pittsburgh franchise in the NHL.

Jones, J. C. H. and William D. Walsh, "Salary Determination in the National Hockey League: The Effects of Skills, Franchise Characteristics, and Discrimination," *Industrial & Labor Relations Review,* **41:4 (1988), pp. 592–604.**

Jones and Walsh look at the extent to which skill differences, labor market structure, and discrimination determine salaries in the NHL.

Kahn, Lawrence M., "The Sports Business as a Labor Market Laboratory," *Journal of Economic Perspectives* **14:3 (Summer 2000), pp. 75–94.**

Kahn reviews the state of research on sports labor markets.

Kahn, Lawrence, "Discrimination in Professional Sports: A Survey of the Literature," *Industrial and Labor Relations Review* **44:3 (April 1991), pp. 395–418.**

Kahn reviews the existing research on discrimination in sports.

Kahn, Lawrence, "Markets: Cartel Behavior and Amateurism in College Sports," *Journal of Economic Perspectives* **21:1 (Winter 2007), pp. 209–26.**

Kahn reviews evidence on the indirect effects of college sports on university operations, such as student applications, alumni contributions, and state appropriations to universities. He also looks at the evidence on whether the NCAA exercises cartel power in the market for college athletics.

Kahn, Lawrence, "Race, Performance, Pay, and Retention among National Basketball Association Head Coaches," *Journal of Sports Economics* 7:2 (May 2006), pp. 119–49.

Kahn estimates racial differences in likelihood of retention, pay, and performance for NBA coaches using a hazard function approach.

Kahn, Lawrence, "Managerial Quality, Team Success, and Individual Player Performance in Major League Baseball," *Industrial and Labor Relations Review* 46:3 (April 1993), pp. 531–47.

Kahn uses MLB data to investigate the impact of managerial quality on team winning and individual player performance.

Kahn, Lawrence, "Free Agency, Long-Term Contracts and Compensation in Major League Baseball: Estimates from Panel Data," *Review of Economics and Statistics* 75:1 (February 1993), pp. 157–64.

Kahn estimates the effects of free agency and arbitration on contract length and pay.

Kahn, Lawrence, "The Effects of Race on Professional Football Players' Compensation," *Industrial & Labor Relations Review* 45:2 (1992), pp. 295–310.

Kahn examines the issue of racial discrimination in professional football and finds that pay difference between players based on race is small after adjusting for performance.

Kahn, Lawrence, "Discrimination in Professional Sports: A Survey of the Literature," *Industrial and Labor Relations Review* 44:3 (April 1991), pp. 395–418.

Kahn reviews the literature of racial, gender and ethnic discrimination in professional sports.

Kahn, Lawrence and Peter Sherer "Racial Differences in Professional Basketball Players' Compensation," *Journal of Labor Economics* 6:1 (1988), pp. 40–61.

Kahn investigates differences in salary based on race for individual NBA players during the 1985/1986 season.

Knowles, Glenn, Keith Sherony, and Mike Haupert, "The Demand for Major League Baseball: A Test of the Uncertainty of Outcome Hypothesis," *American Economist* 36:3 (Fall 1992), pp. 72–80.

Knowles and colleagues argue that fans like to see their teams succeed, but if they succeed too much for too long, interest may be lost.

Krashinsky, Michael and Harry A. Krashinsky, "Do English Canadian Hockey Teams Discriminate Against French Canadian Players?" *Canadian Public Policy (Analyse de Politique)s* 23:2 (1997), pp. 212–16.

Krashinsky and Krashinsky argue that previous findings of discrimination against French Canadian hockey players in the NHL is not justified.

Lanning, Jonathan A., "Productivity, Discrimination, and Lost Profits During Baseball's Integration," *Journal of Economic History* 70:4 (December 2010), pp. 964–88.

Lanning tests for various types of discrimination in Major League Baseball and what led to the slow pace of integration.

Lavoie, Marc, "The Location of Pay Discrimination in the National Hockey League," *Journal of Sports Economics* 1:4 (November 2000), pp. 401–11.

Lavoie looks at wage discrimination in the NHL, using both national origin of the player and the location of his employer as explanatory variables.

Lee, Young Hoon, "The Decline of Attendance in the Korean Professional Baseball League: The Major League Effects," *Journal of Sports Economics* 7:2 (May 2006), pp. 187–2.

Lee explains the decline in attendance at Korean Professional Baseball League games as a result of the emergence of Major League Baseball in the United States as a rival.

Long, Judith Grant, "Full Count: The Real Cost of Public Funding for Major League Sports Facilities," *Journal of Sports Economics* 6:2 (May 2005), pp. 119–43.

Long estimates the cost of governments to build sports facilities, including often omitted costs such as land transfers, infrastructure, and operating costs.

Lowenfish, Lee, *The Imperfect Diamond: A History of Baseball's Labor Wars s*(revised edition), **Lincoln, NE: Bison Books, 2010.**

Lowenfish provides a long run view of player-owner relations in Major League Baseball, using the historical evolution of the game as a backdrop for the current collective bargaining issue.

Madalozzo, Regina and Rodrigo Berber Villar, "Brazilian Football: What Brings Fans to the Game?" *Journal of Sports Economics* **10:6 (December 2009), pp. 639–50.**

Madalozzo and Villar identify variables that determine the demand for tickets to Brazilian soccer games.

Noll, Roger (Ed.), *Government and the Sports Business,* **Washington, D.C.: Brookings Institute, 1974.**

Noll edits a series of papers delivered at a conference on sports and government. The volume covers a wide range of topics including stadiums, discrimination, government subsidization of sports, broadcasting, and antitrust issues.

Noll, Roger and Andrew Zimbalist (Eds.), *Sports, Jobs and Taxes,* **Washington, D.C.: Brookings Institution Press, 1997.**

Noll and Zimbalist have brought together a series of articles by various authors that examine the economic impact of stadiums and sports franchises on local economies. The papers cover topics ranging from methods for measuring economic benefits and costs, the local politics of attracting and retaining teams, and the relationship between sports and local labor markets. Several of the articles are case studies. There is general agreement among the authors that sports teams and stadiums are not a source of local economic growth and employment.

Owen, P. Dorian and Clayton R. Weatherston, "Uncertainty of Outcome and Super 12 Rugby Union Attendance: Application of a General-to-Specific Modeling Strategy," *Journal of Sports Economics* **5:4 (November 2004), pp. 347–70.**

Owen and Weatherston determine the factors that affect game-by-game attendance at rugby matches in New Zealand.

Paton, David and Andrew Cooke, "Attendance at County Cricket: An Economic Analysis," *Journal of Sports Economics* **6:1 (February 2005), pp. 24–45.**

Paton and Cooke estimate the effects of structural changes on the demand for tickets to cricket matches in the United Kingdom.

Pope, S. W. (Ed.), *The New American Sport History: Recent Approaches and Perspectives,* **Urbana, IL: University of Illinois Press, 1997.**

Pope edits a volume of diverse papers, ranging from race superiority in athletics and gender discrimination to marketing sports. The volume focuses less on economic topics than social topics such as class, gender, race, and ethnicity.

Rosen, Sherwin and Allen Sanderson, "Labour Markets in Professional Sports," *Economic Journal* **111:469 (February 2001), pp. F47–F68.**

Rosen and Sanderson use economic theory to analyze a variety of aspect of sports labor markets, including discrimination, property rights, the incentive to win, and collective bargaining.

Rottenberg, Simon, "The Baseball Players' Labor Market," *Journal of Political Economy* **64:3 (June 1956), pp. 242–58.**

Rottenberg argues that the best ballplayers would end up on the teams in the biggest markets regardless of contract status, casting doubt on the claim that the Major League Baseball reserve clause was necessary for competitive balance.

Sanderson, Allen R. and John J. Siegfried, "Simon Rottenberg and Baseball, Then and Now: A Fiftieth Anniversary Retrospective," *Journal of Political Economy* **114:3 (June 2006), pp. 594–605.**

Sanderson and Siegfried review some of the insights Rottenberg made in his seminal article on sports economics.

Schmidt, Martin B. and David J. Berri, "Research Note: What Takes Them Out to the Ball Game?" *Journal of Sports Economics* **7 (May 2006) pp. 222–33.**

Schmidt and Berri look at the change in demand for baseball over the twentieth century, focusing on how the factors that drove demand for baseball changed.

Scully, Gerald W., "Pay and Performance in Major League Baseball," *American Economic Review* **64:6 (December 1974), pp. 915–30.**

Scully uses individual player salary and performance data to measure the relationship between Major League Baseball player pay and marginal productivity.

Scully, Gerald, "The Distribution of Performance and Earnings in a Prize Economy," *Journal of Sports Economics* **3:3 (August 2002), pp. 235–45.**

Scully looks at the PGA and its system of nonconstant pay to players based on tournament performance in order to analyze the efficiency and equity of the method of paying prize earnings.

Scully, Gerald, *The Business of Major League Baseball,* **Chicago: University of Chicago Press, 1989.**

Scully was one of the first economists to apply economic theory to professional baseball. In this book, he reveals how economics can be used to explain the behavior of players, teams, and leagues.

Siegfried, John and Andrew Zimbalist, "The Economics of Sports Facilities and Their Communities," *Journal of Economic Perspectives* **14 (Summer 2000), pp. 95–114.**

Siegfried and Zimbalist analyze the trend toward publicly subsidized sports stadiums in the second half of the twentieth century.

Surdam, David G., "A Tale of Two Gate-Sharing Plans: The National Football League and the National League: 1952–1956," *Southern Economic Journal* **73:4 (April 2007), pp. 931–46.**

Surdam looks at NFL revenue sharing in the 1950s and compares it to MLB. He finds that owners were willing to enact regressive aspects in their revenue-sharing plans, possibly to forestall moral hazard possibilities arising from automatically helping teams that remain poor draws or fail to improve.

Surdam, David G., "The New York Yankees Cope with the Great Depression," *Enterprise and Society* 9:4 (December 2008), pp. 816–40.

Surdam looks at the financial records of the New York Yankees to explain the business practices of one professional baseball team during the Great Depression.

Surdam, David G., "What Brings Fans to the Ball Park? Evidence from New York Yankees' and Philadelphia Phillies' Financial Records," *Journal of Economics* 35:1 (2009), pp. 35–47.

Surdam looks at the financial records of the New York Yankees and Philadelphia Phillies during the Depression to form his hypothesis about what determines the demand for baseball in a depressed economy.

Surdam, David, "The Coase Theorem and Player Movement in Major League Baseball," *Journal of Sports Economics* 7:2 (May 2006), pp. 201–21.

Surdam tests the Coase theorem, which suggests that the distribution of payer talent should be similar before and after free agency. He includes a measure of team performance to refine previous attempts to analyze this theorem.

Vignola, Patricia, "The Enemies at the Gate: An Economic Debate about the Denouement of Negro League Baseball," *NINE* 13:2 (Spring 2005), pp. 71–81.

Vignola focuses on Negro League baseball as a microcosm of African American capitalism and society, and how it ultimately failed.

Whitney, James D., "Winning Games versus Winning Championships: The Economics of Fan Interest and Team Performance," *Economic Inquiry*, October 1988, pp. 703–24.

Whitney focuses on the role of winning championships as a factor in the demand for professional sports.

Yamamura, Eiji, "Game Information, Local Heroes, and Their Effect on Attendance: The Case of the Japanese Baseball League," *Journal of Sports Economics* 12:1 (February 2011), pp. 20–35.

Yamamura uses the Japanese Baseball League to test for the impact of the popularity of individual players on game day attendance.

Zimbalist, Andrew, "Labor Relations in Major League Baseball," *Journal of Sports Economics* **4:4 (November 2003), pp. 332–55.**

Zimbalist analyzes the 2002 labor agreement between MLB players and owners. He explores some of the roots of the difficult relationship between the two sides and analyzes the inefficiency of the labor agreement.

Zimbalist, Andrew, *Baseball and Billions,* **New York: Basic Books, 1992.**

Zimbalist takes a look at the business of professional baseball, using proprietary data to make a number of observations on how professional baseball is organized and operates.

Television

Baker, Matthew J. and Lisa M. George, "The Role of Television in Household Debt: Evidence from the 1950s," *B. E. Journal of Economic Analysis and Policy: Advances in Economic Analysis and Policy* **10:1 (2010).**

Baker and George test whether households with early access to television saw steeper increases in household debt as a result of increased exposure to a new type of advertising. They conclude that television access is associated with higher debt levels for durable goods.

Barnouw, Eric, *A Tower in Babel: A History of Broadcasting to 1933,* **New York: Oxford University Press, 1966.**

In this three-volume series, Barnouw provides an exhaustive history of the television and radio industries as they grew from a dream in the minds of inventors into the social, economic, and political forces of the twentieth century.

Barnouw, Eric, *The Golden Web: A History of Broadcasting from 1933 to 1953,* **New York: Oxford University Press, 1968.**

In this three-volume series Barnouw provides an exhaustive history of the television and radio industries as they grew from a dream in the minds of inventors into the social, economic, and political forces of the twentieth century.

Barnouw, Eric, *The Image Empire: A History of Broadcasting from 1953*, New York: Oxford University Press, 1970.

In this three-volume series Barnouw provides an exhaustive history of the television and radio industries as they grew from a dream in the minds of inventors into the social, economic, and political forces of the twentieth century.

Batten, Frank, *The Weather Channel: The Improbable Rise of a Media Phenomenon*, Boston: Harvard Business School Press, 2002.

Batten uses the Weather Channel to illustrate the rise of niche marketing in the cable television industry.

Baughman, James L., "Show Business in the Living Room: Management Expectations for American Television: 1947–56," *Business and Economic History* 26:2 (Winter 1997), pp. 718–26.

Baughman examines the evolution of the television network design in its first decade, focusing on the development of programming design as a function of profit maximization.

Block, A., *Out-Foxed: The Inside Story of America's Fourth Television Network*, New York: St. Martin's Press, 1990.

Block provides a behind the scenes story of the rise of a television network.

Blumenthal, Howard and Oliver Goodenough, *The Business of Television*, New York: Billboard Books, 2006.

Blumenthal and Goodenough provide a comprehensive guide to the television industry. It serves as a user's guide to the business.

Boyer, Peter J., *Who Killed CBS? The Undoing of America's Number One News Network*, New York: Random House, 1988.

Boyer uses his journalist skills to tell a story about the downfall of the news division at CBS. Ultimately, his focus settles on economics as the primary cause. Ultimately, this is a case study of the economics of running a network news division.

Browne, Nick (Ed.), *American Television: New Directions in History and Theory*, Chur, Switzerland: Harwood Academic Publishers, 1994.

Browne edits a volume of some of the most important writing on television published in *Quarterly Review of Film and Video* up through the mid-1990s. The articles cover topics such as the relation between television's politics and cultural forms, gender, and the impact of changing technology on the industry.

Comstock, George, *The Evolution of American Television*, Newbury Park, CA: Sage, 1989.

Comstock looks at the evolution of the television industry during the 1980s, a period when cable television became a dominant force in the industry.

Conway, Mike, *The Origins of Television News in America*, New York: Peter Lang Publishing, 2009.

Conway provides in-depth coverage of the growth and development of the television newscast from its earliest days.

Day, J., *The Vanishing Vision: The Inside Story of Public Television*, Berkeley: University of California Press, 1996.

Day writes the first history of public television, offering an insider's view of the growth of public television and its uncertain role as a publicly subsidized media giant.

Dupagne, M. and P. Seel, *High-Definition Television: A Global Perspective*, Ames: Iowa State University Press, 1998.

Dupagne and Seel provide a global overview of the technological, political, and economic factors that conspired against the adoption of a single worldwide production standard for HDTV. They look at the impact of the technology, politics, and economics of the innovation of HDTV.

Edgerton, Gary R. and Peter C. Rollins (Eds.), *Television Histories*, Lexington: University Press of Kentucky, 2001.

Edgerton and Rollins examine the power of television to influence culture. They ask why television has become such a respected source of truth and what impact that has, especially on our understanding of the past.

Eisemann, Thomas R., "The U.S. Cable Television Industry: 1948–1995: Managerial Capitalism in Eclipse," *Business History Review* **74:1 (Spring 2000), pp. 1–40.**

Eisemann looks at the cable television industry as an example of Chandlerian growth policy.

Hart, Jeffrey A., *Technology, Television and Competition: The Politics of Digital TV,* **Cambridge: Cambridge University Press, 2004.**

Hart looks at the relations between business and government in an effort to explain why the world television industry evolved into three incompatible standards.

Miller, Ian R., "Models for Determining the Economic Value of Cable Television Systems," *Journal of Media Economics* **10:2 (1997), pp 21–33.**

Miller identifies determinants of the economic value of cable television systems. He calculates elasticities and explains the variation in value for a sample that reflects the industry trend of consolidation.

Sterne, Jonathan, "Television under Construction: American Television and the Problem of Distribution: 1926–62," *Media, Culture & Society* **21:4 (July 1999), pp. 503–30.**

Sterne examines the growth of the television infrastructure in the United States. He denaturalizes the technological and institutional form of broadcast television distribution and considers it instead as a product of liberal ideology, corporate strategy, and audience desires.

Udelson, J. H., *The Great Television Race: A History of the American Television Industry: 1925–1941,* **Tuscaloosa: University of Alabama Press, 1982.**

Udelson traces the American television industry from its inception until its commercialization and demonstrates the prominent role played by the federal government in the history of the enterprise.

Recorded Sound

Bakker, Gerben, "The Making of a Music Multinational: Poly-Gram's International Businesses: 1945–1988," *Business History Review* 80:1 (Spring 2006), pp. 81–123.

Bakker describes how PolyGram grew to become the world's largest music multinational. He argues that it developed a decentralized organizational structure that fit the fast-changing business environment in which it grew.

Barnet, Richard D. and Larry L. Burriss, *Controversies of the Music Industry,* **Westport, CT: Greenwood Press, 2001.**

Barnet and Burriss cover 12 ethical issues facing the music industry in the twenty-first century, from both sides of the issue.

Chapple, Steven and Reebee Garofalo, *Rock and Roll Is Here to Pay: The History and Politics of the Music Industry,* **Chicago: Nelson Hall, 1977.**

Chapple and Garofalo survey the history and economics of the music industry, and the impact of social change and politics on the music market.

De Graaf, Leonard, "Confronting the Mass Market: Thomas Edison and the Entertainment Phonograph," *Business and Economic History* 24:1 (Fall 1995), pp. 88–96.

De Graaf looks at the difference between innovation and marketing in the phonograph industry. He focuses on the failure of Thomas Edison to successfully market his invention, concluding that his strategies for marketing the phonograph were ill suited to the emerging mass consumer market.

Eliot, Marc, *Rockonomics: The Money Behind the Music,* **New York: Franklin Watts, 1989.**

Eliot examines the careers of performers, disc jockeys, and industry executives throughout the history of the recorded music industry to show the influence that commerce has on art.

Gelatt, Roland, *The Fabulous Phonograph: 1877–1977*, **New York: Macmillan, 1977.**

Gelatt looks at the history of the phonograph and its evolution over a century of market and technological advances.

Goldberg, Isaac, *Tin Pan Alley: A Chronicle of American Popular Music*, **New York: Frederick Ungar, 1970.**

Goldberg covers the history of the origin and business of Tin Pan Alley, the New York City music publishing industry in the nineteenth and early twentieth centuries.

Hull, Geoffrey P., *The Recording Industry*, **Needham Heights, MA: Allyn & Bacon, 1998.**

Hull covers the evolution of the recording industry in the twentieth century.

Millard, Andre, *America on Record: A History of Recorded Sound*, **New York: Cambridge University Press, 1995.**

Millard provides a comprehensive history of recorded sound, beginning with the inventors in the nineteenth century through to the evolution of the compact disc.

Mol, Joeri M. and Nachoem M. Wijnberg, "Competition, Selection and Rock and Roll: The Economics of Payola and Authenticity," *Journal of Economic Issues* **41:3 (September 2007), pp. 701–14.**

Mol and Wijnberg use the music industry as a vehicle to discuss the determination of product value and its impact on how firms compete.

Montoro-Pons, Juan D. and Manuel Cuadrado-Garcia, "Live and Prerecorded Popular Music Consumption," *Journal of Cultural Economics* **35:1 (February 2011), pp. 19–48.**

Montoro-Pons and Cuadrado-Garcia analyze the demand for the popular music sector in Spain, considering its double dimension as a supplier of live concerts and pre-recorded music.

Sanjek, Russel, *Pennies from Heaven: The American Popular Music Business in the Twentieth Century*, **New York: Da Capo Press, 1996.**

Sanjek covers the technological and economic revolutions of the twentieth century that transformed the music business, including recorded sound, vaudeville, and the rise of the huge entertainment conglomerate

Suisman, David, *Selling Sounds: The Commercial Revolution in American Music,* **Cambridge: Harvard University Press, 2009.**

Suisman explores the rise of the music business and its impact on the music culture from the origins of recorded sound into the twenty-first century.

Movies

Allen, Jeanne Thomas, "Copyright and Early Theater, Vaudeville and Film Competition," *Journal of the University Film Association* **31:2 (Spring 1979), pp. 5–11.**

Allen outlines the nature of intermedia competition and surveys aspects of business organization that accounted for film's superior competitive abilities.

Acheson, Keith and Christopher J. Maule, "Understanding Hollywood's Organization and Continuing Success," *Journal of Cultural Economics* **18:4 (December 1994), pp. 271–300.**

Acheson and Maule seek to explain why Hollywood has remained the center of the global movie industry and why the relationship between distributors and producers persists in its current form.

Bakker, Gerben, "Building Knowledge about the Consumer: The Emergence of Market Research in the Motion Picture Industry," *Business History* **45:1 (2003), pp. 101–27.**

Bakker finds that film companies became increasingly sophisticated in their methods of trying to obtain knowledge about consumer preferences over time. These changes were caused by the rise in sunk costs as well as technological and contractual changes. The increasing need for quick information led to the use of new market research techniques such as Gallup audience research.

Bakker, Gerben, "Entertainment Industrialized: The Emergence of the International Film Industry: 1890–1940," *Enterprise and Society* 4:4 (December 2003a), pp. 579–85.

Bakker looks at the market for films and finds evidence that product differentiation was important to the success of film companies.

Bakker, Gerben, "Selling French Films on Foreign Markets: The International Strategy of a Medium-Sized Film Company," *Enterprise and Society* 5:1 (March 2004), pp. 45–76.

Bakker explains the success of the medium-sized French film company Les Films Albatros in a global movie market dominated by Hollywood.

Bakker, Gerben, "Stars and Stories: How Films Became Branded Products," *Enterprise and Society* 2:3 (2001), pp. 461–502.

Bakker shows that the high sunk cost and relatively short market window for films led producers to invest in name brand value, much as other consumer goods industries did. They built audience loyalty around stars and stories to lower the cost of delivering information about film quality to potential consumers.

Bakker, Gerben, "The Decline and Fall of the European Film Industry: Sunk Costs, Market Size, and Market Structure: 1890–1927," *Economic History Review* 58:2 (May 2005), pp. 310–51.

Bakker looks toward the United Kingdom for clues to the American domination of the industry during the silent film era. Bakker determines that the escalation of sunk costs during the rapid phase of U.S. movie industry growth resulted in American domination of international film production and distribution.

Bakker, Gerben, *Entertainment Industrialized: the Emergence of the International Film Industry: 1890–1940*, Cambridge, UK and New York: Cambridge University Press, 2008.

Bakker compares the economic development of the film industry in the United Kingdom, the United States, and France between 1890 and 1940.

Balio, Tino (Ed.), *Hollywood in the Age of Television*, Boston: Unwin Hyman, 1990.

Balio edits a collection of papers examining the evolving relationship between the motion picture industry and television from the 1940s to the 1990s, with an emphasis on the institutional and technological histories of the film and TV industries are.

Balio, Tino (Ed.), *The American Film Industry* (revised edition), Madison: University of Wisconsin Press, 1985.

Balio provides a comprehensive history of the movie industry. He shows how the industry evolved over time, covering all aspects of the industry, from production to exhibition.

Balio, Tino, *Grand Design: Hollywood as a Modern Business Enterprise: 1930–1939*, New York: Charles Scribner's Sons, 1993.

Balio covers the history of the movie industry during the Great Depression. He focuses on topics such as colorization, censorship, and the studio system.

Balio, Tino, *United Artists: The Company That Changed the Film Industry*, Madison: University of Wisconsin Press, 1987.

Balio covers the history of United Artists, the distribution company that he argues changed the movie industry.

Boatwright, Peter, Suman Basuroy, and Wagner Kamakura, "Reviewing the Reviewers: The Impact of Individual Film Critics on Box Office Performance," *Quantitative Marketing and Economics* 5:4 (December 2007), pp. 401–25.

Boatwright and colleagues distinguish individual movie critics who are simply good at identifying products with popular appeal from those who act as opinion leaders and engender early product sales.

Brewer, Stephanie M., Jason M. Kelley, and James J. Jozefowicz, "A Blueprint for Success in the US Film Industry," *Applied Economics* 41:5 (February 2009), pp. 589–606.

Brewer and colleagues analyze movie box office gross performance. They make a distinction between information available to the public prior to the release of the film and that available only after the film has opened.

Chingtagunta, Praddep K, Shyam Gopinath, and Siriam Venkataraman, "The Effects of Online User Reviews on Movie Box Office Performance: Accounting for Sequential Rollout and Aggregation across Local Markets," *Marketing Science* 29:5 (September–October 2010), pp. 944–57.

Chingtagunta and colleagues measure the impact of national online user reviews on box office performance of movies.

Chisholm, Darlene C., Margaret S. McMillan, and George Norman, "Product Differentiation and Film-Programming Choice: Do First-Run Movie Theatres Show the Same Films?" *Journal of Cultural Economics* 34:2 (May 2010), pp. 131–45.

Chisolm and colleagues analyze product differentiation in the movie industry and compute two measures of product similarity, which they then use to investigate the determinants of strategic product differentiation in the industry.

Chiou, Lesley, "The Timing of Movie Releases: Evidence from the Home Video Industry," *International Journal of Industrial Organization* 26:5 (September 2008), pp. 1059–73.

Chiou examines the home video industry to provide evidence on whether booms in theatrical movie revenues are driven by the underlying seasonality of demand or the quality of movies released.

Conant, Michael, "The Paramount Decrees Reconsidered," *Law and Contemporary Problems*, 44:4 (Autumn 1981), pp. 79–107.

Conant looks at the Paramount case and the radical changes it brought to the marketing of movies in the United States.

Davis, Peter, "Spatial Competition in Retail Markets: Movie Theaters," *RAND Journal of Economics* 37:4 (Winter 2006), pp. 964–82.

Davis uses data from the U.S. cinema industry to evaluate the form of consumer transport costs, the effect of a theater ticket pricing and quality selection policies on rivals, the effects of geographic differentiation, and the nature and extent of market power in the movie exhibition industry.

Davis, Peter, "Measuring the Business: Stealing, Cannibalization and Market Expansion Effects of Entry in the U.S. Motion

Picture Exhibition Market," *Journal of Industrial Economics* 54:3 (September 2006), pp. 293–321.

Davis uses a data set of theater revenues and documents the extent and nature of business stealing, revenue cannibalization, and market expansion that occurred during the height of the 1990s boom in movie theater construction.

Davis, Peter, "The Effect of Local Competition on Admission Prices in the U.S. Motion Picture Exhibition Market," *Journal of Law and Economics* 48:2 (October 2005), pp. 677–708.

Davis provides empirical evidence on the relationship between local market structure and the prices charged to consumers in the U.S. motion picture exhibition market. He finds a relationship between the geographic distribution of movie theaters in a market and the admission prices that they are able to charge.

De Vany, Arthur S. and W. David Walls, "Uncertainty in the Movie Industry: Does Star Power Reduce the Terror of the Box Office?" *Journal of Cultural Economics* 23:4 (November 1999), pp. 285–318.

De Vany and Walls investigate how risky the business of movies is and whether there are any strategies to reduce the risk.

De Vany, Arthur S. and W. David Walls, "Estimating the Effects of Movie Piracy on Box-Office Revenue," *Review of Industrial Organization* 30:4 (June 2007), pp. 291–301.

De Vany and Walls develop and estimate a statistical model of the effects of piracy on the box-office performance of a widely released movie.

De Vany, Arthur, and Henry McMillan, "Was the Antitrust Action That Broke Up the Movie Studios Good for the Movies? Evidence from the Stock Market," *American Law and Economics Review* 6:1 (Spring 2004), pp. 135–53.

De Vany and McMillan use stock market evidence to evaluate the impact of events in Paramount litigation on firm value.

Dick, Bernard F., *Engulfed: The Death of Paramount Pictures and the Birth of Corporate Hollywood*, Lexington: University Press of Kentucky, 2001.

Dick tells the history of the movie industry from the perspective of Paramount Pictures, addressing technological and organizational challenges that changed the industry.

Einav, Liran, "Seasonality in the U.S. Motion Picture Industry," *RAND Journal of Economics* **38:1 (Spring 2007), pp. 127–45.**

Einav estimated the weekly demand for movies and finds that the estimated seasonality in underlying demand for movies is much smaller and slightly different from the observed seasonality of sales.

Epstein, Edward Jay, *The Big Picture: Money and Power in Hollywood,* **New York: Random House, 2005.**

Epstein takes a look at the twenty-first century version of the movie studio and how the movie itself is only one small part of the total business deal that includes television, video, amusement parks, and soundtracks, to name but a few of the related industries Epstein covers.

Eyman, Scott, *The Speed of Sound: Hollywood and the Talkie Revolution: 1926–1930,* **Baltimore: Johns Hopkins University Press, 1997.**

Eyman covers the history of the arrival of sound to the movies and the impact it had on the industry.

Filson, Darren, "Dynamic Common Agency and Investment: The Economics of Movie Distribution," *Economic Inquiry* **43:4 (October 2005), pp. 773–84.**

Filson builds a model of the movie distribution industry and uses it to analyze investment and other strategies.

Gil, Ricard, "An Empirical Investigation of the Paramount Antitrust Case," *Applied Economics* **42:1–3 (January–February 2010), pp. 171–83.**

Gil looks at the change in production patterns by studios after the forced vertical disintegration of the industry.

Gil, Ricard, "Demand Shifts and Changes in Competition: Evidence from the Movie Theatre Industry," *International Journal of the Economics of Business* **13:3 (November 2006), pp. 407–28.**

Gil examines how demand shifts affect firm behavior in the Spanish movie theater industry.

Gil, Ricard, "Revenue Sharing Distortions and Vertical Integration in the Movie Industry," *Journal of Law, Economics, and Organization* 25:2 (October 2009), pp. 579–610.

Gil looks at the contracts between movie distributors and theaters to analyze how variation in firm boundaries affect economic outcomes.

Glancy, H. Mark, "MGM Film Grosses: 1924–1948: The Eddie Mannix Ledger," *Historical Journal of Film, Radio and Television* 12:2 (June 1992), pp. 127–43.

Glancy provides guidelines to interpreting the financial figures in the Eddie Mannix ledger, lending insight to the financial performance of MGM films during the years 1924 to 1948.

Glancy, H. Mark, "Warner Bros Film Grosses: 1921–1951: The Williams Schaefer Ledger," *Historical Journal of Film, Radio and Television* 15:1 (March 1995), pp. 55–73.

Glancy examines the finances of Warner Brothers studios from 1921 to 1951.

Gomery, Douglas, "Rethinking U.S. Film History: The Depression Decade and Monopoly Control," *Film and History* 10:2 (1980), pp. 32–38.

Gomery provides a historical overview of the studio system, focusing on the monopolization of the production and distribution of films during the Great Depression.

Hand, Chris, "Analyzing Movie Going Demand: An Individual-Level Cross-Sectional Approach," *Managerial and Decision Economics* 26:5 (July–August 2005), pp. 319–30.

Hand provides the first detailed individual theater level analysis of the factors that increase or decrease the demand for movie theater tickets.

Hand, Chris, "What Makes a Blockbuster? Economic Analysis of Film Success in the United Kingdom," *Managerial and Decision Economics* 23:6 (September 2002), pp. 343–54.

Hand uses data from the U.K. film market to predict box office performance of films. Specifically, he estimates the probability that a film will be a blockbuster.

Hanson, Gordon, and Chong Xiang, "Trade Barriers and Trade Flows with Product Heterogeneity: An Application to US Motion Picture Exports," *Journal of International Economics* 83:1 (January 2011), pp. 14–26.

Hanson and Xiang use data on bilateral U.S. movie exports to look at variation on box-office revenue by number of exports and the average sales ratio as trade distance varies.

Hanssen, F. Andrew, "Revenue-Sharing in Movie Exhibition and the Arrival of Sound," *Economic Inquiry* 40:3 (July 2002), pp. 380–402.

The pricing scheme in the movie industry has long been based on revenue sharing. The distributor provides films to the exhibitor in return for a percentage of the box office. Hanssen argues that the arrival of sound altered the incentive structure of movie theater owners, which led to a change in the method of dividing box office receipts between theaters and distributors.

Hanssen, F. Andrew, "Vertical Integration during the Hollywood Studio Era," *Journal of Law and Economics* 53:3 (August 2010), pp. 519–43.

Hanssen finds that the vertical integration of studios promoted efficiency in the industry because they were more likely to alter the run lengths of new releases after the initial run contract was written. This promoted efficiency since the demand for a given film is not known until after it begins to play in the cinema.

Hanssen, F. Andrew, "The Block Booking of Films Reexamined," *Journal of Law and Economics* 43:2 (October 2000), pp. 395–426.

Hanssen focus on the impact of the practice of film distributors packaging films for sale to theaters.

Holbrook, Morris B. and Michela Addis, "Art versus Commerce in the Movie Industry: A Two-Path Model of Motion-Picture Success," *Journal of Cultural Economics* 32:2 (June 2008), pp. 87–107.

Holbrook and Addis analyze films and find that reviewer-and-consumer evaluations and "buzz" respond differently to a film's marketing clout and that these audience responses contribute independently to a film's industry recognition and market performance along two separable paths.

Holbrook, Morris B., "Popular Appeal versus Expert Judgments of Motion Pictures," *Journal of Consumer Research* 26:2 (September 1999), pp. 144–55.

Holbrook finds that filmgoers and film critics emphasized different criteria in forming their tastes for specific movies.

Jewell, Richard B., "RKO Film Grosses: 1929–51: The C. J. Tevlin Ledger," *Historical Journal of Film, Radio and Television* 14:1 (March 1994), pp. 37–50.

Jewell presents information on the financial performance of the RKO production company from 1929 to 1951 based on a ledger kept by operations manager C. J. Tevlin.

Joshi, Amit M. and Dominique M. Hanssens, "Movie Advertising and the Stock Market Valuation of Studios: A Case of 'Great Expectations'?" *Marketing Science* 28:2 (March–April 2009), pp. 239–520.

Joshi and Hanssens study how the release of individual movies impacts the investor valuation of a movie studio.

Jozefowicz, James J., Jason M. Kelley, and Stephanie M. Brewer, "New Release: An Empirical Analysis of VHS/DVD Rental Success," *Atlantic Economic Journal* 36:2 (June 2008), pp. 139–51.

Jozefowicz and colleagues study movie rental revenue in the home video industry for responsiveness to box office gross, production budget, critical ratings, genre, star power, awards, genre, word of mouth, and economic variables.

Jung, Sang-Chul and Myeong Hwan Kim, "Does the Star Power Matter?" *Applied Economics Letters* 17:11 (July 2010), pp. 1037–41.

Jung and Kim investigate the role of superstars in the Korean film industry.

Kenney, Roy W. and Benjamin Klein, "How Block Booking Facilitated Self-Enforcing Film Contracts," *Journal of Law and Economics* 43:2 (October 2000), pp. 427–36.

Kenney and Klein use the exhibition contracts that were the subject of the Paramount Studios antitrust case to examine the role of contract terms in facilitating self-enforcing relationships.

Kenney, Roy W. and Benjamin Klein, "The Economics of Block Booking," *Journal of Law and Economics* 26:3 (October 1983), pp. 497–40.

Kenney and Klein develop a theory that explains why block booking was ruled in violation of antitrust laws. They show that distributors choose the particular contractual arrangement that minimizes the brand name and transaction costs.

Kraft, James P., "The 'Pit' Musicians: Mechanization in the Movie Theaters: 1926–1934," *Labor History* 35:1 (Winter 1994), pp. 66–92.

Kraft looks at the impact of sound motion pictures on the employment of pit musicians in the vaudeville and silent movie industries.

Kraft, James P., "Artists as Workers: Musicians and Trade Unionism in America: 1880–1917," *Musical Quarterly* 79:3 (Autumn 1995), pp. 512–43.

Kraft looks at the development of the labor market for musicians during a period of rapid technological advance in the workplace. He finds that unlike other skilled artisans, whose status power waned during this era, musicians benefitted from working for small businesses whose success depended on the performance of their employees.

Kraft, James P., "Musicians in Hollywood: Work and Technological Change in Entertainment Industries: 1926–1940," *Technology and Culture* 35:2 (April 1994), pp. 289–314.

Kraft describes and assesses the impact of new technologies on musicians in Los Angeles from 1926 to 1940. He finds that musicians rejected the notion that modernization should benefit only entrepreneurs and their customers and sought instead to influence to their own advantage the changing work environment.

Lang, David M., David M. Switzer, and Brandon J. Swartz, "DVD Sales and the R-rating Puzzle," *Journal of Cultural Economics* 35:4 (November 2011), pp. 267–86.

Land and colleagues look at the factors determining sales of individual DVDs in the United States.

Macmillan, Peter and Ian Smith, "Explaining Post-War Cinema Attendance in Great Britain," *Journal of Cultural Economics* 25:2 (May 2001), pp. 91–108.

Macmillan and Smith model the interaction between post WWII supply and demand for the movies. They find that sustained negative shocks decreased the demand for cinema, which led to a steady reduction in the supply of screens, further inducing the decrease in admissions.

Mezias, John and Stephen Mezias, "Resource Partitioning, the Founding of Specialist Firms and Innovation: The American Feature Film Industry: 1912–1992," *Organization Science* 11:3 (2000), pp. 306–22.

Mezias and Mezias use the early twentieth century movie industry to examine the hypothesis that concentration among large generalist firms will be associated with higher founding rates of specialist producers and distributors.

Miksell, Peter, " 'Selling America to the World?' The Rise and Fall of an International Film Distributor in Its Largest Foreign Market: United Artists in Britain: 1927–1947," *Enterprise and Society* 7:4 (December 2006), pp. 740–76.

Miksell looks toward the United Kingdom for clues to the American domination of the industry during the silent film era.

Miksell, Peter, "Resolving the Global Efficiency versus Local Adaptability Dilemma: US Film Multinationals in Their Largest Foreign Market in the 1930s and 1940s," *Business History* 51:3 (May 2009), pp. 426–44.

Miskell attributes Hollywood's domination to its ability to tailor their films to the U.K. market, something the U.K. studios were ineffective at doing for the U.S. market.

Moul, Charles C. (Ed.), *A Concise Handbook of Movie Industry Economics*, New York: Cambridge University Press, 2005.

Moul edits a volume of essays covering all aspects of the business of the motion picture industry including profitability, studio executive behavior, the impact of changing accounting standards, and seasonal demand for tickets.

Orbach, Barak Y. and Liran Einav, "Uniform Prices for Differentiated Goods: The Case of the Movie-Theater Industry," *International Review of Law and Economics* 27:2 (June 2007), pp. 129–53.

Orbach and Einav explore the justifications for uniform pricing and constraints on vertical arrangements between distributors and exhibitors in the movie industry.

Papies, Dominik and Michel Clement, "Adoption of New Movie Distribution Services on the Internet," *Journal of Media Economics* 21:3 (July–September 2008), pp. 131–57.

Papies and Clement analyze the internet market for movie downloads, identifying the drivers of consumer intentions to adopt a legal movie download service.

Pokorny, Michael and John Sedgwick, "Profitability Trends in Hollywood: 1929–1999: Somebody Must Know Something," *Economic History Review* 63:1 (February 2010), pp. 56–84.

Pokorny and Sedgwick present an overview of the development of the U.S. film industry since the advent of sound pictures.

Pokorny, Michal and John Sedgwick, "Stardom and the Profitability of Film Making: Warner Bros. in the 1930s," *Journal of Cultural Economics* 25:3 (August 2001), pp. 157–84.

Porkorny and Sedgwick use Warner Brothers as a case study to examine the economics of the film industry during the Great Depression.

Redondo, Ignacio and Morris B. Holbrook, "Modeling the Appeal of Movie Features to Demographic Segments of Theatrical Demand," *Journal of Cultural Economics* 34:4 (November 2010), pp. 299–315.

Redondo and Holbrook model the appeal of movie features to market segments using demographically detailed movie attendance data for the Spanish film market.

Scott, Allen J., *On Hollywood: The Place, The Industry*, Princeton, NJ: Princeton University Press, 2005.

Scott uses the tools of economic geography to answer the question of why the movie industry is concentrated in Hollywood. He analyzes the history of the industry and explains why it originally moved to Hollywood from New York, and why it is still there.

Sedgewick, John, "Product Differentiation at the Movies: Hollywood: 1946 to 1965," *Journal of Economic History* 62:3 (September 2002), pp. 676–705.

Sedgwick examines how the major film producers retained their dominant position in the movie industry in the post–World War II period by becoming distributor-financiers and reducing their exposure to the risks associated with production.

Sedgwick, John and Michael Pokorny, "Consumers as Risk Takers: Evidence from the Film Industry during the 1930s," *Business History* 52:1 (February 2010), pp. 74–99.

Sedgwick and Pokorny examine the risk environment of film consumption in the United States during the Great Depression when the movie industry was the dominant form of purchased leisure activity.

Sedgwick, John and Michael Pokorny, "The Film Business in the United States and Britain during the 1930s," *Economic History Review* 58:1 (February 2005), pp. 79–112.

Sedgwick and Pokorny analyze the underlying economic arrangements of the film industries of the United States and United Kingdom during the Great Depression for producing and diffusing movies.

Sedgwick, John and Michael Pokorny, "The Risk Environment of Film Making: Warner Bros in the Inter-War Years," *Explorations in Economic History* 35:2 (April 1998), pp. 196–220.

Sedgwick and Pokorny examine the financial strategies used in the process of film production with particular emphasis on the performance of Warner Brothers during the decades of the 1920s and 1930s.

Smith-Doerr, Laurel, "Flexible Organizations, Innovation and Gender Equality: Writing for the US Film Industry: 1907–27," *Industry and Innovation* **17:1 (February 2010), pp. 5–22.**

Smith-Doerr credits the nonbureaucratic configuration of the early movie industry for the success of women writers. This form of organization gave women more visibility and authority than the studio system that eventually arose.

Strick, J. C., "The Economics of the Motion Picture Industry: A Survey," *Philosophy of the Social Sciences* **8:4 (December 1978), pp. 406–17.**

Stick provides one of the first overviews of the economic literature pertaining to the movie industry. He notes that little economic analysis was actually applied to the movie industry. This is no longer true.

Suarez-Vazquez, Ana, "Critic Power or Star Power? The Influence of Hallmarks of Quality of Motion Pictures: An Experimental Approach," *Journal of Cultural Economics* **35:2 (May 2011), pp. 119–35.**

Suarez-Vazquez experimentally tests how individual moviegoers are influenced by critical reviews and the role of box office stars.

Sunada, Mitsuru, "Vertical Integration in the Japanese Movie Industry," *Journal of Industry, Competition and Trade* **10:2 (June 2010), pp. 135–50.**

Sunada examines the vertical integration of the Japanese movie industry, estimating an admission price equation and a movie-going demand equation.

Thomas, Jeanne, "The Decay of the Motion Picture Patents Company," *Cinema Journal* **10:2 (Spring 1971), pp. 34–40.**

Thomas examines the causes of the failure of the Motion Picture Patents Company, focusing on three major areas: federal litigation, competition from independent companies, and the breakdown of the cartel as a result of the behavior of its members.

Walls, W. D., "Superstars and Heavy Tails in Recorded Entertainment: Empirical Analysis of the Market for DVDs," *Journal of Cultural Economics* 34:4 (November 2010), pp. 261–79.

Walls presents an empirical analysis of the market for DVDs.

Waterman, David, Sung Wook Ji, and Laura R. Rochet, "Enforcement and Control of Piracy, Copying, and Sharing in the Movie Industry," *Review of Industrial Organization* 30:4 (June 2007), pp. 255–89.

Waterman and colleagues review strategies that movie distribution companies have used to cope with piracy and illegal sharing of their movies.

Stage Shows

Bernheim, Alfred L., *The Business of the Theatre: An Economic History of the American Theater: 1750–1932*, New York: Benjamin Bloom, 1964.

Bernheim provides an early historical overview of the business of the live performance industry.

Clevinger, Donna L. and George S. Vozikis, "A Historical Review of Early Entrepreneurial Theatrical Activity in a Growing Railroad Center," *International Entrepreneurship and Management Journal* 3:2 (June 2007), pp. 159–69.

Clevinger and Vozikis look at the role of transportation on the spread of entertainment, finding the railroad to be a significant determinant of the growth of the American theatre.

Di Meglio, John E., *Vaudeville U.S.A.*, Bowling Green, OH: Bowling Green University Popular Press, 1973.

Di Meglio writes a history of the vaudeville industry, chronicling its roots, rise, and ultimate demise with the rise of the movie industry.

Erdman, Andrew L., *Blue Vaudeville: Sex, Morals and the Mass Marketing of Amusement: 1895–1915*, Jefferson, NC: McFarland and Co., Inc., 2004.

Erdman reveals the often racy, sexually charged nature of the vaudeville stage, examining the ways in which big-time vaudeville nonetheless managed to market itself as pure, safe, and morally acceptable. He compares the industry's marketing and promotional practices to those of other emergent mass-marketers in the late nineteenth and early twentieth centuries.

Gragg, Larry, "A Big Step to Oblivion for Las Vegas? The 'Battle of the Bare Bosoms': 1957–59," *Journal of Popular Culture* 43:5 (October 2010), pp. 1004–22.

Gragg addresses the evolution of the Las Vegas entertainment scene in his research on the growing use of nudity during the 1950s as a means of attracting customers during a period of over-expansion of hotels.

Isaacs, Edith J. R., *The Negro in the American Theatre*, New York: Theatre Arts, Inc., 1947.

Isaacs looks at the contribution of African Americans to the American theater during a period of time when segregation and discrimination were commonplace.

Leavitt, M. B., *Fifty Years in Theatrical Management*, New York: Broadway Publishing Co., 1912.

Leavitt provides an insider's view of the business side of the American theater industry at the turn of the twentieth century

Milford, T. A., "Boston's Theater Controversy and Liberal Notions of Advantage," *New England Quarterly* 72:1 (March 1999), pp. 61–88.

Milford looks at the puritanical influence on early American theater.

Poggi, Jack, *Theater in America: The Impact of Economic Forces: 1870–1967*, Ithaca, NY: Cornell University Press, 1968.

Poggi takes a look at the rise and fall of various types of theater over a century.

Pompe, Jeffrey, Lawrence Tamburri, and Johnathan Munn, "Factors that Influence Programming Decisions of US Symphony Orchestras," *Journal of Cultural Economics* 35:3 (August 2011), pp. 167–84.

Pompe and colleagues examine the factors that affect programming decisions of symphony orchestras by creating an objective index of the propensity of a symphony orchestra to perform the standard repertoire.

Snyder, Robert W., *The Voice of the City*, Chicago: Ivan R. Dee, 2000.

Snyder shows how entrepreneurs created a near monopoly over bookings, theatres, and performers on the vaudeville circuit during its rise to prominence and its death.

Taubman, Howard, *The Making of the American Theatre*, New York: Coward McCann, Inc., 1965.

Taubman traces the rise of the American theatre from Colonial times into the mid-twentieth century, noting the forces that revolutionized the industry in the twentieth century.

Toll, Robert, *On with the Show! The First Century of Show Business in America*, New York: Oxford University Press, 1976.

Toll covers a wide range of show business, including vaudeville, burlesque, the circus, and the legitimate theater.

Sullivan, Edward J. and Kevin B. Pry, "Eighteenth Century London Theater and the Capture Theory of Regulation," *Journal of Cultural Economics* 15:2 (December 1991), pp. 41–52.

Sullivan and Pry use the eighteenth century London theater market to study the capture theory of regulation. They find that the Licensing Act of 1737 restricted competition and successfully maintained the interest of three London theater companies.

Radio

Aitken, Hugh, *Syntony and Spark: The Origins of Radio*, Princeton, NJ: Princeton University Press, 1985.

Aitken, an economic historian by trade, surveys the earliest days of radio, with a particular emphasis on "spark" receivers and detectors.

De Long, Thomas A., *The Mighty Music Box: The Golden Age of Musical Radio,* **Los Angeles: Amber Crest Books, 1980.**

De Long portrays the history of musical broadcasts on radio and looks at the impact of radio on the development of the music industry.

Douglas, George H., *The Early Days of Radio Broadcasting,* **Jefferson, NC and London, England: McFarland Pub., 1987.**

Douglas concentrates on the radio industry during the 1920s. He covers the development of the commercialization of radio, programming, regulation, the manufacturing of equipment, the rise of networks, and radio as a medium of entertainment and news.

Douglas, Susan J., *Inventing American Broadcasting 1899–1922,* **Baltimore: Johns Hopkins University Press, 1987.**

Douglas explores the origins of a corporate media system that today dominates the content and form of American communication.

Fones–Wolf, Elizabeth, "Creating a Favorable Business Climate: Corporations and Radio Broadcasting, 1934–1954," *Business History Review* **73:2 (Summer 1999), pp. 221–55.**

Fones–Wolf looks at the use of radio by corporate America during the period 1930 to 1950 for public relations campaigns aimed at improving their image. She concludes that radio was the most influential medium by which they could reach the public, which succeeded in helping business improve its status in American society.

Godfried, Nathan, "Struggling over Politics and Culture: Organized Labor and Radio Station WEVD during the 1930s," *Labor History* **42:4 (November 2001), pp. 347–69.**

Godfried conducts a case study of station WEVD to look at the relationship between organized labor and radio during the Great Depression.

Kruse, Elizabeth, "From Free Privilege to Regulation: Wireless Firms and the Competition for Spectrum Rights before World War I," *Business History Review* 76:4 (Winter 2002), pp. 659–703.

Kruse studies the evolution of property rights in the radio broadcasting spectrum.

Lewis, Tom, "A Godlike Presence: The Impact of Radio on the 1920s and 1930s," *OAH Magazine of History* 6:4 (Spring 1992), pp. 26–33.

Lewis focuses on the social impact of radio during the period 1930 to 1950. He describes the early radio broadcasting as a mix of culture, education, information and entertainment and looks at the role of radio on American culture in the decades between the wars.

Lewis, Tom, *Empire of the Air: The Men who Made Radio*, New York: Harper Collins, 1991.

Lewis traces the lives of the three visionaries behind the modern radio industry: Lee de Forest, Edwin Howard Armstrong, and David Sarnoff.

Liebowitz, Stan J., "File Sharing: Creative Destruction or Just Plain Destruction?" *Journal of Law and Economics* 49:1 (April 2006), pp. 1–28.

Liebowitz examines the history of music file sharing, the history of record sales, various explanations for the change in record sales over time, and an analysis of the economics of file sharing.

Liebowitz, Stan J., "The Elusive Symbiosis: The Impact of Radio on the Record Industry," *Review of Economic Research on Copyright Issues* 1:1 (June 2004), pp. 93–118.

Liebowitz shows that radio airplay of music does not benefit overall sale of recordings. By way of association, he also demonstrates the negative impact of television on the movie industry.

Lippmann, Stephen, "The Institutional Context of Industry Consolidation: Radio Broadcasting in the United States: 1920–1934," *Social Forces* 86:2 (December 2007), pp. 467–95.

Lippmann looks at the early concentration of firms in the radio industry. He finds that this concentration was the result of institutional shifts in legitimate organizational practices and the political environment in which broadcasters operated.

McChesney, R. W., *Telecommunications, Mass Media, and Democracy: The Battle for the Control of U.S. Broadcasting: 1928–1935,* **New York: Oxford University Press, 1993.**

McChesney details the emergence and consolidation of the commercial broadcasting industry, focusing on the political battles behind the regulation of the airwaves.

Websites

Academy of Motion Picture Arts and Sciences http://www.oscars.org/

American Film Institute http://www.afi.com/

American Vaudeville Museum http://vaudeville.org/

BaseballReference.com http://www.baseball–reference.com/

BLS American Time Use Survey http://www.bls.gov/news.release/atus.nr0.htm

Box Office Mojo http://boxofficemojo.com/

Broadway http://www.broadwayworld.com/

Broadway league http://www.broadwayleague.com/

Bureau of Labor Statistics homepage http://www.bls.gov/home.htm

Hollywood Box Office http://www.hollywood.com/boxoffice/

Internet Broadway database http://www.ibdb.com/index.php

Movie database http://www.imdb.com/

MPAA http://mpaa.org/

Museum of Broadcast Communication http://www.museum.tv/collections section.php?page=3D16

National Association of Theater Owners http://www.natoonline.org/

Nielson http://en–us.nielsen.com/content/nielsen/en_us/industries/media.html

Playbill http://playbill.com/index.php

Stage and vaudeville http://memory.loc.gov/ammem/vshtml/vshome.html

Theaters http://www.tcg.org/tools/facts/

TV history http://www.tvhistory.tv/TV%20Program%20Stats.htm

Time Use/Leisure and Work

Bowden, Sue and Avner Offer, "Household Appliances and the Use of Time: The United States and Britain since the 1920s," *Economic History Review* 47:4 (November 1994), pp. 725–48.

Bowden and Offer provide an interesting view on technology and the use of time in the household. They look at the falling cost of electronic entertainment media and their role in the household budget, and conclude that electric appliances did not shorten housework hours until television viewing expanded in the allocation of household time to the point where its marginal utility fell to that of housework.

Chandler, Alfred, "How High Technology Industries Transformed Work and Life Worldwide from the 1880s to the 1990s," *Capitalism and Society* 1:2 (2006), pp. 1–55.

In a sweeping look at how high technology industries transformed work and life, Chandler uses the example of the rise and fall of RCA to illustrate the new science of the electronics industry.

Cole, Arthur H. and Dorothy Lubin, "Perspectives on Leisure-Time Business," *Explorations in Entrepreneurial History, New Series* 1:3 (Supplement, 1964), pp. 1–38.

Cole and Lubin provide an overview of the growth of the leisure industry and the existing research on the topic.

Costa, Dora, "The Wage and the Length of the Work Day: From the 1890s to 1991," *Journal of Labor Economics* 18:1 (January 2000), pp. 156–81.

Costa investigates the relationship between wages and the length of the workday from the late nineteenth to the late twentieth century.

Dulles, Foster Rhea, *A History of Recreation: America Learns to Play*, New York: Appleton-Century-Crafts, 1965.

Dulles looks at the earliest origins of recreation and entertainment in America.

Garrett, Thomas A., "War and Pestilence as Labor Market Shocks: U.S. Manufacturing Wage Growth: 1914–1919," *Economic Inquiry* 47:4 (October 2009), pp. 711–25.

Garrett looks at the effect of the influenza pandemic and World War I on U.S. manufacturing wage growth.

Gould, E. D., "Cities, Workers, and Wages: A Structural Analysis of the Urban Wage Premium," *Review of Economic Studies* 74:2 (April 2007), pp. 477–506.

Gould uses a dynamic programming model to analyze the reasons behind the higher wages earned by urban versus rural workers. His work supports the interpretation that cities make white-collar workers more productive and suggest that workers may consider moving to the city not only in terms of locational choice but also as a form of human capital investment.

Higgs, Robert, "A Revealing Window on the U.S. Economy in Depression and War: Hours Worked: 1929–1950," *Independent Review* 14:1 (Summer 2009), pp. 151–60.

Higgs looks at the U.S. economy from 1929 to 1950 based on hours worked.

Hunnicutt, Benjamin, "Historical Attitudes toward the Increase of Free Time in the Twentieth Century: Time for Work, for Leisure, or as Unemployment," *Society and Leisure* 3:2 (November 1980), pp. 195–218.

Hunnicutt examines the political, economic, and intellectual events surrounding the increase in leisure time during the first four decades of the twentieth century, how its use changed, and how it was viewed by society.

Maoz, Yishay David, "Labor Hours in the United States and Europe: The Role of Different Leisure Preferences," *Macroeconomic Dynamics* 14:2 (April 2010), pp. 231–41.

Maoz attributes differences in the valuation of leisure in the United States and Europe during the twentieth century to differences in labor hours. He noted that U.S. annual hours per worker declined in general over the time period, but not always at the same rate as in Europe.

Robinson, John P. and Geoffrey Godbey, *Time for Life: The Surprising Ways Americans use their Time*, University Park: Pennsylvania State University Press, 1997.

Robinson and Godbey look at the results of the Americans' Use of Time Project.

Shaw, Douglas V., "Making Leisure Pay: Street Railway Owned Amusement Parks in the United States: 1900–1925," *Journal of Cultural Economics* 10:2 (December 1986), pp. 67–79.

Shaw looks at the complementary goods of transportation and entertainment by examining the ownership of amusement parks by street railways during the latter part of the nineteenth century. Economies of scale in the generation of electricity as street railways converted from horse power to electric power required efficient use of the capital plant, which involved running as many loaded cars as possible over the tracks. Railway interest in amusement parks arose from a desire to encourage use during nonpeak hours.

Shpayer-Makov, Haia, "Relinking Work and Leisure in Late Victorian and Edwardian England: The Emergence of a Police Subculture," *International Review of Social History* 47:2 (August 2002), pp. 213–41.

Shpayer-Makov looks at the connection between leisure and work in her study of public sector employers in late nineteenth century England who organized formal recreational activities for their employees.

Vandenbroucke, Guillaume, "Trends in Hours: The U.S. from 1900 to 1950," *Journal of Economic Dynamics and Control* 33:1 (January 2009), pp. 237–49.

Vandenbroucke looks at the impact of the length of the workweek on the consumption of recreation. He attributes the decrease in the length of the U.S. workweek in the first half of the twentieth century to technological progress, which increased wages and decreased the cost of recreation, making it possible for the average worker to afford more leisure time.

Whaples, Robert, "Winning the Eight-Hour Day: 1909–1919," *Journal of Economic History* 50:2 (June 1990), pp. 393–406.

Whaples looks at the quest by American workers for an eight-hour day, which finally happened around 1919.

General

Baumol, William J. and William G. Bowen, *Performing Arts: The Economic Dilemma*, New York: Twentieth Century Fund, 1966.

Baumol and Bowen provide an economic analysis of the major attributes of the performing arts. They demonstrate why the cost per performance and per attendance has always risen faster than the economy's rate of inflation, and why it is not likely to change.

Cairncross, F., *The Death of Distance: How the Communications Revolution Will Change Our Lives*, Boston: Harvard Business School Press, 1997.

Cairncross writes about the ways the communications revolution will tilt the balance between large and small, rich and poor, as it transforms business and government decisions. He argues that this revolution will be the single most important economic force shaping society over the first half of the twenty-first century.

Caves, Richard E., *Creative Industries: Contracts between Art and Commerce*, Cambridge: Harvard University Press, 2000.

Caves explores the organization of creative industries, including the visual and performing arts, movies, theater, sound recordings, and book publishing. To explain the logic of these arrangements, he draws on the analytical resources of industrial economics and the theory of contracts.

Coase, Ronald, "The Economics of Broadcasting and Government Policy," *American Economic Review* 56 (May 1966), pp. 440–47.

Coase examines the formulation of government policy toward broadcasting and considers the conclusions that should be drawn in making future policy recommendations.

Felton, Marianne Victorius, "Evidence of the Existence of the Cost Disease in the Performing Arts," *Journal of Cultural Economics* 18:4 (December 1994), pp. 301–12.

Felton examines the experience of 25 large U.S. orchestras over a period of 21 years, measuring inputs and outputs, including productivity, compensation, ticket prices, and attendance.

Frey, Bruno S., "Superstar Museums: An Economic Analysis," *Journal of Cultural Economics* 22:2–3 (1998), pp. 113–25.

Frey defines superstar museums, identifies their origins, and discusses their development over time.

Green, Abel and Joe Laurie, Jr., *Show Biz: From Vaude to Video*, New York: Holt, 1951.

Green and Laurie provide a detailed history of popular theatre, radio, film and television from 1905 to 1950.

Halberstam, David, *The Powers That Be* (reprint), Urbana: University of Illinois Press, 1990.

Halberstam writes a historical account of the rise of the modern media as an instrument of political power.

Haupert, Michael, *The Entertainment Industry*, Westport, CT: Greenwood Publishing, 2006.

Haupert writes an economic history of the American entertainment industry from the late nineteenth century to the dawning of the twenty-first century.

Heilbrun, James and Charles M. Gray, *The Economics of Art and Culture*, New York: Cambridge University Press, 2001.

Heilbrun and Gray cover the economics of the fine and performing arts as well as public policy toward them.

Heilbrun, James, "Keynes and the Economics of the Arts," *Journal of Cultural Economics* 8:2 (December 1984), pp. 37–49.

Heilbrun review Keynes' activities as a lifelong entrepreneur for the arts and examines his writings that deal with the economics of art and culture.

Hilliard, Robert L. and Michael C. Keith, *The Broadcast Century,* Burlington, MA: Elsevier, 2010.

Hilliard and Keith provide a history of the broadcasting industry, focusing on the technologies that have emerged in the twenty-first century and the profound impact they have had on the broadcasting industry in political, social, and economic spheres.

Holler, Manfred J., and Barbara Klose-Ullmann, "Art Goes America," *Journal of Economic Issues* 44:1 (March 2010), pp. 89–112.

Holler and Klose-Ullman use the art market to examine the effects of conspicuous consumption on the growth of the American art market between 1870 and World War II.

Kotler, Philip and Joanne Scheff. *Standing Room Only.* Boston: Harvard Business School Press, 1997.

Kotler and Scheff apply marketing principles to the performing arts industry. They review all of the key marketing functions—from segmentation to pricing to public relations—in the context of arts management, illustrated through numerous examples.

Matlaw, Myron (Ed.), *American Popular Entertainment: Papers and Proceedings of the Conference on the History of American Popular Entertainment*, Westport, CT: Praeger, 1979.

Matlaw edits a compilation of academic papers on the history of the American entertainment industry.

Pratt, George, "No Magic, No Mystery, No Sleight of Hand," *Image* 8 (December 1959), pp. 192–211.

Pratt looks at the first 10 years of the film exhibition business in Rochester, New York.

Rosen, Sherwin, "The Economics of Superstars," *American Economic Review* 71:5, (December 1981), pp. 845–58.

Rosen applies economic analysis to explain the existence of superstars in some markets, such as entertainment and sports.

Schwartz, Evan I., *The Last Lone Inventor*, New York: Harper Collins, 2002.

Schwartz details the history of the invention of television, focusing on the rivalry between inventor Philo T. Farnsworth and RCA president David Sarnoff.

Snowball, Jeanette D., *Measuring the Value of Culture: Methods and Examples in Cultural Economics,* **Berlin: Springer-Verlag, 2010.**

Snowball documents the use of methods that put a value on cultural goods, including theater, museums, archeological sites, and libraries. She considers the advantages and disadvantages of each method, using case studies to illustrate how they work.

Stoeber, Rudolf, "What Media Evolution Is: A Theoretical Approach to the History of New Media," *European Journal of Communication* **19:4 (December 2004), pp. 483–505.**

Stoeber combines Schumpeter's distinction between invention and innovation with evolution theory to argue that the emergence of new forms of media are not merely the consequence of new technology but also "social institutionalizing," whereby the new technology takes on new possibilities and is adapted in new ways by society. The technology that provided text messaging, for example, begat a whole new way of communicating and social networking possibilities. Stoeber casts his lens on a variety of media ranging from the Gutenberg printing press to the latest innovations of the twenty-first century.

Towse, Ruth (Ed.), *Cultural Economics: The Arts, the Heritage and the Media Industries,* **2 vols, Cheltenham, UK: Edward Elgar, 1997.**

Towse edits a collection of articles on a range of economic issues related to the various aspects of the cultural sector of the economy: the performing and creative arts as well as the heritage and media industries.

Vogel, Harold L., *Entertainment Industry Economics: A Guide for Financial Analysis* **(5th ed.), New York: Cambridge University Press.**

Vogel writes a financial guide to various sectors of the entertainment industry, including television, movies, broadcasting, toys and games, gambling, theme parks, and stage shows.

Glossary

Bilateral monopoly A market in which there is one producer and one consumer, thus each side of the market is a monopoly.

Cartel A market in which a few firms cooperate to monopolize a market.

Comparative advantage When one party can produce something at a lower opportunity cost than another.

Diminishing returns The decrease in the additional amount of output obtained from adding one additional unit of input to a production process.

Elasticity of demand The additional quantity demanded due to a change in price. This is measured as the percentage change in quantity demanded divided by the percentage change in price.

Kinetoscope An early version of a movie projector in which one person at a time could watch the movie by viewing it through a peephole in the top of the kinetoscope.

Labor exploitation Paying workers less than their marginal revenue.

Marginal cost The additional cost of producing one additional unit of a good.

Marginal revenue The additional revenue earned by selling one additional unit of a good.

Marginal revenue product The revenue earned by the marginal product of a worker.

Marginal product The additional output produced by the hiring of an additional unit of input.

Monopoly A market in which there is only one firm that produces all of the output.

Monopsony A market in which there is only one buyer of all the output.

Oligopoly   A market in which only a few firms produce all the output. While there is no firm number of firms that make up an oligopoly, each firm in an oligopoly controls enough of the market so that it can influence the market price.

Opportunity cost   The foregone opportunity when a choice is made.

Price discrimination   A market in which the producer of a good is able to charge different prices for the good to different buyers of the good. The prices charged are in line with the buyer's willingness to pay.

Prisoner's dilemma   A bargaining situation in which two parties are not likely to cooperate even when it appears it is in each of their best interests to do so.

Utility   An economic term used to explain what satisfaction or need fulfillment consumers get from consuming a good or service.

Vaudeville   An entertainment market consisting of a variety of live stage acts. Vaudeville flourished in the United States in the early decades of the twentieth century. It disappeared shortly after sound came to the movies.

Zero sum game   A situation in which the gains of one party are offset by the losses of the other party.

Index

About the Author

Michael Haupert is Professor of Economics at the University of Wisconsin—La Crosse. His research interests include the sports and entertainment industries, particularly their economic history. He has published numerous articles on the economics of professional sports, and is the author of *The Entertainment Industry* (Greenwood Press, 2006).

14 DAY LOANS
NO RENEWALS

Overdue charge is 10 cents per day,
Including Saturdays, Sundays and holidays.